FRONTING UP

THE SEAN FITZPATRICK STORY

with

Steven O'Meagher

Moa
Beckett

ISBN 1-86958-110-5

Published in 1994 by
Moa Beckett Publishers Limited
28 Poland Road, Glenfield.
PO Box 100-749, North Shore Mail Centre, Auckland 1330.

Typeset by Jazz Graphics, Auckland.

Printed in China through Colorcraft Ltd.

To Bronnie

Source Notes

SEAN FITZPATRICK is the primary source for the views and thoughts expressed in *Fronting Up*.

In addition, the author conducted interviews with dozens of people who have known, played with and/or against, or in some other way offer a perspective of Sean. Their time, assistance and contributions were very much appreciated.

Sean did not censor or influence any of the comments attributed to those quoted.

Chapter quotes were taken from the following publications:

Allen, Fred. *On Rugby*, Cassell, 1970
Barrow, Graeme. *All Blacks vs Springboks*, Heinemann, 1981
Bockris, Victor. *Keith Richards*, Penguin, 1992
Botham, Ian/Roebuck, Peter. *It Sort of Clicks*, Collins, 1986
Chester, R.H./McMillan, N.A.C. *The Encyclopedia of New Zealand Rugby*, Moa, 1981
Gifford, Phil. *Grizz – The Legend*, Rugby Press, 1991
Haden, Andy. *Boots 'n' All!* Rugby Press, 1983
Heller, Peter. *Tyson*, Pan, 1989
Howitt, Bob. *Inga – The Winger*, Rugby Press, 1993
Jones, Stephen. *Endless Winter*, Mainstream, 1993
Knight, Lindsay. *The Geriatrics*, Moa, 1986.
Laidlaw, Chris. *Mud In Your Eye*, Reed, 1973
Lewis, Paul. *Brothers In Arms*, Moa, 1991
Masters, Roy. *Inside League*, Pan, 1990
Newcombe, Barry/Probyn, Jeff. *Upfront*, Mainstream, 1993
Palenski, Ron. *Graham Mourie – Captain*, Moa, 1982
Parker, Julia and Derek. *Gemini*, Sun and Moon Library, 1993
Robinson, Derek. *Run With The Ball*, Collins, 1984
Thomas, Paul. *Running On Instinct*, Moa, 1991
Thomas, Paul. *Straight From the Hart*, Moa, 1993
Wheeler, Peter. *Rugby From The Front*, Paul, 1983

Rugby Almanac series
Rugby Annual series
Rugby World & Post
Listener
Rugby News
Esquire
New Zealand Herald
Auckland Star
Sunday Star (and *Star-Times*)
Observer
Mail on Sunday
Sportspages Almanac 1992
Sunday Telegraph
Sunday Times

CONTENTS

INDIVIDUALS WHO FEATURE IN *FRONTING UP*

Abo	*Ian Abercrombie*	Auckland hooker
Andrew Harvey		school friend
Andy	*Andy Haden*	former All Black; Auckland captain
Anna	*Anna Voss*	sister
Ant	*Ant Strachan*	North Harbour, All Black halfback (1992–93)
BBJ	*Brian Fitzpatrick*	father; former All Black (1951–54)
Bernie	*Bernie McCahill*	Auckland, All Black midfield back (1987–91)
Boro	*Kevin Boroevich*	King Country, Wellington, North Harbour, All Black prop (1983–88)
Bob Dwyer		Wallaby coach
Bronnie	*Bronwyn Fitzpatrick*	wife
Brother Richard Dunleavy		teacher, Sacred Heart College
Bryce Bevin		University team-mate
Buck	*Wayne Shelford*	North Harbour, All Black number 8 (1985–90)
Doc	*John Mayhew*	All Black doctor (1988–93)
Grant Dickson		University, Auckland team-mate
Drakey	*John Drake*	Auckland, All Black prop (1985–87)
Ernie	*Earle Kirton*	All Black selector (1988–94)
Fats	*Peter Fatialofa*	Auckland, Manu Samoa prop
Foxy	*Grant Fox*	Auckland, All Black first-five (1984–93)
Frybee	*Richard Fry*	University team-mate
Harty	*John Hart*	Auckland (1982–86); All Black coach (1987–91)
Hika	*Hika Reid*	Bay of Plenty, All Black hooker (1980–86)
Jeff Probyn		England prop
JK	*John Kirwan*	Auckland, All Black winger (1984–94)
John Allen		Scotland, Springbok hooker
JR	*Jamie Joseph*	Otago, All Black flanker (1992–94)
Julie	*Julie McDiarmid*	sister
Kevin Putt		Waikato, Natal halfback; All Black trialist
Kirky	*David Kirk*	Auckland, All Black halfback captain (1983–87)
Laurie	*Laurie Mains*	All Black coach (1992–94)
Louise Fitzpatrick		mother
Mark	*Mark Fitzpatrick*	brother
Mark Greatbatch		school friend
Neil Gray		All Black manager (1992–93)
Nick Farr-Jones		Wallaby half-back, captain
Pascal Ondarts		French prop
Peter FitzSimons		former Wallaby; journalist
Phil Kearns		Wallaby hooker
Pieter Muller		Springbok centre
Postie	*Craig Innes*	Auckland, All Black (1989–91)
Purvy	*Graham Purvis*	Waikato, All Black prop (1989–93)
Richard Becht		journalist, TVNZ
Rimu	*Arran Pene*	Otago, All Black number 8 (1992–93)
Rob	*Robin Brooke*	Auckland, All Black lock (1992–94)
Rocky Patterson		broadcaster
Sisso	*Paul Sissons*	Steinlager liaison
Stevie	*Steve McDowell*	Auckland, All Black prop (1985–92)
Stephen Jones		journalist, [London] *Sunday Times*
Thorbs	*Peter Thorburn*	All Black selector (1992–93)
Uli Schmidt		Springbok hooker

N.B. *dates in brackets are years between first and last All Black involvement*

BOOK I

Fall and Rise

Laurie would have lost faith in me long ago if he thought my views off-beam – the All Black coach seeks my immediate post-game reaction (here in a Super 10 game against Natal).

CHAPTER ONE

The End of the Golden Weather

"Getting old is a bitch." – Jimmy Connors

WHAT THE HELL AM I doing here?

As I ducked another gob of spit, this one aimed at my face, I asked myself this question yet again. Unfortunately, it wasn't the first time I'd done so in the past six weeks.

It was mid-July, 1991. The location: Buenos Aires, Argentina. The All Blacks were an hour away from kick-off in the second test against the Pumas – the last act of an over-long, unfortunate, ill-fated tour – and once more we found ourselves under attack from an angry, hostile, Latin crowd.

Since arrival we'd endured insults and jeers from the rugby "fans" of Argentina. Now, as we were walking from the team bus to the dressing room *before* the test, they started spitting.

Adults spat at our feet. Teenagers spat on our blazers. Even little kids were in on the act; they climbed up barriers separating the team from the crowd and as we walked below they spat down.

Welcome to rugby, Argentina-style. In over 20 years I'd never been so disenchanted with the game. The tour was a sign of what troubles lay ahead. Before the end of the year, my bad experiences would get far worse. In Buenos Aires it didn't seem possible.

Argentina is a difficult country to tour for many reasons. It's very poor, with a great contrast between the haves and have-nots. Slum areas are widespread, the worst I've seen. New Zealanders have no idea just how large the country is, how long it takes to get places. There's not much to do, not many diversions or much entertainment. You spend so much time on dreary bus trips or in second-rate hotels that you never fully relax. It drains you – I imagine even the best tours there must be pretty grim.

When your team's unhappy – and in 1991, that described us to a T – Argentina becomes a nightmare, the perfect breeding ground for disharmony and tension.

The tour was meant to be the first stage of our build-up to retain the World Cup. As an exercise in achieving an effective rugby style, uniting the team, and resolving any internal problems, Argentina was a disaster.

The rugby, with a couple of exceptions, was very average. It did nothing to help either our form or reputations. The crowds were consistently hostile; apart from the welcome-to-the-ground spit at Buenos Aires, at other times they threw bottles, oranges, even stones at us.

The games were a joke. Their players were off-side most of the time, stifling our backs. The refs let them do it, and there were always one or two gorillas in their teams looking to take your head off.

I was 28 years old, a veteran of over 40 tests for the All Blacks, a member of what everybody was calling the world's greatest team – but suddenly rugby wasn't fun any more.

It's all too easy to blame other people when things go wrong, instead of asking "what could I have done better?" The reality was that the All Blacks in 1991 were living on glory. And though it wasn't all his fault, Grizz Wyllie, our coach, the one who set the direction of the team, was struggling. There had been a few public incidents, followed by a few private ones, which had undercut his reputation with the players.

As a coach he seemed to have run out of fresh ideas. His team-talks were repetitive, his training sessions stale.

Lane Penn, the assistant coach in Argentina, was a good man to have around. He did what he could to help the team. He constantly spoke of the pride we must have to wear the All Black jersey, how we weren't performing to our full potential ... sentimental stuff.

As much as we respected Lane, however, he was always in Grizz's shadow – he didn't have the real power to bring about change.

That tour, everyone, including me, seemed out of sync. In Argentina, an All Black team which had done so much right for the past five years lost its way.

We had the bizarre situation of the All Black props being

bracketed for a test instead of being dropped. We had players sticking together in small groups, mixing only with those of the same age, same union or same outlook on life. We had constant talk coming from New Zealand that a new coach was needed.

Things came to a head in the coastal city of Mar del Plata.

CRAIG INNES

> 'Argentina was awful, everybody hated it. The young guys were all absolutely terrified of Grizz, and everyone was playing for themselves.
>
> The training was all the same. It was all routine, with no flair in it.'

JOHN KIRWAN

> 'Sean was a little bit of a fence-sitter, like I am. I'd rather keep the peace than create a fuss and Sean was the same. Within the team, we'd walk away from something rather than confront it.'

I was rooming with JK when he and Colt Crowley confronted the team's management one day. It was late in the tour. At that stage, as just a player, I was ignoring the off-field signs and trying to concentrate on the rugby. In the back of my mind I still believed we were the best team in the world, and sheer talent would carry us through to the World Cup.

JK wasn't prepared to risk it. He was pretty close to Colt, who'd been an All Black since 1985, so they got the management – Gary, Sturge and Grizz – together, and JK spoke from his heart. He had Grizz on about his coaching, Gary about his captaincy. He didn't hold back.

It was a brave thing for JK to do. He came back to our room and told me that Gary was furious, that he eye-balled him during the meeting. But JK told him he had to say what he felt for the good of the team. He's very staunch like that, and I respected him for his action.

Things were that serious. Both JK and Gary were good friends of mine and to see the situation reach this level was really sad. But it wasn't a personality thing between them – JK's feelings summed up what the team felt.

Everything that could go wrong was going wrong. I wished it was like the good old days again when we had the world at our feet. But life's not that simple. As an All Black you learn pretty quick that nothing precious comes easily.

JOHN KIRWAN

> 'The reality of that side was that there were two schools in that team, operating to two separate sets of standards. That's why I spoke out – I couldn't accept that. None of the senior guys like Fitzy or me were ever bawled out like the newer, younger ones were.

It was a major problem in the team. And once one edge falls off, the whole thing eventually tips over.'

I HAVE NO HESITATION in describing the 1987 All Blacks as a freak team. People often ask what made that side so good. The short answer: unbelievable natural ability. In my career I've never seen another team approach it.

Even now I'm not sure why things came together as sweetly as they did. I don't think anyone does. Destiny, perhaps. One minute everyone was in doom and gloom because of the All Blacks' form in 1986. Then, almost out of the blue, we had the greatest rugby team side around. John Gallagher, who'd been a centre the year before, was now our answer at fullback. Michael Jones was plucked from nowhere; AJ came back from oblivion to play inspired rugby. After quietly doing his business for years, Drakey turned into the world's number one prop and Foxy kicked everything in sight . . . we were a team with perfect balance. There wasn't a weakness anywhere.

Rugby players aren't shrinking violets, but in 1987 everyone suppressed their egos. We were happy. Cavalier feuds were forgotten; players competing for the same position wished the other guy good luck, and meant it. There was no back-stabbing or player politics; it was a unique situation.

And we were driven by a hunger for success. The more victories, the deeper the pride in our achievements. No one wanted it to end. Winning was like a drug.

I'll never forget the day we drew against Australia in 1988 – the one blot on our record in 50 games. This was a calamity; you'd have thought we lost by 30 points. Personally, I was devastated. I probably had only a couple of bad throw-ins that day but I thought my performance was utterly hopeless. The other guys felt the same way about their games. Collectively we were shattered. We considered ourselves failures.

The team session that night was so tense. There was almost a stand-up fight between a couple of the guys. Everyone was on edge. John Hart was over there, commentating for TV, and I remember telling him later that none of us deserved to be All Blacks any more.

Every player in that side was superb at what they did. *Every* player. That's why I tried so hard to get John Drake to reconsider his decision to retire in 1988 – I didn't think we could survive without him.

". . . [they] set about restoring New Zealand's rugby fortunes by adopting very simple but precise methods. Under their tutelage the All Black game became quicker, more determined, more spirited. Greater levels of fitness, intelligence and motivation were

sought. Pressure was applied to opposing teams who were knocked off balance."

– A description of the 1977 All Blacks, *The Geriatrics*

We were very successful – but we weren't supermen. Nothing's totally new in rugby and we didn't discover any magic formula for greatness. We just tapped into this country's rich rugby heritage, had players of great athletic ability and kept on working hard. All the time. There was one simple reason we were so consistently successful: we practised really high standards. Everyone had immense personal pride. Foxy, for instance, would turn up at training an hour before the rest of us just to work on his kicking.

We knew when to have fun, and when to raise a sweat. I remember when we played Wales during the World Cup in Brisbane. A friend of mine lived there, a bit of a wild man. On the Wednesday night my mate took Gary Whetton, Murray Pierce, John Drake, Steve McDowell and myself out for a few quiet beers. The plan: a few rounds and then we'd go. But the barman said, "Next one's on the house", and this carried on a bit more . . . and a bit more . . .

The next day at training we were so hungover. Crook as anything. But we still trained as hard as ever. Harder, probably. Although we felt dreadful we pushed ourselves that extra step because we were determined not to let the team down.

And on Sunday we gave Wales a good old-fashioned walloping.

BUCK SHELFORD

'The rest of the world was still preoccupied with set-piece rugby. But we played a very basic style: in a nutshell we kept people on their feet instead of the ground.

Everything was built around support play. You had to be fit – fitter than you'd ever been – and have the ball skills.

That was it.'

No single person deserves the credit for inspiring the golden weather era of All Black rugby in the late 1980s. The praise should be spread among the 1987 World Cup management.

Andy Dalton is one who's never quite got the public recognition that he deserved. Can you imagine how disappointed he was when injury cost him a place in the World Cup? But he never showed it to us during the tournament. His almost-fatherly manner, his astute off-field advice was brilliant. I'm surprised he hasn't gone on further as a coach. He knows so much about the game, and what makes people tick – the most important aspects an All Black coach needs.

BJ Lochore, the boss in '87, inspires some of my fondest rugby memories. But it's his motivational skills, his speaking from the heart, which sticks out more than his coaching ability. My first test, for instance, against France in 1986, almost reduced me to tears. A year later, before the World Cup final, his words were immensely powerful.

The most important individuals, tactically, were BJ's "assistants", Alex Wyllie and John Hart. They did brilliant jobs. Cleverly, they looked after the Canterbury and Auckland guys they knew so well. On test day, Harty would pop in to say a few words, check your motivation, add a bit here or there . . . Grizz was doing the same thing with his players. It wasn't parochial, it made sense. Thanks to Harty's drills, the backs were so slick. And Grizz's work with the forwards was inspired.

After we won both the World and Bledisloe Cups in 1987 the All Blacks never looked back. A pattern was established, everyone knew exactly what they had to do. That was the secret of our success.

BOB DWYER

> 'In the first international against New Zealand, in 1990, Peter FitzSimons made his test debut for us. In our dressing room afterwards he said, 'I don't think the All Blacks are such bad blokes. In every ruck or maul at least four or five of their blokes kept telling me, 'Well done, Fitzy, keep it up Fitzy, nice tackle Fitzy . . . '
>
> We thought he was having us on, but he's saying this straight-faced. Then one of the guys pipes up: 'You dumb bastard, Fitzy. They were talking about Sean Fitzpatrick.''

Jim Blair's role in getting us super-fit has been discussed a lot. While Jim's fitness techniques were great, he was lucky to have such a talented group of players to work with. It was his finest hour – but everything came naturally to us. And we trained hard.

Then there was Harty's influence. Jim did well for Auckland by working closely with Harty. Hart would ask Blair for a drill that developed, say, low body position. Jim would come up with an answer and then Harty would oversee it during practice. In recent years Jim has had to devise and run his own grids with Auckland. It's not as effective. He's a fitness guru, not a rugby coach. I don't think it's a coincidence that Jim's found it more difficult to relate to other coaches since working with John Hart.

It's a bit of a myth how fit we were. It's too often overlooked that we were basically a young team. I was in my early twenties, I was building for a living, I was very healthy. Michael Jones, JK, Foxy, Kipper – they were very young too. Most of the side were in their physical prime. Compared to the training I've experienced in recent years, the 1987 side wasn't that fit, actually. We were fitter than the opposition: that's what mattered. We always knew we'd outlast anyone in the final 20 minutes of a game.

Today, aged 31, I'm probably 10 per cent fitter than in 1987. I can finish a game fresher, I'm probably stronger too. But fitness techniques are a lot more sophisticated than in 1987.

JOHN KIRWAN

> ‘Player for player we weren't as good as the All Blacks are now. But as a team we were better. We gutsed a lot of our success, we hung in there all the time. And in a tight situation, you need gutsers every time.’

The talent. The strategy. Superior fitness. Essentials for any great team. But they count for nothing if you don't have the character to call on when you're under pressure. And no matter how dominant you get, you still feel the pressure.

I think we were a brave team. Physically and mentally. We didn't panic if things went wrong.

Any time it seemed we could be in any danger of losing – like against France in 1989, when they scored 17 points in 15 minutes – we turned up another gear to win. Our critics later said we took it a bit easy on them, but give credit to the French. Most other teams wouldn't have kept them out. We did because everyone believed totally in themselves, and each other. We never doubted we would win. That made us great: our unshakeable faith.

That belief was our downfall in 1991. We hadn't done enough hard work to warrant us having such faith.

In 1989 everyone was still training as hard as they could. I really believed if I slackened off Warren Gatland would get my place, so I played out of my skin. Call it self-motivation, whatever. It's really a matter of setting your own standards and not falling short.

Our confidence had nothing to do with ego. It was fully deserved. In tense situations, with the crowd on the edge of their seats, the team stayed calm. We knew we'd pulled big games out of the bag before, so we could do it again. That's the importance of past successes. It's proof that you can come through pressure situations. It's a two-way deal. The All Blacks drew confidence from our record. The opposition were demoralised by it. Even if they were leading, or the momentum was with them, you sensed their doubts. You knew they were thinking, 'When will they come back into the game?' Because the All Blacks always came back.

So much has been said about the 1987-1989 era it's easy to get carried away with superlatives and praise. But even as someone who was right there, right in the middle of it, I realised the team was special.

I was happy with my form during these years. I believe I deserved to be there. I never took my place for granted though. Being an All Black mattered too much to assume anything.

> *"[On the 1990 tour of France] the number of players from the Auckland union increased to 14, the greatest number of players from any union to be included in a New Zealand team . . . the percentage of 45 per cent is also the highest."* – 1991 *New Zealand Rugby Almanack*

THE BASIS OF THE All Blacks' success was simple: it carried on the approach Auckland used for its domestic success. I'm not being parochial in saying this – it's a fact. There was nothing in the All Blacks' methods that didn't have some connection with Auckland. Support play, fitness, attitude to training – you name it, Auckland had done it first. The individual skills of a guy from another team, like Wellington's John Gallagher, only added more options to the dozens that existed. Foxy could have carried a notepad with him in games, he had so many choices already available.

The benefit to the All Blacks of having a strong Auckland team at its core was obvious. Playing for Auckland in big games like the Ranfurly Shield or First Division nail-biters taught us how to cope with pressure, about dominating teams, about breaking them. When we pulled on an All Black jersey we were already match-hardened to big-time rugby.

For me, Auckland's glory days were the three seasons between 1986 and 1988. After that the decline set in, although that wasn't obvious in 1990.

At our peak, we loved beating teams by as many points as we could. Sometimes we'd size up the opposition and say, "Right, today's going to be perfect. We're going to score 80 points." And if we didn't score at least 40 points in the first half we were really disappointed.

Our goals were as specific as that: 40 points each half. If we fell behind our target we'd just crank it up a gear. I remember times when Auckland was up by 50 or 60 points and the guys sprinted back to halfway with a minute to go saying, "We've *got* to score another try, we have to get there." It was a superb attitude. And it rubbed off onto the All Blacks.

Even as a player in '86 and '87 I'd look around the Auckland dressing room and think, 'This *is* special, I am damn lucky to be here.'

KEVIN BOROEVICH

> 'Basically, Auckland's players were fitter mentally and physically than the rest of us. Their skill factor was higher because they were fitter. As a result, winning became a habit for them, they were on a roll. They never believed they could lose. In guys like Fitzy they had a sophisticated player who was also physically very hard.'

John Hart built Auckland. But when Maurice Trapp and Beegee Williams took over we were more successful than ever. That first season we won every game, we set a new record for Shield defences, there were always heaps of All Blacks in the side.

None of us understood the consequences then, but our success weakened Maurice and Beegee's hold over the team.

If you put yourself in their shoes it must have been hard for Trapp and Williams. How do you follow an act like Harty? They were very laid-back coaches, believers in self-motivation for players. They were completely the opposite to Hart, who had to control everything. And they were good for a while. In 1987 it was very relaxing to go along to training and not be yelled at . . . to be asked for input instead of being told what to do.

But how do you control grown men who have been successful for so long? Eventually, you can't.

In training the senior players' influence grew stronger and stronger. Everyone seemed quite happy about it.

ROCKY PATTERSON

> ‘On radio I made a couple of comments about the coaches' style.
>
> Beegee said to me, 'Rocky, I think you're being unfair to Maurice and me. You don't understand what we're trying to do. When you take over a successful team like we did you can only go down.
>
> 'We have a different philosophy to John Hart. We want the team to have a big part in the decision-making.' ’

The coaches would say, “Right, away you go, guys. Gary, you take the forwards, Foxy you take the backs”. Maurice and Beegee then sat back and watched.

They provided motivation, the team talk before the game and a managerial roll.

Gary's ability to sum up the necessary tactics, or what needed to be done, was impressive. He'd take two or three minutes to get his point across.

> *“It is so hard to get yourself up the next year when you have already achieved your goal. Once that feeling of exhilaration and the realisation that you have actually done it has passed, there is a certain void afterwards.”*
>
> – Michael O'Connor

SELF-MOTIVATION HAS ITS drawbacks.

Around 1990 I discovered after, say, 60 minutes of a game and we're up by 30-40 points, that I'd start to switch off. It wasn't a deliberate thing . . . but I knew it was happening. So did a lot of the other guys, the experienced ones like Foxy and JK and Gary.

We thought we had it under control, that we wouldn't slacken off when playing for the All Blacks.

But bad habits are bad habits. Eventually, with most of the team playing for the All Blacks as well, they became part of the way we played the game. And we probably became a bit withdrawn because we got so much criticism. People expected so much. You can't turn in world-class efforts every week, it isn't mentally possible. Top players aren't machines.

We were often compared to the great Auckland team of 1984. A big thing was made of how the Eden Park crowd would drift towards the opposite end of the ground at half-time to watch the boys run in some more tries.

But in 1984 Auckland was young, fresh, highly motivated. Neither they nor the All Blacks yet totally dominated the game. Everything about rugby was exciting.

In 1990 our attitude at playing a mediocre team was, "Here we go again." We'd still say, "We've got to win by 30 points," but it was hollow. We'd get to 20 points and subconsciously the team would think, "We've had enough of this. This is boring."

We had stacks of confidence. One year, when we played Waikato, we had special T-shirts made: "Waikato milked and creamed." They were handed out to the team straight after the match. We'd had them printed days earlier – the idea we might lose hadn't even been discussed.

PETER THORBURN

> 'I was coach of North Harbour at the time and I was very aware of Auckland's dominance. I think Auckland were the catalyst to drag New Zealand rugby up in the early '80s but also, by becoming so predictable, they dragged it down.
>
> If anyone had them on about their style their argument was 'Just look at our results'.'

Foxy was in charge of Auckland's backs, the one responsible for calling the shots. As a tactician he was excellent; his rugby brain is superb. As a player he expects more than most. I think the twin roles of playing and coaching got to him at times. Brett Iti was one who found his standards difficult.

I know it hurt Foxy when Brett went to league and made a few cracks at him. Foxy had put a lot of time in with Brett, working on his game, and I think he helped make him a better player.

Foxy admits he's a perfectionist, and diplomacy wasn't always his number one priority. But he used the highest standards on himself.

On Friday nights he'd wash his bootlaces and leave them to dry. He'd roll them up neatly, then he'd clean his boots. They were spotless.

Then he'd spend ages talking over defence tactics with the loosies. A lot of it wasn't new but he wanted nothing overlooked. Attention to detail was the key. In every game.

It's the nature of the man. Nothing is ever done half-hearted. Playing golf with him is an adventure. Every putt is approached like he's taking that last-minute penalty against the Lions. If he's having a bad day . . . well, he probably won't finish the round. He'll throw his clubs in his bag because he's so angry at himself and pack up and go early.

A person with such standards isn't going to look calmly away when other people aren't trying. Someone who insists that a practice ball be pumped to exactly the right air pressure isn't going to say nothing when a player keeps passing left when the call is right.

"For the junior players . . . of which I was one, all was not always well. There existed a very distinct division in the team between the older, experienced group of players . . . and the younger, completely inexperienced, and by consequence more fragile group."

– Chris Laidlaw, *Mud in your Eye*

WHEN A NEWCOMER MADE the Auckland team he would discover a world where, for many of the guys, their lives were totally built around rugby.

Harty had started this tradition where the mums and dads of the players were heavily involved on the social side. It carried on with Maurice and Beegee too. Initially it was a great idea, but it got to the stage where every Saturday night we used to have a dinner for the whole team and their families at Eden Park. And if you didn't go there was an unspoken but subtle pressure: "Why aren't *you* going? Aren't you part of this team?" It got past the point of being fun.

Eventually I said to Gary, "Mate, we can't have these dinners every Saturday night. People have other things to do, other people to see . . . "

All the young guys, the 19- and 20-year-olds, just wanted to get to the pub and meet girls. They were bored stiff. Bronnie and I didn't want to be there every Saturday night either. It's always been important for me to spend as much time as I can with people who aren't involved with rugby.

PETER FATIALOFA

'I believe anyone could have coached that Auckland side after Harty left. Guys like Fitzy and Foxy and Geedub and them got to a level where probably, from my point of view, they weren't approachable. They'd been together for so long that they probably had their own hardness about themselves. There was about six or seven of them. Geedub was always speaking. Fitzy was in the background, he wouldn't say much.

They probably got too carried away with running the team to realise that not even they are bigger than rugby.'

CRAIG INNES

'Sean was one of the first guys to make me feel relaxed in the Auckland team. One Sacred Heart old boy to another. There weren't many other of the older guys like him.

Auckland had this seniority thing where you had to work your way up the ladder. I was only 18 or so, still pretty young, so

I knew to keep my place. Inga found it harder than me. His natural personality is to do a fair bit of yapping but after a few games and a few looks from the older guys he quietened down . . .'

I never thought the seniority thing was a big issue in the Auckland team. However, I know some players did.

The young guys in particular didn't always know how to relate to Gary's captaincy style. Gary was moody – he would often fire off a comment if he wasn't happy with someone. It didn't bother me, I'd give back as good as I got. He was a friend, I knew he was motivated by making the team as efficient as it could be.

Gary was influenced by a long line of strong personalities, individuals not afraid to say what they thought – people like Haden and Hart.

He believed it was up to a newcomer to leave their mark. If they couldn't . . . well, he wasn't going to hold their hand, no matter how young they were. It's a competitive attitude. Gary believed rugby teams are built on respect, and respect must be earned by the quality of your rugby.

Not every youngster was shy. Take Matthew Ridge. From the first minute he was in the squad Ridgey acted like the team was picked just for him.

I used to give him a friendly thump or two at training because he was a smart little bugger. He loved it, he'd always bounce back up and try and have a go at me. "Come on Fitzy, come on you big ugly hooker, is that the best you can do . . . "

I've done a few promotions with Ridgey since and he's still as cocky as ever. But his loss to rugby was huge – especially off-field. He was good for the other young guys. His attitude was simple: he wouldn't take anything from us oldies, he gave back anything he got with interest.

BUCK SHELFORD

'The player power of the Auckland team rubbed off onto the All Blacks. It was inevitable. Sean was tied up in the Aucklanders thing but he wasn't one of the main ones. Gary Whetton, Grant Fox, Alan Whetton called the shots . . .

Player power in Auckland extended to even the wives. Everyone was used to getting everything they wanted.

None of this would have mattered, but by 1990 politics had taken over from the rugby, unlike the team of 1987 who were driven by only their on-field performance.

The politics took lots of different forms but it was most noticeable in the fitness. Players were not putting in the graft. The basic attitude at training was 'a short time's a good time' and instead of doing 10 scrums we'd only do five . . . '

STEVE McDOWELL

'The Auckland team's always been political, always had rifts. Some people can handle it, some can't. I could, so it didn't bother me.'

CHAPTER TWO

Passing the Buck

"You arrive at the top due to drive and ambition; it's very hard to maintain that drive and ambition when you've made it."
– Ian Botham

WHEN I LOOK BACK on both the All Black and Auckland teams of 1990, I realise we did get too big for our boots. I see it more clearly in hindsight – there are signs of what we did echoed in many young players today. You can see them believing their own publicity. Pick up a paper or a magazine and they'll probably be featured in it – and they're only at the start of their careers. They're already enjoying the perks rugby brings them . . . the danger is obvious: they're young so they forget there's no such thing as a free lunch.

There's one guy in the Auckland team, *very* talented, a big future ahead of him. But before one of the Super 10 games this year he arrived late for a Friday night team meeting. He said he got stuck in the motorway traffic – he'd been at a promotion.

I asked him what he was doing at a promotion instead of concentrating on his preparation for a game that the All Black selectors were attending. He didn't have a satisfactory answer. Hopefully, he realised his priorities were wrong. It's not totally his fault, either. No one's ever sat him down and told him that you only get the promotions and free cars if you produce the results on the field.

That's what the All Blacks of 1990 forgot. But in our defence we'd produced the results for so long that it was almost inevitable we'd get complacent.

The year before the World Cup we basically trained and lived exactly the same for the All Blacks as we did for Auckland. There wasn't enough variety in our approach. Even an outsider, like Ian Jones, slipped into the same mode. We knew we'd slipped down a cog or two in standards but even then no one seemed to be in our league.

Probably there should have been more changes in the side. There was only one significant one: the dropping of Buck.

BUCK SHELFORD

> ‘By 1990 the pace of our game was definitely starting to wane. Four or five years under the same coaching regime and you start to hear the same things and do the same things. You lack motivation . . .
>
> I thought I played pretty good football before I was dropped but they said I wasn't doing the work. I looked at the tight five: Gary, Jonesy, Fitzy, Stevie, Loey. *Everyone* wanted to run with the ball instead of what they were there to do – the basics.
>
> Players were less and less motivated. The World Cup wasn't on our minds at all – it was well over a year away, it didn't feature in our thinking.’

Buck's fall sent shock waves through the All Blacks. It wasn't entirely unexpected – there had been a lot of talk doing the rounds – but once it actually happened we were stunned at the impact. We withdrew into our shell as a result.

In his prime, which I consider was 1988–89, Buck was superb. On the tours of Australia and the UK he played great rugby. He wasn't a particularly good speaker off the field but he had such a mana about him it didn't matter.

Simon Poidevin spoke at the launch of Buck's book, which happened after he was dropped, and he couldn't believe Buck wasn't in the All Blacks any more.

The Aussies feared Buck, he said. He wasn't a dirty player but he was so aggressive. How could you drop a player like him?

Game after game I saw Buck spare his body nothing. He soaked up punishment. His back was scarred from lying on the ball during games. He commanded total respect from everybody.

Buck was fair, but hard. If he saw someone doing something wrong he'd warn them. Once. In 1989 against Newport he thumped this Welsh lock. That night at the team dinner I was sitting beside the Welshman – who now sported this big gap in his mouth from a few missing teeth. "I've got no complaints," the guy said, "he did warn me."

Buck was a great trainer. And you could see why the public admired him: here was this good-looking, strong, fine-featured guy who commanded attention by his presence.

The style the public loved so much wasn't so evident with the All Blacks, however. He never spoke to us like he did North Harbour. That famous TV scene of him yelling and shouting at the North Harbour team to produce more effort never occurred with the All Blacks.

In that respect he was like Grizz; they both had this tough-guy image in the public eye, but with the All Blacks it never appeared. It didn't have to; he led by example, in every game, so we naturally followed.

With hindsight, the dropping of Buck coincided with the wheels falling off the All Blacks. But the absence of Buck wasn't the reason for the team's subsequent failure.

> *"Midway between the first and second World Cups it has to be said that everything in the New Zealand garden is rosy."* – Editorial, 1989 *New Zealand Rugby Annual*

THE NEW ALL BLACK captain, Gary Whetton, was completely different to Buck. There was nothing really new in what he said after taking over – Gary had always offered a lot at team talks.

Because he was taking over from a legend – and he knew it as well as anyone – I think Gary found the role difficult. He knew the public never accepted him like they did Buck. It probably hurt him that all those years of service he'd given to New Zealand rugby weren't acknowledged by people.

I think this was a huge shame – for him, and New Zealand rugby. Gary was a superb, underrated lock. One of the greats. Although he didn't seem a hard, rugged forward in, say, the Buck mould, he certainly knew how to look after himself. And he was incredibly athletic, at his peak the best number two line-out jumper in the world.

Gary and I traced our friendship back to 1984. He spent a bit of extra time with me and encouraged me when I seemed to be Auckland's permanent reserve. "Stick with it, Fitzy," he told me over and over again. "Your time will come."

I believe Gary's captaincy was misunderstood, both from within and outside the team. He would be the first to admit he was from the old school of doing things. I don't think the younger guys, for instance, got close to him.

He was extremely articulate, but he was also quite shy.

GRANT FOX

> 'John Sturgeon and Gary Whetton both put the team first, to the detriment of how it appeared to outsiders.
>
> Gary *cared*. Sure, he could be moody. You could walk past him in the corridor and he might not say 'hi' because he was preoccupied with some matter. But that was him. I accepted that. He wasn't always good at externals . . . but he cared passionately about the All Blacks.'

Alex Wyllie and John Hart were opposite men on the same side. They worked well together at the first World Cup – wonderfully so. But that was their heyday as a team.

When John Hart took the All Blacks to Japan later that year most of us assumed he'd be coach the following season. When Grizz got the job instead I was surprised, like most players. But no one was too upset. No one ever thought, 'Oh no, we're in trouble now.' Grizz was respected.

For a start, he had a good track record as Canterbury's coach. He'd also inherited a great All Black team. And he soon showed the All Blacks that as a coach he was fair, honest in his dealings with players, and had seen everything on a rugby field.

As a bloke, especially in public, Grizz was pretty gruff. He called a spade a spade every time. Despite his image, if you got him one to one, he was really shy. I doubt in the five years I knew him we ever sat down and had a real heart to heart – no pun intended. You'd share a beer with him, swap a few words, but nothing intimate.

Socially, especially around 1990, Grizz let a few things slip. He was under pressure to keep producing results, and had one or two more big nights than he probably should have. That side of his nature was always there, but he was lucky to have a good All Black manager in John Sturgeon to cover for him.

Sturge was the peacemaker. He didn't drink whereas Grizz did, but they both had a lot in common. That's why Sturgeon never wanted to be John Hart's manager. Harty is a one-man band, he does everything himself.

He was the ideal foil for Grizz. He wouldn't hesitate to say, "Shut up you grizzly, grey-headed old bugger" if Grizz was in a bad mood.

We found their routine hilarious. At team meetings Sturge would ask the guys to speak. "Gary, have you got anything to say?"; "Doc, have you?"; "Foxy?" . . . Finally, he'd turn to Grizz and say, "Well what about you, you grizzly old bugger?" Everyone would just crack up laughing. Then Grizz would throw Sturge back a quick one-liner and we'd laugh again . . .

PETER THORBURN

> 'When dealing with top players, man management is much more important than having the best coaching skills.'

Like every player, I'd heard about Grizz's Hitler-style training methods with Canterbury. But as All Blacks we never had an old-fashioned bust-your-guts session. Not one. We never had to run round the paddock a thousand times just to prove how tough we were. Perhaps we should have, because gradually we lost any fear of him. He wasn't the bad old Grizz we were brought up to believe in.

Admittedly, a couple of times he tried to push us, but we successfully stopped him. The older players had too much influence over him, he couldn't overrule them.

He did have a go at some players – the new guys, the young ones, and the Canterbury players whom he knew. He'd also have a go at Loey, but that didn't count because they were family. For guys like me, from Auckland, there was never any abuse.

Liaison guys copped it from Grizz. He was always very aggressive with them. And he had a short temper if they didn't do what he wanted. In Wales, when our dressing room door was locked, instead of waiting for the key he just barged it off its hinges.

Physically, you wouldn't want to tangle with him. He was really powerful. His finger jabs were like getting poked with a truncheon. If you ever got a whack on the arm or across the back from Grizz – his way of saying "gidday" – your whole body shook. He did it to everyone, big or small; size didn't come into things. That was his way.

In 1990, when the selectors dropped Buck and the All Blacks lost three games, I think the strains of the job really got to Grizz. That was the year the Rugby Union wanted Grizz to take an assistant coach to France and he refused. As players, we knew what the Union wanted and I suppose it affected the way we responded to Grizz.

Slowly, our doubts set in about Grizz. At first it was nothing major – but then if you're a coach, and your team starts drifting away from you . . . well, you've got to stop it or it spreads. But Grizz did nothing.

What he should have done, especially after JK and Colt spoke to him in Argentina, was what Laurie Mains has done a couple of times: confront the team. For example, the day after we lost against England last year, Laurie spoke to the guys about putting Mike Brewer in the reserves. He told them he'd felt a lot of tension and undercurrents in the squad since making that decision, and he wouldn't stand for it. What was it all about, he wanted to know?

Pervy spoke up, then Liam Barry. Finally, Laurie said his piece. I'm not saying everyone agreed but at least they understood and were in the picture. It cleared the air.

In 1990, with all the rumours flying around about "Harty for coach" and everything, Grizz never once addressed the issue. And when our form dropped off, he let things slide.

I don't know why. Maybe he was nervous. Maybe, because the test team was still successful, he thought, 'Why should I change?'

After all, we cleaned up France in both tests – it's the old story: if it ain't broke, why fix it?

Maybe we were just as guilty in our thinking as Grizz. The senior players all agreed losing hadn't made us a bad team, it just exposed our lack of depth. As long as the top 15 stayed injury-free, in form and hungry, we were certain we were still the best in the world.

There was one problem with this approach: key guys like Foxy did get hurt, not everyone's form remained consistent, and we certainly lost the most important thing which had driven us for so many years: our hunger.

> *". . . Hart laughs at the stories he's heard of imagined differences between the two and how they couldn't get on."*
> *"Alleged personality clashes between Hart and Wyllie were largely from the imaginations of outsiders, too."*
> *". . . perhaps the greatest disagreement . . . between Hart and Wyllie was over their choice of food."*
>
> – Ron Palenski, from the same article, 1991 *New Zealand Rugby Annual*

A FEW MONTHS OUT from the 1991 World Cup, we lost to Australia in Sydney. This was probably Grizz's last chance to keep full control of the team, because now Harty was called back to "help out".

Before the team assembled, Harty got me into his office for a chat. He told me he'd already spoken with JK and Gary and Foxy and now he wanted my input. We talked about what the team needed to do to improve. I was very careful what I said. I wasn't going to bag Grizz. Harty asked me how the team was going and I told him the truth: "Not that great." By now I was really worried about my, and the team's, form. The build-up for Sydney had been ideal, superb. And still we'd lost. The rock-solid confidence we'd lived on for so long was shaken after our indifferent tour of Argentina and now this defeat.

I had mixed feelings about Harty's return. Personally, he was good for my confidence: he knew how to build me up again when I had some doubts. But I couldn't see him and Grizz operating smoothly. Though Grizz was nowhere near the coach he had been in 1988 and 1989, it didn't require a genius to see that he and Hart could never work together. They were total opposites.

I think Hart's a great motivator and a great coach, but his weakness is that he plays too many people off against each other. Through sheer strength of personality he manipulates players. At times this approach creates insecurity and disharmony among the team. No doubt Hart rationalises his methods by saying that the end justifies the means but they certainly create friction. Having said that, he probably brings out the best in most players and certainly achieves results.

Harty is political. He manipulates people very cleverly. He'll admit this – it's his way of ensuring no one gets complacent. It's effective, but not a comfortable experience. When I was playing for Auckland I know Abo felt the same way because we'd discuss it. Harty would say something to Abo and then he'd say something else to me. We'd find out there were two different versions by comparing stories.

I played only 13 games for Auckland in Harty's period of coaching, nine of which came in his last season.

But he was the best Auckland coach I've known. He knew how to get the most out of each player, what to say and what not to. He is a complex man – there isn't just one John Hart – but for me, like most of the team, Harty seemed to press the right buttons.

In 1991, I hoped – we all hoped – he'd do it again.

BUCK SHELFORD

> 'The overriding thing of John Hart is his ego. He wants to be number one, to put his successes on his CV. It's his corporate culture mentality – the survival of the fittest.
>
> It's why he says one thing to one, a different thing to another. He does it to keep producing the best.
>
> But it's ego too. He always wanted to promote 'his' guys – JK, Kirk. Jason Hewett was another. If they didn't measure up – well, you didn't hear much of them after that.'

Even with Harty's input for the second test, we still shouldn't have won. The skids were on, we were on a downhill slide, but we dug deep and gutsed out victory.

Grizz seemed shell-shocked by Harty's return. Joe Stanley joined the team late as a reserve and couldn't believe how much Harty was saying. Basically Grizz was already in the shadows and Harty was the number one coach in all but name.

It was like Japan in 1987 again. Then Hart was certain he had the inside running for All Black coach. That tour Grizz was basically a spare-parts man. Harty ran everything. His methods weren't to everyone's liking. He was hard on Loey, for instance, and Richard wasn't happy about it. He smouldered away, angry at his treatment.

Richard's a larger-than-life personality, a real character. The way he talks now is the way he talked when he first got into the team. People then said, "Who is this guy?" The more we got to know him, the more we understood it was just his way. Loey being Loey.

But in Japan Hart was mean to him. He told Richard his handling skills were terrible, and as if to prove it at training he'd kick the ball 100 miles in the air and go, "Come on, Richard. Catch the ball." And of course Loey would drop it – with everyone watching.

We retained the Bledisloe Cup with victory in Auckland but, like in Sydney, I was very disappointed in my performances. I was doing just enough, but you can't kid yourself. Every player knows when he's cutting corners or going through the motions, and that was certainly true with me.

Against Australia I'd stand at the front of the line-out and watch as Nick Farr-Jones got a bad ball tapped back to him and still have time to fetch and clear it. In the good old days I would have nailed him.

BUCK SHELFORD

> 'With Auckland, Fitzy could hang off all the time. He was always coming in last to rucks and mauls off the second and third phase. In the All Blacks he was more in the thick of it, he had to push and do the hard work more.'

Everyone slackened off. It was contagious. We took it for granted that All Blacks didn't have to do that extra bit, we didn't have to run that extra mile or didn't have to train every day. We'd take a day off, or take two days off and justify it with a weak excuse.

In 1991, the Aussies were the better team because of their mental approach, in particular their hardness and will to win. They didn't have the better players, but they wanted to beat us more than we wanted to beat them, basically. That's what it came down to.

I'd lost enthusiasm. It had been a full, stressful year, and there was still the World Cup to go. I said to my brother Mark one morning, "This is hopeless. What am I doing here?"

And he said, "Just get out of it. If you're not enjoying it any more, get out."

> *"With five minutes to go we could sense we'd got them. I can't remember Sean's reaction specifically, it was more a team thing. Maybe it was something on their faces, a look which said, 'We can't win this . . .' "*
>
> – Phil Kearns

LOSING THE WORLD CUP is the biggest disappointment of my career. The reasons for our failure have been analysed and dissected pretty thoroughly now, and hopefully New Zealand rugby has learned from the experience.

But failure is a bitter teacher. Even now, it rankles the way we lost. So, with the advantage of hindsight, what should the All Blacks have done differently in 1991?

Our lack of top fitness should have been discovered earlier. We lacked a comprehensive training programme like we have now under Laurie. In our build-up to the Cup most individuals weren't putting in enough hard work, but they were getting away with it. We definitely weren't as fit as we should have been.

Possibly we were distracted by the commercial opportunities that the new IRB regulations allowed. It's simplistic to blame our decline entirely on this, but it was a factor.

The pursuit of money slowly eats away at the team. It's very gradual; you don't even realise you've become too busy doing that extra function instead of going for that run you promised yourself. All that great food and drink that's laid on, too . . . you tell yourself it doesn't hurt to have a couple of beers, that little snack . . .

Being in demand affected our attitude. We got a bit superior. I always tried to give my best, that's what I was paid for.

But some of the guys had the approach at functions, "How long to go before we're out of here?" There's no point in offending somebody. You might make 'x' dollars out of the day, but you've lost goodwill.

It's such short-sighted thinking; as soon as you stop being an All Black, who wants to know you? As one sponsor told me, "If you're not in the All Blacks, you're not worth having."

People said the All Blacks were arrogant in 1991. I think there's some truth to that claim, but it's probably been exaggerated. I'm sure if we'd won the World Cup, for instance, no one would have said boo about our standards. There were instances of unacceptable behaviour. John Hart refers to some in his book. It's fair to say success went to our heads, we didn't do the little things, the PR touches, all that well. If someone asked for an autograph we'd snap, "Who's this for?" instead of saying, "Sure, no problem, who can I make it out to?"

The coaching situation should definitely have been settled with one person clearly in charge. Whoever was coach needed to feel secure. Grizz had run his course by the end of 1989, but no one knew it then. If he'd been replaced at the end of 1989 there would have been an uproar. The players wouldn't have been happy, either.

By the time everyone realised Grizz had run out of gas it was too late.

At the World Cup, he and Harty played out a private game in public. At team meetings they'd make a joke out of deferring to the other one – "Do you want to speak? Is it my turn today?" – but they couldn't hide their real feelings. In press conferences they'd contradict each other.

The tension between them unsettled the team. And because we weren't playing well in the early games, and the media was getting stuck into us, we weren't happy. No wonder we weren't a PR hit at the World Cup; the contrast with four years earlier couldn't have been more noticeable.

CRAIG INNES

'In training there was always a lot of talk from Harty about we must do this, do that. But when it got on to the field we always went back to the safest options. It got to the stage where you wouldn't want to pass. Everyone was very conscious of what might happen if your pass *didn't* come off . . . You felt like robots.

It was a confidence thing. I think the guys just lost confidence in themselves. People asked me later, 'Why didn't the backs throw long passes?' The only way you can do things like that is if you have confidence.'

PETER THORBURN

'The All Blacks trained against North Harbour a couple of times [before they left] and it was noticeable they were getting slower and slower.

As a side gets older, and the decision-makers get older, the play gets tighter. Tight rugby means you don't have to go such long distances to the breakdown.

It happens to every team, in every era. It's subconscious. I know; I played till I was 37, I did it myself.'

JEFF PROBYN

'In our squad sessions before the tournament we talked and talked about the All Blacks. It's all we ever talked about. We were told if we wanted to be successful we had to emulate every aspect of their lives: to eat, think, train, be a New Zealander. We watched videos on them. We tried to train and play like them.

But we imagined they were better than they were. It wasn't until well through that opening World Cup game that we suddenly discovered they had two arms and two legs.

After that game their supermen image was broken.'

When things go wrong, New Zealand's rugby public demands scapegoats. After our defeat at Dublin, they wanted answers. The reason we lost was because we never really found consistent form at any time in the tournament – or when we played to our capability it was only in bursts.

The semifinal against Australia was over by half-time. They led 13-0. After that they just shut up shop and defended, which they did very well.

I know there's a lot of buck-passing, and laying of blame on individuals' performances that day. This overlooks the main issue: the whole team was not playing to its potential.

I can still picture the look of elation that spread across Phil Kearns' and Tony Daly's faces when the final whistle went, their sheer joy, the ecstatic yell they gave, "yeeehaaaaaaaaaaaa . . ."

I felt numb. I walked off the field by instinct. Somehow I found Kearns and made a point of saying, "Well done. Congratulations. Best of luck for the final." I meant it too; Australia were the best side and they deserved to win the World Cup.

In our dressing room nothing seemed to happen much for five or six minutes. I think Grizz said something to the team, Harty had a few words with individual players . . .

We had a team session, but none of the players got drunk. There's nothing to celebrate if you haven't won. Most of the team split up and did their own thing because there were so many wives and family there. It was about 10 o'clock when I went out to dinner with Bronnie, Anna my sister, and her husband George, who were all over there supporting us.

I was glad to be where no one recognised me. The team's hotel was swarming with New Zealanders over to watch the game. The last thing I wanted were endless postmortems of what might have been. It probably helped that we went to a Chinese restaurant for dinner.

George ate steak.

I was in bed by about midnight.

BOB DWYER

'I've always thought that the New Zealand team and its supporters are much the best losers in the world. Sure, the team are really, really shitty when they lose, I mean like really shitty, but as a group they don't want to detract from your win in any way. They act very graciously.

I think it's right for them to feel shitty – but I've often said that it's probably because they haven't had time to get used to losing too often.'

CHAPTER THREE

Captaincy

"There's only one thing more painful than carrying on. Giving up."
– Anon

LIKE ME, MOST OF the guys tried to forget the World Cup as soon as possible. It was great that we didn't go straight back to New Zealand but across to Italy for JK and Fiorella's wedding instead.

A few of the boys kept saying, "Imagine the flak that's going on back home." I didn't really think a great deal about it. The World Cup was history as far as I was concerned. Anyway, I'd decided to retire.

I didn't need the hassles a second longer; I'd had a gutsful.

I knew it was a hasty decision, that I didn't know how I'd feel again next year. I didn't care. I threw away my boots.

When I told Bronnie she had her doubts — she knows me too well. "Give it time," she said. "You've got to give it another go, you've got to see if you really do want to retire."

Back in New Zealand, over summer, the wounds of the World Cup started healing. After Christmas, I had this nagging doubt about my decision so I suppose that shows I wasn't too sure if I was doing the right thing. Each day I felt less and less comfortable with the idea of being a "former All Black". Originally I had planned to retire when

I was 26. When I got to 25 I made it 28. Now I had retired it didn't feel right. I suspected I was taking the easy way out.

There was no single reason why I changed my mind. It was a combination of things. Around this time I visited Sydney on business and I saw a picture in the paper of Tony Daly, "the *World Champion* Wallaby". Little things like that stung . . . so did the praise Kearns was getting. They all added up, they all motivated me to play on.

> *"The councillors recognised that one of the most stunningly successful eras in the near-century-long history of the NZRFU had come to an end, a not particularly satisfactory end at that. Not only had Wyllie and Hart's team bombed out in the semifinal in Dublin but there were serious misgivings about the players' public relations."* – 1992 *New Zealand Rugby Annual*

THE NEWS THAT JOHN HART was knocked back as All Black coach and a new panel had been chosen for 1992 was obviously political. Clearly the New Zealand Rugby Union was trying to get rid of what they saw as the dead wood from the World Cup.

In some ways Harty had dug his own grave. What counted against him most was our failure in Dublin. The Rugby Union aren't known for their tolerance of losers. As the saying goes, "To err is human, to forgive is not company policy."

I wasn't that thrilled with the choice of Laurie Mains as the new coach. I wondered if he had the goods to do the job. He and I later had a great laugh about this. I told him, "Look at your record: you had Otago for 10 years and everyone thought it was great that you'd won *one* national championship.

"But to me that result was hollow, because Otago didn't beat a full-strength Auckland team . . . I had big doubts you'd make a successful All Black coach."

LAURIE MAINS

'I was inheriting a team who were extremely insular and somewhat arrogant collectively, a team who had been under enormous pressure to keep winning, a team whose attitude was quite clearly not right.

My first requirement was to make them honest again. I don't see everything players do in a game – I'd be naive to think I can, or else have a colossal ego – so I rely on them to play honestly. When it comes to how much work they'll do in a maul or a scrum, or if a player makes that effort to get across to make that extra tackle . . . at the end of the day, only the player knows if he's giving 100 per cent.

I needed a team of honest All Blacks. It was up to me to foster it in them, which was quite a challenge – you're dealing with a wide diversity of personalities, not all of whom react the same way.

I've never been one to believe motivation by fear is smart. The results you get are very short-term. Worse, it doesn't give you the honesty, the real commitment needed in the last quarter-hour.

We did a lot of research on the established players in the All Black team, we talked to a lot of players, the management of the team, former players – and from these totally diverse groups we heard some very consistent messages.

Our conclusion was that some players were detrimental to the side. We wanted to have players desperate to be All Blacks. We also realised we didn't have that many world-class players in New Zealand.

When we discussed Sean, my assumption was that he was pretty uncomplicated, fiercely competitive, a great player who somehow had lost the plot in a minor way. In 1991 I felt he slipped from his standards to the point where other hookers were almost as good. I didn't know him. In all previous dealings with him he'd struck me as polite and courteous. On the field there were some little things I didn't like – he talked too much to the opposition, let himself down at times being too aggressive – but I put most of this down to his intensely competitive nature.

But I was certainly prepared to give him a chance.'

PETER THORBURN

'There was a lot of goodwill from the older guys because they all wanted to survive as All Blacks. I think Sean was aware of surviving too, but he also saw 1992 as an opportunity to shrug off the image he'd got, rightly or wrongly, from the past 18 months.'

"If you leave players to their own devices, you're bound to get a few bludgers."

– Don Furner, former Australian league coach

THE FIRST TIME I heard directly from Laurie was when he rang to ask if I'd be playing again. This was in late January. When I told him yes, he said I'd have to get a lot fitter and play a more expansive role than in 1991.

Laurie said, "I want the All Blacks to play a very fast type of game and if you want to be in the team, Sean, you have to get fit . . . see you at the trials."

His call encouraged me. He was open, friendly. I was glad I'd never bagged him – Laurie wouldn't forget things like that.

Clearly Laurie wasn't his biggest fan, but I thought Gary was still the best lock in the country at the time, that the selectors just had to pick him. But then Laurie started ringing most of the people he wanted for the trials and he didn't ring Gary or AJ.

We had dinner with the Whettons around this time and it was a bit of a joke among us that Gary and AJ hadn't been rung. Yet. We still believed we'd all get a trial. No one had made the connection: they weren't wanted.

I was getting up early and doing a lot of running. I surprised myself how much satisfaction I got. You could really sense it was a new era dawning. Any time I was tempted to slacken off, Phil Kearns' reputation as the world's number one hooker nagged at me – and I kept on running.

PETER THORBURN

'Our insistence on fitness was a way of getting some hardness into the players. It was a myth that the All Blacks in 1991 were fit.

Jim Blair did brilliantly with his fitness work with Grizz in 1983. But perhaps familiarity bred contempt, because by 1991 he was tailoring fitness programmes around 45 minutes a day. That was all the players said they could spare. Instead of doing running they were doing gym work.

But rugby's first and foremost a game of running and you can't substitute for it. It's like a bank account: if you don't put in, when you need it there's nothing to draw upon.

In our fitness tests it was interesting to see guys like Fitzy, Dowdy, Loey – all the big men, the props and hookers – really going for it it, burning and hurting.

The thing was these guys enjoyed it. You could see the pleasure/pain on their faces . . . the effort was hard, but the satisfaction of having done the work was obvious too.'

LAURIE MAINS

'I was assessing Sean, to see whether I felt his motivation was there.

I got pretty good vibes. My basic message to him was: hit the roads . . .

Later, he proved one of the players who had best picked up on our need for aerobic fitness. He had listened – but there were still players who believed they could get fit for rugby in the gym. They hadn't done the running. Sean had.'

PETER THORBURN

'I went through every issue of *Rugby News*, went through every provincial team and made a list of any player I thought showed promise or ability. It was a huge list. I also wrote a strategy for what I saw as our ideal player in each position. I took these notes to our selectors' meeting. Earle and Laurie had brought along their ideas and players. We went through a lot of names.

The public imagine a lot of bartering goes on. I can't speak for previous panels but this one didn't. Perhaps a bit of subconscious mental bartering occurs, but there was never any talk of how many players each union got.'

At previous trials Grizz would consult me about props or other hookers, but this time in Napier I was basically a nobody. The message was clear: no matter who you were or what you'd done in the past, you had to prove yourself all over again.

Laurie was after knowledge: he wanted to learn as much as he could about the players, what we were like as people as well as observe our rugby skills. He admits now he knew little about me. He didn't know how I trained, how I mixed, what I was like off the field. All the time at the trials you could see Laurie watching you out of the corner of his eye. Or he'd be talking to Earle and Thorbs. Occasionally you'd see Bruiser talking to Laurie, the two of them standing together. Things were very different to when Gary was captain.

KEVIN PUTT

‘I'd come back from South Africa just to have a trial and there was definitely more buzz around than in previous years. For people on the fringe, like me, you knew you stood a chance.’

ARRAN PENE

‘There were no promises made – it's not Laurie's way to give that sort of encouragement.’

It was well known that Mains wanted Bruiser as his captain. Bruiser was a natural leader.

And Bruiser organised everything. That was the way that everyone viewed him: the organiser.

I respected him as the choice for captain. I certainly didn't want the job.

LAURIE MAINS

‘Before I start talking to a player he has to get my respect. I quickly suss out if players are bullshitting me.

In 1992, I didn't know enough of the players to trust them.

Brewer was someone I knew backwards. With Otago, he developed as a captain as I developed as a coach. I could say whatever I wanted to him and I valued his judgement.’

During the trials Laurie asked if I would be prepared to captain the All Blacks during the tour of Australia. Mike was the Saturday captain of the All Blacks, Laurie said, but he wanted me to captain the team in some midweek games. I realised there was no one else experienced enough to captain the side. I said yes.

This lack of quality players was something I'd spoken about with Stevie; I found it hard to accept having guys playing in the same team as me who weren't the best in their position. Looking at some of the hopefuls I thought, “What are you doing here?” I felt they were imposters. At Napier there seemed to be too many players who shouldn't have been there . . . players with obvious talent, but who hadn't served their apprenticeships.

I looked at the locks in the trials and thought, "Where is Gary Whetton, why isn't he here?" At the loosies: "Where's Alan Whetton, one of the best blindside players in the country . . . ?"

There were players like Jamie Joseph at Napier. I had nothing against Jamie but I wasn't convinced he had the goods. The week before the trials he played for Otago against Waikato and he let Kevin Putt score four tries on the blindside.

You could see the selectors' attitude – they were building for the next World Cup. My attitude was: I don't play to win one game in 1995. And there was no way I was going to go through the next three years losing games just so some greenhorn lock could get the experience to become a world-beater. *Maybe*.

As people the new panel made a good impression. I got on well with them all. Thorbs you had to respect because he was obviously a very good coach for North Harbour. Earle was a character who backed up his decisions with reason, even if I didn't always agree with them. And Laurie just took charge from the outset. You were left in no doubt there was a new system in place, or who was boss.

Still, I had real question marks about the selectors' thinking. Imagine if we'd lost every game in 1992 and at the end of the year they said, "It's OK, we're building for the next World Cup."

LAURIE MAINS

> 'I talked over one or two things with Sean and a couple of others, but really, they weren't going to get much option to change things.'

EARLE KIRTON

> 'We looked all around the parish for advice. John Drake. Andrew Haden. Pole Whiting. Lin Colling. Brian Lochore. All part of the old 'AB' fraternity. It keeps you from developing tunnel vision.'

PETER THORBURN

> 'We knew this was the year to experiment. The public would allow us a certain latitude because we'd lost the World Cup and accepted we had to rebuild. Take the choice of Eric Rush as a wing. It wasn't an illogical thing to do. Earle was the guy who suggested it. He argued he was the fastest player in New Zealand, and that we lacked fast wings . . .'

In the first trial game I thought I'd done quite well. I captained one side and we won easily. The selectors said I'd played better than in the World Cup. Then they named the main trial sides: a shadow test XV and a "best-of-the-rest" team. I was in the shadow test team, but whether it was intentional or not, the selectors set us up.

They put Stevie in the "Rest" team to get him going, and it worked. He played a blinder and his side drilled us.

It was during this game that an incident happened which changed my whole career. Brewer smashed his calf. I heard him say, "It's gone, I've stuffed my leg."

As he lay there, and the seriousness of his injury hit home, I realised Mains had lost his captain. Suddenly, the All Blacks needed a leader. They were announcing the new team straight after the match and I was the obvious choice.

LAURIE MAINS

‘I felt devastated for Mike but knew he has this tremendous philosophical strength, that he would handle it – and come back.

It was also a hellish and traumatic experience for me. It was bloody pressure time. We were about to make a lot of changes in the team, introduce some controversial selections, and the last thing I needed was to lose the one person with the most affinity between myself and the established All Blacks.

Hell, it was the New Zealand centennial, and here was I, a pretty average All Black, charged with the responsibility for representing the great All Blacks of the past 100 years. That was pressure.’

EARLE KIRTON

‘We thought, 'What do we do now?' Laurie agreed Sean was the obvious choice, but he was worried about having a captain in the front row, and someone who was from Auckland. I said I had no qualms, Thorbs was quite happy too.

Laurie got onto BJ who thought he'd probably be a good captain.’

LAURIE MAINS

‘With Mike gone I'd lost my decision-maker but Earle and I felt confident we could cover that as coaches.

I chose Sean because in him I knew I had a leader by example, and that's what I wanted most. I had other, more tactic-oriented players I could have chosen, but no one seemed to have such total respect from the other players.’

JOHN KIRWAN

‘If you go through the players available, who else was there except Sean and Bruiser? There were one or two potential captains, but very few who could dominate their position as Sean could his.

With all due respect to Sean, I think the selectors probably took a bit of a punt and were pleasantly surprised at the way it worked out.'

Mike's injury was a really big blow to Laurie. He'd planned so much around him. What people forget is that Laurie was unproven too. He doubted himself as All Black coach as much as I doubted myself as captain.

I really didn't want to be the All Black captain. It wasn't something I'd ever considered. Now that I had it, I didn't feel good about it. I was excited, but nervous too. I didn't want the pressure of public speaking and the pressure of looking after a new team . . . I wanted to sit back, recapture my form and not have any responsibilities.

If I'm honest, I doubted my own ability. I didn't know if I could do the job, if I could be a good motivator or handle people.

It's not like I had a track record as captain. A couple of trial teams, once for Auckland in a nothing match, the Colts eight years before . . . that was it in first-class rugby. I'd seen Buck and Gary in the job, seen very closely the pressure an All Black captain gets put under.

I didn't think the on-field tactics would be a big worry. The media side of things wasn't too daunting, either. The responsibility was leading the All Blacks in the New Zealand Rugby Union's centenary year. The best players in the world were in the country to play us in three tests – what a time to take over a rookie team . . .

There were 10 new All Blacks announced. When I looked at some of the names in the squad I thought, "I can't believe it, *I've* got to do something with these players."

Everything was a blur. I called home: my family were thrilled. Dad cried on the phone. Bronnie was really excited.

JK and Stevie were among the first to lend their support when the team was announced. They both said, "If we can do anything to help, just ask."

Later on I took a bit of stick from Gary and AJ, but it was all good-natured. John Hart wrote me a letter saying "Congratulations".

I never heard from Alex Wyllie.

CHAPTER FOUR

Some Days are Better than Others

"Failure is not an option." – Anon

AFTER THE TRIALS we went straight to Christchurch to prepare for the first test against the World XV.

At our first team meeting I wasn't sure what was going to happen. I needn't have worried: Laurie just took over the whole thing. In previous All Black teams Gary would say whatever he wanted to, then Sturge would say his bit, Grizz his . . . but here in Christchurch I sat on the edge of my seat, feeling really nervous.

I had it pretty clear in my mind what I was going to tell the team when Laurie finished talking and said, "Right, let's go."

That was my first "talk" as All Black captain. I didn't get to say a word.

As a series, the games against the World XV didn't deserve test billing. As a stepping-stone towards the recovery of All Black rugby, on the other hand, the series was ideal for the team, Laurie – and me.

That first week, as the team went through the basics, I felt lonely, full of doubt, uncertain. I was sceptical about the quality of my team-mates, I wondered how I would establish a relationship with the new coach.

There were several positives: everyone had an excellent attitude, Laurie was clear in his commands, and the spirit in the team seemed great. That helped me a lot. There were no smart-arses. They were good. Early on I made it really clear, for instance, that everyone had to be on time to any formal team functions or meetings. And they were.

Looking around the squad there were only a few faces I could totally rely on: JK, Stevie, Foxy, Loey. No one else had really proved themselves. Some had played tests or been on a few tours but there weren't many stars. Even an older guy like Buncie, who'd been at the World Cup with Samoa, had never proved to me he could actually do it. I remembered the years he couldn't break into the Auckland team.

It was the lack of noise I noticed the most. No one said much, not even characters like Richard Turner, or Ant Strachan, whom you normally couldn't shut up. Everyone just wanted to play for the All Blacks. Nothing else mattered. You could see the intensity on their faces.

There were signs this was a different breed of player. They were pretty fancy off the field. That's what Bronnie noticed when she first met them. "They're very smooth aren't they?" she said. It was all that slicked-back hair.

Most of them were so young. Little things reminded you of this. We had to fill out these questionnaires for publicity. One question was, "Who did you idolise as a kid?" Jamie Joseph answered, seriously, "Sean Fitzpatrick".

A lot of them wore expressions like Blair Larsen. You could see on his face that he didn't think he was meant to be here.

In truth, they were a bunch of promising players who now found themselves called All Blacks. They never expected it. They were thrust into the media spotlight, called on for interviews and asked for their autographs. They knew they were seen as "the answer" to the World Cup disaster. But it's one thing to know why they were there; some clearly wondered if they ought to be . . .

ARRAN PENE

'Sean was very encouraging to new guys like Jamie and me. He asked us, even as new boys, what we thought.'

"I think that our rugby players have come to hold out their hand a bit too much, they have come to expect too high a quality hotel, they have come to expect too much to be laid on for them . . . without doing the hard work first." – Laurie Mains, *20/20* interview

IN THE FIRST FEW days Laurie didn't really ask much of me. He realised I didn't need any extra pressure, so he took as much on his shoulders as he could. I really appreciated that. There wasn't a lot of confidence around. Everyone was doubting everyone. The players were doubting me, I'm doubting them, Laurie's doubting me, I'm doubting him . . . I doubted whether I was doing the right thing by being captain.

I wanted Laurie to tell me if I was doing a good job. But Laurie's not the sort of guy who gives that sort of feedback in a couple of days. Mike Brewer had warned me at the beginning of the week, "You won't get too close to Laurie because he likes to keep away from the team a bit." Bruiser was right; Laurie was pretty standoffish.

Laurie told me, "I'll have good times with the team, I'll share a few beers with them, but I don't want them to get too close to me. I need to be aloof from the team, especially in these early days."

That's his style. You'll see him at nights after a game but then he'll just quietly leave the team to enjoy themselves. It's a good system. It means he keeps his authority with the guys all the time and he doesn't try to be one of the boys. Occasionally he lets his hair down, but only at the right times. Almost from the start I found myself warming to him. He wasn't the dour bugger his critics said. At the end of the first week I felt more reassured about him and our relationship got better from there.

Laurie put a lot of emphasis on fitness. In fact this was probably the hardest training I've endured.

At the first practice he said, "In this team there are going to be no shortcuts. *Everyone* will do the 'shit work', I don't care who you are. I don't want anyone shirking. And we're starting *now* . . ."

He produced the ruck machine. When I saw it I wondered if we were going back to the dark ages of coaching. The ruck machine looks like a scrum machine mounted on a sledge and covered with tackle bags. We had to pound into this for about 20 minutes. By the time of the Irish series we were up to 40 minutes. It's a killer. The guys loathed it so much, there was talk of coming to training with chainsaws.

PETER THORBURN

'Every coach has his own way of teaching – reminding – players that rugby's a hard, physical game.

You must create the understanding in a team that hard work is positive. Laurie's '150s' [a gruelling series of 150-metre sprints] are infamous because they are his way of getting some hardness into the bastards.

But the hardness must have a secondary purpose too. We wanted the players to feel satisfaction from *their* hard work. If they don't they resent you.'

The skill levels of some of the players concerned me. By All Black standards they were abysmal. Every second pass was dropped.

The backs in particular were a real worry. Walter, Eroni and Frank could not kick accurately. Earle was continually teaching them basics like punting. I couldn't believe that All Black backs needed basic kicking practice.

For the past five years I'd taken it for granted that every player in the All Blacks was the best player in the world in his position. The 1992 players were nowhere in their class. Hika Reid used to say, "The only reason Fitzpatrick's so good is because he plays in great teams." At the time I'd thought, "Hard luck, pal."

I now had more sympathy for him.

In hindsight I was an anxious, inexperienced captain, critical of my new team and wanting them to be successful at everything *immediately*. I didn't appreciate that Laurie had his own methods, that not every training session would involve heaps of scrums or the dreaded ruck machine. Laurie was determined to stamp his own mark on the team. He was looking at the wider picture. Then I didn't know what it was, or know him well enough to ask.

There was a very clear demarcation line between the players and Laurie. If you mucked around when he wanted you to concentrate, or didn't try hard enough when he asked for 100 per cent effort, he showed his tough side.

That's what happened with Richard Turner. Richard was a bit of a clown. He always liked a laugh.

For some reason, Laurie didn't rate him much. At training he sometimes abused Richard: "What do you think you're doing?" he'd yell, or, in front of the team he'd ask him a question like, "Why did you make that mistake?"

In his dealings with Richard the team saw another side of Laurie's character. If you're not performing, or you break his rules, or he thinks you're not applying yourself, you don't get picked. Richard got dropped after the first test, came on as a replacement in the next . . . but that was it. He hasn't featured in the All Blacks' thinking until 1994. He's had to fight his way back. It's not easy.

PETER THORBURN

> ‘Richard was a classic example of someone who wanted to be an All Black so badly he played when he possibly shouldn't have. He had a cracked bone in his thumb, a cracked bone in his wrist, a huge bruise on his thigh and couldn't really play the game at pace.’

"Some days are better than others." – Bono

THERE WAS AN INCREDIBLE amount of tension before the first centennial test. In fact the build-up was very similar to what I experienced with the Baby Blacks. It was a situation of going into the unknown.

The pressure was intense. Normally I'm a good sleeper but that week there were a few sleepless nights. In one radio interview I said it was strange not rooming with a team-mate, that as captain I was finding it lonely in my own room. A couple of days later a big teddy bear arrived; obviously, somebody felt sorry for me . . .

There was a lot of public goodwill towards the team, which was a pleasant change from '91. We received letters and hundreds of faxes from all over New Zealand. John Sturgeon came to see me and he was just over the moon I was captain. It was great to chat with him, it helped relieve some of the stress.

The pressure was mounting every day.

After training I'd sit in my bedroom twiddling my thumbs, thinking of what I had to do . . . about the speech I had to make in front of hundreds of great All Blacks . . . about the team talk . . . about the game.

I wasn't concerned about my captaincy on the field. I knew if I played well, I'd lead well.

Because we were a new side, Laurie knew he could lay down the law without much resistance. He did away with traditions he considered harmful, like too many team sessions. There were other changes. Number one was improving relations with the media. They were at an all-time low in 1991.

On the Friday before the test there is a media function. The All Black captain is asked as a courtesy but never goes.

However, Laurie and Neil Gray thought it would be good if I went along. It was one of the best things I did all season. I was only there for five or 10 minutes but I shook everyone's hands and you could tell the journos were impressed. Their attitude seemed to be: "Wonderful. Great start. The All Blacks are off on the right foot. What a nice change."

That one visit probably benefited us enormously in the long run. Relationships between the All Blacks and the media were better in 1992 than they had been for a long time.

Before the test Gary phoned me. I think it was pretty hard thing for him to do; he felt bitter about the way he'd been dropped. I really wanted Gary to call. I really wanted to know I had his support. It meant a lot that he did.

It was a strange atmosphere. Everyone was really nervous, as you are before any All Black international. But Christchurch wasn't quite like a normal test, either. Before the game we were given special caps to mark the first 100 years of New Zealand rugby and had a picture taken with the World XV players. I'd never mixed with the opposition before a test like this, and found it very difficult to do. But most of the new All Blacks didn't seem too concerned. That worried me. It was a sign the guys' minds weren't focused – too many were more interested in trying their caps on, wondering what they looked like.

It was probably the most unusual test match preparation I've ever been part of. The whole thing felt unreal. Especially once the test began and I found my first All Black team down by 19 points.

GRANT FOX

> ‘Sean was impressive. He didn't panic. He wasn't angry or abusive to anyone. He simply told the team we were all letting ourselves down.
>
> It was, ‘C'mon guys, get stuck in . . .', not, ‘Get stuck in you bunch of useless bastards . . .'
>
> He was authoritative, calm, cool-headed. That's how he earned our respect so quickly.’

We hauled them back a bit in the second half but this was the worst possible start: All Blacks 14, World XV 28. I couldn't believe it. The dressing room was very quiet.

Setbacks tell you a lot about people and the thing I liked about Laurie that day was his positive attitude in defeat. He didn't turn round and have a go at anyone.

Basically he said, “We've lost, the result is crook, but there are a lot of good things to build on.”

I tried not to show it but I was shattered by the defeat. Adding to my gloom was an injury I'd sustained. I can't remember exactly how it happened but I got smashed in the hand . . . somebody stood on it in a ruck.

At first I thought it was broken. The bone was sticking up, and it really hurt. There was never a chance I'd come off, not with Fergie McCormick and the other All Blacks watching from the stands, but for the remainder of the game my hand was bloody sore.

After the test it swelled up very badly and Doc Mayhew told me to get an X-ray. As I was waiting to get X-rayed, the week's pressure got to me. I hoped the X-ray would show that my hand was broken . . .

That way I could pull out with honour . . .

That way I wouldn't have to captain a bunch of losers any more . . .

That way I could run away and hide.

Looking back I can't believe I wanted out so badly. But I felt incredibly embarrassed with so many old All Blacks watching such an inept display. Part of me wondered if it was my captaincy at fault. Maybe another captain would have inspired the guys better . . .

The X-ray results showed heavy bruising. My hand was okay.

> *“Sean Fitzpatrick, the captain of New Zealand, was probably the most fierce competitor . . .*
> *“For Fitzpatrick, the stakes were incredibly high. He had to live up to a whole history of All Black superiority and the blessed memories of his predecessors.”*
>
> – Stephen Jones, *Endless Winter*

FORMAL BLACK-TIE DINNERS were held at each centenary test for every former All Black who could make it. At every dinner, the guest list ran to hundreds.

When someone makes their All Black debut it's traditional to acknowledge this in the captain's speech. In Christchurch there were three debutants who started the game, but I was so nervous I forgot Arran Pene's name – he'd come on as a replacement.

I said, "I'd like to congratulate these young players on making their All Black debuts today: Frank Bunce . . . Mark Cooksley . . . Richard Turner . . . and . . . and . . ." and I stood there, my mind blank. Disaster. I couldn't remember the fourth player's name.

A few people started to laugh and I'm thinking, 'Oh God, how embarrassing . . .'

Behind me some guy goes, "Greg Cooper." Then someone else yells, "No, it's not Greg Cooper," and next thing everyone's yelling some name at me. Finally, while I'm dying a hundred deaths with everybody watching me, I hear from the back: "*Arran Pene.*" And in a really small voice I said, "– and Arran Pene."

It hadn't been a great day.

The next morning the selectors decided to bring another lock into the team because Cooksley was hurt.

I couldn't believe some of the names they were throwing around. I sat there thinking, "Why don't you call Gary Whetton in?" but said nothing. One selector mentioned Gary's name but another said, "There is no way we're bringing Gary in, he's the least fit lock in the country at the moment."

I wanted to disagree but I wasn't confident enough in myself then as captain to speak up. But I'd say it now if a similar situation occurred, and have done so over a couple of players. Then it wouldn't have been right. None of us knew each other well enough to understand if there were hidden agendas.

The selectors were like the team, still testing each other out. Thorbs can be stubborn: if he doesn't like somebody he really doesn't like them.

Earle has some pretty strong views too, and he and Thorbs had some lively discussions. Laurie mostly listened. But when he had his say, he knew what he wanted. They all had very firm opinions.

In Wellington we just had to win the test. A second loss was unthinkable. Laurie was determined to go for form only and so players like JK and Foxy got dropped. Graeme Bachop too.

Our win in Wellington saved the series, possibly the entire season. And part of our inspiration came from the Prime Minister, Jim Bolger.

At a function at Parliament the night before the game, Nick Farr-Jones, the World XV skipper, and I met with the PM privately for 15 minutes.

He talked to Nick about how great his team was and how bad

the All Blacks were. Kirky was there too. He'd written a speech for the occasion.

The PM cracked a joke: "Sean, you can borrow David for a couple of days if you want a half back."

Later, when the Prime Minister addressed both teams he didn't use Kirky's speech but said exactly what he told us in private: how unfortunate it was that "we" lost the first test – to a World XV who weren't even a "real" opponent . . . how "we" used to be world champions and now "we're" no longer this and that. It went down like a lead balloon.

Afterwards, back at our hotel, Mains was livid. He walked in to the team room and said, "Right, you've heard all you need to hear. We better win this game tomorrow . . ." Then he walked out.

The next day we cleaned out the World XV 54-26. Everyone played well for us. In the dressing room afterwards the guys were so happy because it was the first time they felt worthy to be called All Blacks . . .

Then Jim Bolger came in, straight after the game. He had a big smile on his face. He said, "Well done, guys, I knew you could do it."

ARRAN PENE

> ‘Bolger tried to be humorous. 'What a generous team we were to give 80 per cent of the ball to the opposition', this sort of thing. He's been in our dressing room a few times since, and now he's got the message about what you say.’

After the victory, the personalities emerged. Everyone couldn't wait for the show-down at Auckland.

The change in attitude of senior players from the World Cup was dramatic. You had a guy like JK really thrilled to be chosen for the Auckland test. *Really* happy. He accepted his position was now like everyone's – under review. And even though he'd been a great player for years, I knew he was under real pressure to keep his place. The selectors had their doubts about him. JK took up the challenge and responded superbly.

"They've obviously strengthened their team up a bit . . ."

– Sean, in a TV interview, at the news of Gary Whetton's inclusion in the World XV side for the third test

WHEN GARY AGREED TO play for the World XV *against* the All Blacks because their locks were injured, I couldn't believe it.

Everyone asked me to comment. My stance was, "It's up to Gary. It's his decision."

Privately, I wished he'd sat the game out. I didn't think he had anything to gain by appearing. But as a friend I never thought I should call Gary and say, "Don't play." I had to respect his decision, even if I didn't necessarily like it. And it was *his* decision.

Peter Bush

time of Golden Weather – we've just beaten Australia to retain the Bledisloe Cup, Auckland, 989.

Olympix

wo outstanding All Blacks, two very different captains – Gary and Buck.

Mendoza, Argentina, 1991. As a build-up for the World Cup, the tour was a disaster.

After running every team off their feet four years earlier, by 1991 the All Blacks weren't fit enough.

Sean Fitzpatrick collection

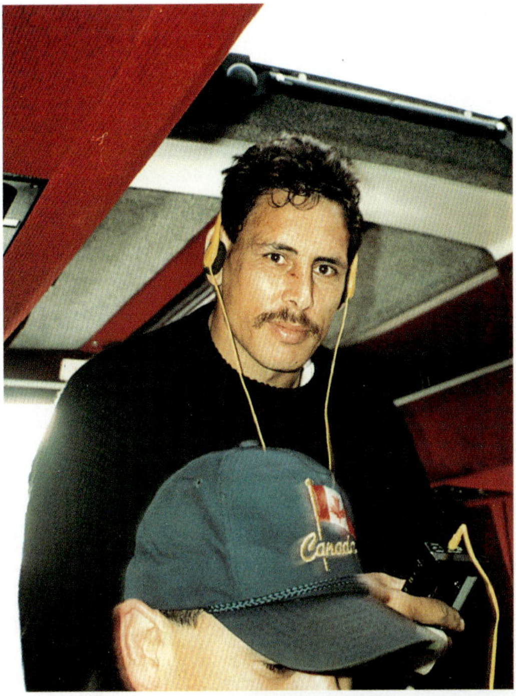

"He commanded attention by his presence" – Buck.

Olympix

Zinzan Brooke justified my faith in him with a superb tour in 1992.

Peter Bush

"In '92 we picked a bunch of greenhorns." The pressures of selection weigh heavily upon Earle "Ernie" Kirton.

RIGHT: After winning the World XV series, I wanted to remain All Black captain.

OVERLEAF: Up the middle against the Wallabies . . . one of the best series I've ever played in.

BELOW: Running onto Ellis Park receiving the loudest cheer I've ever heard from an opposing crowd.

Peter Bush

Colorsport

XXXX

Facing the U.S.A. with Graham Purvis and Steve McDowell, at the 1991 World Cup.

A great competitor – Phil Kearns, the best all-round hooker in the game today.

I spoke to AJ about it too. In the end, Gary did what he wanted to.

In my opinion, even after the centennial tests, Gary was still the best lock in the country. By far. But he should never have played in that game against the All Blacks. After 58 tests for his country Gary had nothing to prove. He could only end up the loser. I felt sorry for him, to go out on a sour note like that after all he'd done for New Zealand rugby . . . He deserved better.

Afterwards, he and I never talked about it. I'd receive the odd few digs at Auckland training but it was harmless stuff, just cracks like, "So, Caveman, how's your buddy Laurie?"

I've called on Gary a number of times since becoming captain because I really value his advice. He's got a great rugby brain on his shoulders, and it wouldn't surprise me if he becomes a successful coach. Tactically, he can sum up play very quickly. He has uncanny instinct for when to keep it tight, or let the ball out. His on-field combination with Foxy was devastating. They thought as one.

Thankfully, Gary's appearance didn't affect the result, even though we had to learn new line-out codes in a hurry. We won convincingly, scoring four tries to one. Our game wasn't flawless but there were genuine reasons for optimism now.

As I answered questions at the Auckland post-game press conference I realised we'd come a long way in a short time.

Those seven days made me as captain. I felt more confident in the role, I hadn't made any major mistakes, and while I wasn't enjoying captaincy, not like I enjoy it now, I discovered something within me: I wanted to remain as All Black captain. I didn't want to stand aside and let Bruiser walk back in and pick up the reins.

In my eyes Laurie had gone from being a coach I doubted to one I could trust, one who knew what he was doing and where he wanted the team to go. Best of all he was decisive. That's what this young All Black side needed.

LAURIE MAINS

> 'I had a long, hard think after the World XV series. I made the decision to keep Sean as All Black captain by the time Ireland visited. I'd been very happy with the way Sean performed in the centenary series and, given the need for stability, he was the only choice.'

If Laurie and I had fallen out at any time in 1992 it would have been after the All Blacks' performance in the first test against Ireland, a few weeks later.

The Irish – a team of nice guys of very average ability – had nearly beaten the best 15 players in New Zealand. Supposedly the best 15.

My doubts about the team resurfaced. I was furious with the guys for playing so poorly, and worse, their casual attitudes. And I told Laurie in no uncertain terms that he better get the right players pretty quickly.

The signs were abundantly clear at practice. Earlier I'd played for Auckland against Ireland – we demolished them by 50 points. But when the All Blacks got together we were hopeless.

I can't remember being involved in such a poor test build-up. Errors dominated everything. We'd work on our kick-offs but they were wildly off-target, our handling was bad, our attention too easily distracted . . .

What made it hard was knowing Auckland players like Foxy and Gary could do the job and weren't getting picked.

In the past I'd never had to worry about simple things like who was going to take the kicks at goal. Foxy always kicked them. But in that first Irish test Greg missed a few kicks. That put the pressure on the rest of the side, and with Ireland playing out of their skin, the result was always in doubt. If Greg had kicked two or three of those earlier goals we would have been out of danger.

I could *tell* the guys everything I knew but clocking up test miles was the only way they'd really learn.

It was frustrating because I'd made it quite clear the series wouldn't be a walk-over, that the worst thing that could've happened was Auckland's massive win. The guys all went, "Yeah, we understand", but deep down, I think they were still reliving the World XV victories. They hadn't appreciated yet that in test rugby the opposition, no matter who they are, are more intense, more committed, they raise their game. And the Irish had played like men possessed.

LAURIE MAINS

> ‘After the game Sean made one or two comments about certain players' attitudes. He was frank and honest.
>
> I'd already hooked into a few guys for their lax attitudes that morning of the test . . . I could tell the attitude wasn't right in the physio room. There was too much laughter and mucking about. On test day you don't want to hear your players laughing.
>
> Sean's comments were the first time he started to complement me. Before, in the World XV series, he'd been supportive. Now he was contributing.’

For once I had to agree with the critics who slammed our performance. The one consolation, though, was that I knew the Irish couldn't get much better. We would.

Choosing the team for the second test was a big challenge for Laurie, because the players in most danger of losing their places were obviously his selections. One of Grizz's problems was he never dropped out-of-form players.

In the new team, Laurie did exactly what he promised – chose form players. That's why it's so easy to respect the guy. He's straight up and down.

When we assembled in Wellington for the second test I noticed right away there was a very different attitude among the guys. The public abuse following our narrow victory had shocked a few of the guys too. Everyone was back to earth about the realities of test rugby. Axing six players removed any lingering doubts.

LAURIE MAINS

> 'Personal feelings don't come – or shouldn't come – into selecting the All Blacks. My role is to do the best I can for New Zealand rugby, not for individual players.
>
> It's all about honesty. I use that word a lot with the players. I expect it of them, but it's important I am seen to be honest too. I'd said there would be changes if players didn't perform, and if I hadn't followed through I'd effectively have told them the coach doesn't have to obey the same set of rules as his team. It would have confused them, as well as showing me up as a hypocrite.'

In Wellington, Laurie told me I was going to captain the All Blacks for the rest of the year. From this point I really started to feel the confidence an All Black captain needs. Laurie told me he respected me, that he planned to build this team around my leadership.

Mike Brewer was healed, and in the second test team. He was excellent. I didn't really think there'd be any awkwardness between us but I suppose in the back of my mind there was a thought that Laurie might be bringing him in to get some feedback.

In a number of ways Bruiser said to the guys what I wanted to, but couldn't always do so without coming across like a dictator. And the guys like hearing it from someone else anyway.

At training the new caps like Olo and Robin fitted in brilliantly. The old guys like Jonesy and Bruiser backed them up. It was a great team performance. On Saturday, on a really grotty Wellington afternoon, we finally clicked as a unit. Poor old Ireland. We had victory by 50 points, scored nine great tries and that night I thought, 'Yeah. Now we're making progress.'

CHAPTER FIVE

"...Not Many Dead"

"If coaching were simply a matter of putting down on a piece of paper 10 points to improve, we'd all be world-beaters. Correcting faults takes time; instilling good habits takes time . . ." – Buck Shelford

USUALLY, AUSTRALIA IS THE ideal place for inexperienced All Black teams to tour. The weak midweek opposition allows a chance to blood new players, there's not the same media pressure as in the UK, it's a great country to visit, the weather's usually excellent and there are lots of Kiwi supporters.

As events revealed, we didn't have it all our way this trip.

I was more than happy with the composition of the team which flew out to Perth for the opening game. Laurie consulted me over some of the tour positions, but all selections except one were his.

The exception was Zinny. It became a test of Laurie's faith in me. Zinny didn't have a clue he was the focus of such attention.

LAURIE MAINS

'Originally Zinzan wasn't in contention for the tour. But Sean and I were trusting each other more so when he asked me where Zinny stood in the scheme of things I told him exactly where: not very high. I said if we took seven loose forwards, his chances were no more than 50-50. So he asked me what reservations I had and I told him.

So Sean looks me straight in the eye and says, 'Zinny hasn't ever been asked to play for the All Blacks as he does for Auckland. I *know* he's good enough to do the work you ask.'

I then looked him straight in the eye and said, 'OK, I'm going to give you this one, Sean. But it's quid pro quo: I don't know Zinzan very well so *you've* got to play your part in making it work, of making him accept my style of play. You've said he's got the goods . . . well, he's now your challenge.' '

Another big issue was Foxy. Without him the backline hadn't functioned properly. All season the backs' kicking had been erratic, especially Walter's. After another poor training session in Wellington before the Irish test I finally said to Laurie, "What are we going to do? This kicking is beyond a joke."

I believed we needed Foxy's tactical authority. Walter was running well but against Australia I knew we needed someone who could kick in pressure situations. Ireland were nowhere in Australia's class. Foxy had taken his dropping with grace and shown a ton of character. There had been no whingeing, no moans. He even helped Wog with his kicking. I knew Mains really respected him for that.

But Foxy had doubts. He was asking me all the time, "What's happening Fitzy, am I doing the right thing?" I knew Grant was considering not going on tour. I told Laurie this: "You've got to speak to Foxy, tell him what you're doing."

So Laurie told Foxy his plan. He said he wouldn't be in the second test against the Irish either. "We don't want to expose you yet, Foxy," Laurie said, "because *you're* going to play in the first test against the Aussies. That day we have to win, and you're essential to our plans. Be patient. We don't want to tip our hand to Dwyer that you'll be involved."

When Foxy told Gary of their plan, Gary was sceptical. "Make sure you get it in writing," was his advice.

I'm not sure if I fully agreed with the selectors' strategy either, but the experiment with Walter had two pluses: it showed people that while he's a great player, Walter's not a test first-five. And by keeping Foxy in the reserves, it got him really hungry again.

LAURIE MAINS

'That tour we picked a few true-blooded All Blacks but by and large we were taking away a large bunch of bloody greenhorns.'

EARLE KIRTON

'No one knew better how green they were, or was more worried about their greenness, than the selectors.'

In Perth, all our thinking was geared towards playing the Wallabies; South Africa was in the back of our minds. Privately I doubted we'd go through unbeaten, but the thought of losing the Bledisloe Cup was devastating. I was confident we'd win the series, but picking up the first test was vital.

The training was even harder than in Christchurch. It bore no resemblance to anything we'd done in 1991 – this team would have run rings around that side in terms of fitness. Guys had taken Laurie's warnings to heart and there were no shirkers. The contrast to the World Cup side was astonishing; people were really trying.

Laurie might ask, "Sean, how many more '150s' do we need to do?" If I said, "I think the boys have had enough, Laurie," he'd say, "You're right, they look knackered. So we'll do some more."

Motivation was simple: everyone wanted to be a good All Black and early on test places were dangled in front of the team. But once the test side was formed, the other players still pushed them. It was astonishing. John Brody, our old liaison man from the tour in '88, visited us and couldn't believe how full-on everything was.

LAURIE MAINS

'The first chance I really had to train the All Blacks my way was in Australia. I wanted them hurting in training, hurting through putting in honest work.

Sean stamped his mark on the team in an interesting way. He noticed a couple of the guys not doing the exercises properly, dropping behind, stopping short. So he stopped training and had them on about it.'

EARLE KIRTON

'Fitzy was the first to show anger at any slackness. He'd say, 'Someone's cutting corners . . .' This was like a general warning. In private, to us, he might say, 'Inga's bloody losing it, he's not on the job, keep him working . . .' '

LAURIE MAINS

'Now this was new to these guys. Fitzy wouldn't stand for any shirkers. The rest of the team saw it but instead of picking on the slow ones, they started helping them. I tried not to show how happy I was but this was *exactly* what I'd hoped to see – initiative is the only way to build real team spirit.'

EARLE KIRTON

'Laurie and I play the good guy/bad guy role. I'm almost the 'joke' to the Auckland guys with my scarf, for example . . . but the thing is 'the boss' gives me a lot of leeway. He only pulls me back if I go off target.'

GRANT FOX

'The All Blacks rediscovered their physical hardness, their aggressiveness. It had drained away in 1991, teams weren't scared of us any more. I think this team redressed the balance.'

PETER FITZSIMONS

'When I played against the All Blacks for a scratch team down in South Australia, I thought, 'This is not an *All Black* side'. Usually when you play the All Blacks you never see the ball, it's so tightly hidden; it's like searching for a needle in a haystack.

But in South Australia I got my hands on the ball 15, maybe 30 times. I was shocked. Either I'd suddenly become a great mauler, or their system had wound down a bit . . .

Four days later against New South Wales I couldn't get over the change in them. They were fast learners. I spoke to Nick Farr-Jones and told him the All Blacks looked like wild mongrel dogs again. Nick just said, 'I think we'll beat them.' '

"There are very few new things in this world, very few. That's why people that are young, if they're smart, try to profit from the experience of an older guy so they won't have to go through all the pain and suffering. But a certain amount of pain and suffering is good, because it makes a person think they've learned."

– Cus D'Amato

THE 1992 BLEDISLOE CUP series was one of the most enjoyable I've played. We lost 2-1 but the games were so close it could have been a series whitewash to either side.

You could argue we lost the first test by a terrible bounce of the ball when JK was about to score, and in the second test Foxy's last minute dropped goal missed by the smallest of margins. Two narrow losses . . . but so nearly two scalps for us.

But it's points on the board which matter. We lost the test series because of two things: inexperience, and our inability to handle the pressure, which is a type of inexperience anyway.

We made too many costly mistakes. It wasn't the young guys' mistakes either – the senior players gave away penalties, took the wrong options, knocked on, threw the dumb punch. The same patterns were repeated in each test: we'd be hard on attack and then we'd give away a penalty and let the pressure off.

Laurie had stressed for weeks that to have any chance of taking the series, we *had* to win the first test. "After then," he said, "they'll realise how quick we are, how much we've improved since the World Cup and the centennial games."

He was dead right. The Aussies couldn't believe how quickly

we'd got our act together. The second test they were better; they deserved victory, just as we dominated the third. But that's test match rugby and we weren't as good as them at dealing with that level of pressure then.

PHIL KEARNS

'Both teams had great respect for each other, and it was a great series to be involved in. It could have gone either way, neither team was really better than the other.

Through 1992 Sean coped better with the captaincy the longer he had it. Maybe in his first couple of tests [against the World XV] he wasn't as dominant a figure as he usually is but I think he probably had a fair bit on his mind.

Whether somebody had a chat to him or not I don't know, but when the All Blacks played us in the tests he was back to playing really well. He was just leading by example, which I think he does naturally anyway, and in the South African test he had a great game.

So mark him as a bit of a slow starter in the first two games. After that it was business as usual.'

Everyone agrees: the series was a great spectacle. As an advertisement for the game it could hardly have been improved. The players enjoyed it as well as the crowd. It had a few controversial moments, but we didn't dwell on these. We were more concerned with what a rookie team achieved. It took the whole series before the younger guys realised they did deserve to be on the same field as guys like Nick Farr-Jones and Campo. Considering it was played under new rules, and against the world champions, I was more than satisfied with the overall performance.

What I was furious about was the disaster against Sydney at Penrith, a few days before the third test.

It's fair to say I wasn't prepared for what took place at Penrith. Apparently, Earle described it as "an aberration". I call a 17-40 loss for the All Blacks outright humiliation.

LAURIE MAINS

'There is no other word for it: we were shit on the night. OK, the ref didn't help but he didn't cost us the game. It was very difficult for the test team and Sean and Earle and I watching in the grandstand. Our pride hurt. A lot. But it also made those watching even more determined to win the test on Saturday.'

EARLE KIRTON

'At full-time we said, 'Let's save this until after the test.' But Sean was grey-faced.

He handled it more hard-nosed than us. He got really stuck into the guys.'

LAURIE MAINS

> 'The dressing room was deathly quiet. I let them stew. But Sean was livid. He was fuming. Individuals, he said, hadn't shown guts. I said, 'Forget it, let's concentrate on the test. They'll keep.' '

After the game I was ropable. I asked Stevie, who'd captained the side, "What the hell happened? Why do you think we lost?" He said, "Too many young players in the team."

I said "Steve, you should have beaten Sydney hands down." He said, "There weren't enough experienced players. We needed guys like Michael Jones." I said, "You know that's not a good enough reason, there's no way the test guys could have played so close to the test."

Experience wasn't the answer anyway. One of the team's most experienced players, a back, was acting like a real outcast because he wasn't in the test team. He was setting a bad example to the younger guys, hitting golf balls at the driving range on the day of the game instead of preparing for the match.

And inexperience doesn't excuse some of the young guys for showing an unacceptable lack of guts. Afterwards I deliberately didn't stay in the dressing room too long.

As far as I was concerned, there weren't *any* excuses for the loss. There were one or two reasons: the wives and girlfriends had flown across that day to meet up with the team for a few days, we were gearing up for the tour of South Africa, the third test was on everyone's minds. But the calibre of our team against Sydney doesn't explain such a heavy loss. When you look at players like Ellis, Cooper, Wright, Larsen, Earl, McDowell, Purvis you're talking real talent . . .

I know a lot of former All Blacks were disappointed that Pat Lam and Glenn Taylor were flown across for just one game. I sympathise with that attitude, but the situation was too close to the test to allow the first-choice guys to appear. This was a Wednesday night game, and the test was on Saturday.

I felt the same in 1987 when the New Zealand team to Japan was given full All Black status. Some of that side didn't deserve the honour. They were one-time tourists.

It was really interesting seeing some of their faces again at the Centennial dinners.

There were players like John Buchan, the Canterbury hooker. We had our moments during Auckland-Canterbury Ranfurly Shield challenges, but he seemed to have a chip on his shoulder, especially towards Auckland players. A prop from Wairarapa Bush, Robbie McLean, went to Japan with us and also never played for the All Blacks again. He was at the Wellington dinner. But Robbie was a nice guy, he tried hard and you can't take it away from him. He was an All Black. To tell the truth, as I've got older I've probably mellowed a bit.

No matter how good or bad a player is, once you are an All Black no one can take that away from you, not even from guys who have played five minutes.

It's a fact of life that some of the players who have worn the All Black jersey you don't rate. But they're still All Blacks, they've still done something that thousands of people never will. It's not the player's fault he got selected – you just hope he won't be picked again.

The All Blacks who *really* annoy me are those with ability but who don't give it 100 per cent, either at training or in games. Inga was like that.

GRANT FOX

> 'There's a saying within the All Blacks: 'It's better not to have been picked than to be a bad All Black.' '

JOHN KIRWAN

> 'Fitzy and I have discussed this issue many times. We're from the old school of All Blacks. Even though I'm not yet 30, there's a big gap between my era and guys who are, say, 22 or 23.
>
> I wonder if my generation of All Blacks has taught the next as well as we could have; it's not their fault if they slip below accepted All Black standards of behaviour because they haven't been told how to act.
>
> When Fitzy and I first made the team the older players were a huge influence in our lives. They drummed home to us that becoming an All Black was a lifestyle thing.'

It hurts me when the All Blacks lose, it really does. It's difficult – no, it's impossible – to describe what being an All Black means. It ignites a feeling that I don't think anyone has ever accurately captured in words. Not even other All Blacks can sum it up, but it's there every time you pull on the jersey.

Young players have so many more options these days. Becoming an All Black still means a great deal, but staying there is another matter . . . I've got my doubts it still matters as much. JK and I both think it's unlikely this generation of All Black will match our long careers. Not because they don't have the talent, but because they don't have the desire.

The most common aim these days seems to be to play five or 10 tests, hopefully a World Cup, and that's enough. Matthew Ridge wished he'd played a single test before switching to league – but that was all he wanted.

The modern player tends to need a lot of nurturing. He wants solutions given to him on a plate, he's less likely to experiment himself finding out what works and what doesn't, like we've all done.

You can't cut corners. It takes years and years of hard work to become, and then remain, an All Black. I know guys who've made great personal sacrifices to become an All Black. But too many guys today won't sacrifice for even 10 weeks. They like their booze too much, or they don't like getting out of bed when it's dark to go for that run. So they survive on raw ability and never push themselves, never find their true potential.

One of the best ways of seeing who's got the right attitude is by watching how an All Black responds in defeat. After the Sydney loss, for example, not every player was hurting. Some almost shrugged it off.

But that night one or two of the older All Blacks in the team were so angry, they wanted to play every other game on tour rather than let some of those imposters wear the All Black jersey again.

I shudder to think what would have happened to morale if we'd followed up the defeat by Sydney with a loss in the third test. Once we won, the tour was saved. We restored pride. And though the record books show Australia wasn't the greatest of tours, results-wise, as a learning curve it was vital.

The morning after the test I got up about 6 am and went for a walk along the beach. I remember sitting on a park bench and writing a few notes about what we'd achieved. We'd come a long way since that first test against the World XV. We now had the core of a test team, which was a fantastic achievement in four months. I doubt many other countries – *any* other country – could've turned things around so fast.

"All Blacks beat NSW – Not Many Dead"

– Newspaper banner after New Zealand defeated New South Wales in a "rugged, bruising encounter"

"Now I know that the haka means 'see this elbow, you're going to get it in your nose'. " – Australian TV commentator

THE MEDIA ATTENTION WAS the biggest eye-opener for me. It was constant, the most publicised rugby I'd experienced in Australia. Even the crowds gave us a hard time, which was a surprise. Normally there is loyal, and vocal, Kiwi support at games. This time, with Aussie as world champs, they gave us heaps. I quite enjoyed it actually. It showed they still feared us, still respected us.

In hindsight, I think we made an error in not making more of an effort with the Aussie media. Laurie made it quite clear he never gave much weight to the general press conference. He'd go through the motions but he'd invite the New Zealand media to have their own press conference with him later. The Aussies were a bit put out I think, because Laurie never gave anything away at the main press conference.

Laurie was certain the Australians deliberately orchestrated a media witch-hunt against us. I don't know if I'd go that far, but I'm sure Dwyer wound their press up against us. He's a wily bugger.

Everything went mad after the All Blacks-New South Wales game when five New South Wales players went off hurt. It was good hard rugby, a bit of stoush involved, but nothing really dirty. More to the point our supposed team of greenhorns scored six tries and our scrum was like a rock. Loey played a blinder. There was a feeling in our team that the Aussies targeted him from then on.

The actions of Simon Poidevin, a good friend of Dwyer's, made us suspicious. For years he's had our total respect for the person he is, on and off the field. Poido's never ever spoken out against anything that's happened on the field before. I can recall Buck Shelford almost ripping his head off and Poido's said nothing.

But he came out all guns blazing in the press after the All Blacks-NSW game. From that game on the Aussies branded us a dirty team. It was rubbish.

Then came the Carozza thing with Loey – and after that it was all on . . .

"He's still angry. I head-butted him in the elbow."

– Paul Carozza

NICK FARR-JONES

'I thought, 'Here's a guy who probably has a programme in his mind and when he puts his rugby boots on and goes out to play, the programme just activates.'

And it's not necessarily the fault of his character, it's just the way he's been brought up playing the game.

I don't believe the incident was over-dramatised, and it annoys me that New Zealand cried wolf.

Let's just say that it's well-known I wear contact lenses. In my whole career I've lost them during a game maybe five times, and four of them have been against New Zealand.'

PHIL KEARNS

'Sean handled the Loe thing the way I'd expect any captain to handle that situation. He supported his player to the hilt and so as far as I'm concerned he did a great job. I'm sure he and his mates felt exactly the same way as the rest of the world did about what happened . . . however, I wouldn't have expected anything other than Sean to back up his player.'

The media influences public opinion so much that loyalty to your team is essential. A lot goes on in private that people don't know about but, in public, it's very important for the captain to support a senior player like Richard. It doesn't mean you condone things – but you don't isolate a team-mate, either.

Loey is a mate. Off the field he talks a lot – a lot. He's very proud of being an All Black. He enjoys meeting new people. He's similar to

AJ in that he's a very open guy, someone you can take anywhere and he'll happily chat away to strangers. He has a lovely wife, lovely kids, is a loyal team man.

On the field Richard's proved himself one of the great All Black props many times. He is *tough*. One time in Australia he smashed his head into a scrum machine. Most people would have broken their necks; his was just sore. His strength is phenomenal, which is why he's such a great mauler. He doesn't do any weights, it's all natural. It's not for me to comment on his discipline. As a captain I can't control him – I can't control any player. I can tell them what's expected of All Blacks but at the end of the day, responsibility is up to the individual.

Another controversial figure in the series was the Wallaby number 8, Sam Scott-Young. His suggestion to ban the haka was stupid. Off the field I won't give him the time of day. He's one of those players who seems to need psyching up by saying dumb things in public. On the field he does enough of them – it was a joke within the All Blacks that Sam was always good for 10 points a game.

Every Aussie I spoke to said he's just a fool. Even his team-mates say he speaks first, thinks later.

Again, we believed the fuss was deliberately orchestrated by Dwyer. But we had a laugh when Scott-Young wrote us a letter saying he was sorry.

PHIL KEARNS

> ‘Sam has a tendency to open up his big mouth a bit too often and all of that stuff about the haka was a load of rubbish. Sometimes Sam doesn't think before he says things and it was just one of those situations when the press got onto it and it all just got out of control.
>
> Obviously, that kind of thing doesn't do anything for trans-Tasman relations, but really, it was something trivial blown out of all proportion.’

The controversies took the gloss off Australia's victory. It was a shame. The quality of the rugby deserved better.

We didn't have time or the inclination to dwell on such matters. Less than 24 hours after beating Australia, we flew out to South Africa. The Richard Loe and Sam Scott-Young incidents seemed totally irrelevant as we left for a country where, if you believed some of the talk going around, the All Blacks risked wearing a bullet.

CHAPTER SIX

Africa

"Glory may be fleeting, but obscurity is forever." – Anon

SOUTH AFRICANS WERE All Black crazy.

From the moment we checked in at Sydney Airport, during the flight over Australia and across the Indian Ocean, right up to arrival in Johannesburg, the South African Airways people treated us like kings. The pilots let some of the guys ride up in the cockpit, the cabin crew passed out bottles of champagne, even the other passengers were excited to have us on board.

When we flew into Johannesburg it was after midnight. Incredibly, several thousand people were present. The All Blacks were pretty nervous as we walked into a jam-packed arrival area. I remember one guy had this huge banner which read, "Sean – Uli is waiting." Another said, "All Blacks. We are going to crush you."

Hello South Africa, we thought, and climbed on the bus.

NEIL GRAY

'It was awesome to see the numbers who turned up to welcome us. From the first moment, they were all quite convinced the Springboks were going to beat us.'

Everything about our visit to South Africa reeked of politics. The tour itself was a last-minute arrangement between the SARU and the NZRFU once it became internationally acceptable to play sport with them again.

You couldn't ignore how explosive the real political situation was. It's hard to believe it was only two years ago. I've been back twice since for Super 10 games, and the place has changed dramatically.

Back then, de Klerk was still in power, blacks couldn't vote and even Mandela was treated with great suspicion. And we knew the All Blacks presented a big political target for any nutters who wanted to make a name for themselves or their cause by blowing us up. The ANC showed how seriously they took the possibility by meeting regularly with manager Neil Gray to update the situation.

If any of us had any doubts that South Africa was serious stuff, they were dispelled on the bus ride from the airport. This guy was standing at the front of the bus. You could see he wasn't a rugby official. We wondered what he was doing until he opened up his coat to reveal a big gun. "Hi," he said, "I'm with security. There are 16 of us here to protect you. We'll be with you every moment while you're in our country."

During the ride in we had a police escort. At the hotel we were warned not to step outside unless one of the security guards came with us. An entire floor of the hotel was blocked off just for the All Black party. No one could reach it without a security clearance.

At 2am we had a press conference. There were a few questions on apartheid but we were well briefed: I said we have no comment to make and delivered the good old cliche that we were in South Africa only to play rugby and we'd leave politics up to the politicians.

Then, thankfully, it was time for bed.

The next day was meant to be a quiet one. It had been a long flight and we hadn't had that much sleep after the third Australian test either.

South Africa was a very short tour: five games, only one test. But I was determined that we got through unbeaten. I saw the games as crucial in turning a satisfactory season into one which gave us real confidence for the future. Defeat was unthinkable; not only would it destroy the gains we struggled for in Australia, it would probably finish off several careers. Maybe mine. I know I wouldn't have fancied returning to New Zealand to explain a "Played four, lost three" test record.

Perhaps Laurie had a rethink about this prospect too. Something got into him. After warning us to take things gently because of the dangers of over-training at altitude, he proceeded to give us this huge blow-out.

It was a killer. Everyone struggled and quite a few legs went wobbly. One of the props threw up, and one of the bigger backs didn't last the session. There were nose bleeds – common at high altitude. We were exhausted but it was good, it cleared a few cobwebs away.

We got off to a rocky start with their media. Laurie was really on the defensive. I'm not sure if it was a throwback to his '76 All Black tour but he didn't trust their media at all. And he was fuming after an article came out that morning. It quoted Bob Dwyer, quoting Laurie, as saying how arrogant and cocky Laurie thought the South Africans were – and how the All Blacks would sort them out . . .

Laurie just hit the roof when he read this. So after the first training run, Laurie told Ric Salizzo, who was our Press Officer, that he wasn't going to give any interviews. Eventually the issue was resolved but Laurie made it quite clear there would be no second chances. In front of all the journos Laurie said, "OK, before we start, let's get the ground rules clear. Anyone who ever misquotes me, *ever*, will never come to another press conference I give."

This big guy from Cape Town stood up and said, "Look, we will never misquote you. It's a blessing to finally have an international rugby team in South Africa. For years all we've had to write about is Currie Cup games. We are thrilled you are here."

They were as good as their word. South African rugby writers, I believe, are the most knowledgeable in the world. But you could see Laurie's little pep talk had an effect.

Because we were stuck in hotels for security reasons so much of the time, we got to know our guards really well. They turned out to be characters.

They were very macho. One guy had white-blond hair, cold blue eyes and a pink face. His name was Cuban. Another guy was called Clint, apparently in honour of his hero, Clint Eastwood. They all carried arms of one kind or another. They loved their guns and never went anywhere without them. They opened bottles of beer with their guns. One guy even used to swing his .45 pistol around his finger, like an old time cowboy.

There were bomb checks every day. Some of the locals seemed to think we were a bit over-protected. Our hotel was in Johannesburg's northern suburbs, about 10km out, and we weren't allowed in the inner city. We did visit Soweto but it was very low-key. It wasn't what I expected at all – neither was South Africa. On one hand you had scenes of great wealth and beauty; on the other fenced-off shopping malls, barbed wire fences and guns, guns, guns.

We didn't see much of the country. Laurie was ultra-concerned about altitude, so to ensure we were properly acclimatised we spent most of our time well above sea level, making quick trips from Johannesburg and back. Again, we were probably over-cautious.

This policy meant no visit to Kruger Park, which is traditional for All Black teams. It was a big disappointment, but we were there with a job to do: beat the Springboks. It's situations like this which can split an unhappy team. The guys showed their character, trained really hard, and the team became really close, closer than at any other time on tour.

"I'm sure there are modest people in South Africa, but we didn't meet any." – Anon

I COULDN'T GET OVER how one-eyed South Africans are. They are even more fanatical than the Welsh. At every game they put aside their "Great to have you in South Africa" backslaps and started hating us – and then after the games they switched back to being our friends. Their change in attitude was amazing.

Their fans are very schizophrenic: they love you because you're rugby people, and they would always cheer us when the team bus arrived at a ground. But they're very arrogant about their abilities, too. I spoke to quite a few New Zealand supporters on tour who found them the same.

They believe so much in themselves, that only they have the world's great players – everyone else is second best. After about five minutes you get really sick of it.

Typical was the guy who asked Foxy for his autograph. "I'd like to wish you well for the test," he said, "but I can't because I hope you lose."

Foxy told him that if that was his attitude, then unfortunately, he couldn't oblige with a signature but he could offer him some free advice instead.

Everywhere we went we got the same talk: "Is this the best beach, or what?" "Is this the best meat?" "The best weather?" "The best rugby?" Etcetera, etcetera, etcetera.

A black man used to ring and just beg me to make sure that we beat the Springboks. He said, "If you don't beat them you'll hurt the blacks. The whites will think they are still the best . . ." The closer it got to the test the more frequently he called. After we won, he rang me at 7am the next day. He was crying with joy.

Louis Luyt, Mr South African Rugby, invited us to a private function. He heard we were looking for somewhere discreet to have a bit of a party and he offered us the use of his house. It was amazing. He extended the invite about 2pm, we turned up about 6pm – and he already had these spits going, drinks laid on for us, the works.

His house wasn't your average roof and four walls either.

Luyt is a big man in every sense. A big build, big jaw, big voice. You can see he's very powerful over there. All the locals bow and scrape around him.

His offer was greatly appreciated. We needed a chance to let our hair down and get away. The security guards put down their guns long enough to join in too. We all got on the rum and Cokes together.

We saw Danie Craven once. Though he still ran South Africa's rugby show, he was just a little old man. Bald-headed. Frail. At the function where we met him, he got off to a very good start with the guys by giving us some gold bars.

Rumours were going round that they were worth about 25,000 rand [$NZ16,000] each, but we later had them valued at about 300 [$NZ190].

Craven made a very strange speech.

He said, "New Zealand and South Africa are very competitive rugby countries. When you come here you are cheated, but every time we go to New Zealand we are treated like dogs. In 1981 it was just disgusting . . ."

He kept going on about 1981. "The way we were treated was disgusting. Those protesters, they should have been rounded up and shot." That's what he said. We thought, "Who is this guy?"

And still he wasn't done. " . . . we were treated like animals. We had to sleep on the floor, we had to sleep on squash courts – and all because of those protesters."

Finally he finished. That was Danie Craven. He wasn't senile; he meant everything he said.

The All Blacks couldn't escape a high profile. And once Australia flew in for their simultaneous mini-tour, the situation became crazy.

We met the then President, F.W. de Klerk, at a State reception for all three teams. This was probably the most tense moment of the trip. It was three days out from the test, at a place called Gold Reef City. Shaft Fourteen – 220 metres underground. To one side, in a VIP area, were the All Blacks, Springboks, and Wallabies. De Klerk was there, so too was Steve Tshwete of the ANC and Chief Buthelezi, the Zulu leader. TV carried the thing live.

But it was nerve-wracking. You knew this would be the ideal time for someone to drop a bomb and grab a lot of headlines. Luckily, the barbecue they'd laid on caused the tunnels to fill up with smoke, so most of us used this as an excuse to move upstairs. I was very aware of how extremely charged and political everything was, and didn't like being part of it. You felt set up.

> *"South Africa has, over the years, been the [world's] most successful rugby nation. They lead the All Blacks in tests and series, have scored four Grand Slams in Britain . . . The All Blacks have been more successful at home against European sides than have the Springboks, but in other areas the Springboks lead."*
>
> – Graeme Barrow, rugby writer

KEVIN PUTT

'I think people tend to exaggerate the different styles of play between the two countries. Rucking is the only thing that's really different: Kiwis are keen to play the ball on the ground, whereas South Africans tend to play it up in the air more.

South Africa doesn't have huge forward packs like they're supposed to. Where they really differ from New Zealand is in loose forwards. They breed loosies big over there.'

We flew down to Durban on Friday for our first game against the Currie Cup champions, Natal. At the airport we were welcomed by a Zulu performance, and then we were driven through the city. The streets were lined with cheering people. Durban was brilliantly fine, very much like Brisbane with its heat and humidity. This was the South Africa we'd all grown up hearing about, the South Africa that Laurie and Earle had been inspired to come back and defeat. I talked about it with Foxy who'd been here with the Cavaliers. They loved the place, and enjoyed a great time.

As the Natalians welcomed us, I began to understand why. For some reason, Johannesburg hadn't seemed like South Africa – as JK said, it felt more like a city in Argentina. Durban was the real thing, part of the image of South Africa I imagined as a kid. I thought of Joe Morgan scoring his famous solo try for the All Blacks against the Springboks on the '76 tour. I was only 13 at the time but I was in awe of the whole All Black-Springbok tradition. It was a marvellous feeling to know that in just 24 hours, our All Black team would be part of that history. I felt excited, and on edge.

The team was apprehensive. At this stage there was still so much uncertainty about the power of South African rugby. They'd been in isolation for so long that no one – not us, not them – knew how much effect this would have. In Australia we'd heard all the stories from Laurie and Earle of how previous All Black teams had been sandbagged in various ways. In South Africa, everyone had a warning for us: How bad the local refs were. How massive the players. How they'd do anything to win. How drugs were rife.

You couldn't separate fact from fiction, which was why everyone was so keen to get that first game under our belt.

That night Laurie and I had a meeting with Freek Burger, the referee, Ian McIntosh, Natal's coach, and Natal's captain, Wahl Bartmann. Wahl confirmed the stereotype perfectly: he is a man-mountain, typical of the Natal forwards who outweighed us by 6kg a man.

We chose a virtual test team. The score reached 22-all at one stage, but we pulled away well at the end. Ant Strachan scored a stunning try and JK and Inga were all power on the wings.

JOHN ALLEN

'Natal never thought we could beat them. Our problems were in our heads and the All Blacks knew that. And once we showed a weakness, that was it: bang, bang, bang. They cleaned us up.

Sean coerced the ref with a couple of decisions. He was talking so much. He was such an irritant, but a perfect gentleman about it. I got so pissed off I asked him, 'Why don't you invite the ref to tea?' ’

Natal was a huge result for us. Most importantly, it popped a few balloons about South African superiority. We played a smart game at the line-out and our general speed around the park was so much faster than theirs. We scored four tries; they got a dodgy penalty try. Despite their size, we knew that their big slow men were metres behind the play. Players like Robin Brooke were smaller, but far more athletic, more skilled, better all-round players.

Psychologically, we were very encouraged. Natal had been building for this game for weeks and had given their best – and though we won, we hadn't played to our full potential. We still had lots left in reserve.

In the other provincial games we never looked likely to lose. It was heartening to see the team thrashed by Sydney come back so well against Orange Free State. Ian Jones was an inspiration that day. The Free State lost their rag and tried to hit us out of the game but they failed to knock us off our stride. The final two matches also produced good results.

In our last week we visited Sun City, a couple of hours out of Johannesburg. It's a giant holiday resort/amusement park set in a volcanic crater, with a machine that makes artificial waves among its many sights. We played nine holes of golf and tried not to think of rugby. We stayed at a nearby game park which was memorable for its lack of animals and abundance of rocks. The guys joked the place sold so many postcards of elephants because you never got to see any.

That night we went touring in these big open-deck trucks. It was a marvellous experience. We travelled through the night, our path lit by giant spotlights. Then we stopped in the middle of nowhere and ate around an open camp-fire. It was a great way to let off steam; the test was now only a couple of days away.

When we got back to Johannesburg, we found the city struck by test fever. It's all anybody talked about. I was interviewed heaps of times, the papers were chock-full of news about "Saturday's big game". That week, the test seemed to be the only thing happening in the world.

In training, we worked on countering their lifting which they were so blatant about. We practised a number of different line-out options, which worked well in the test. Laurie and Earle had spent a lot of time thinking about tactics, delving deep into their understanding and experiences of South African rugby. We respected the South Africans, but we weren't afraid of them. And we knew how inexperienced they were. Half of their side had never played a test. Naas Botha, Danie Gerber and Uli Schmidt were their big guns. On the other hand, this was our ninth test of the year and by now our guys were test-hardened.

We weren't immune to nerves. The day before the test there was a big argument among some of the test pack. It was a sign of the pressure we felt under.

That night Laurie told me he was worried. "Something's not right, the feeling in the team's not right," he said. I wasn't too concerned. The players were in good form; everyone knew what they had to do.

One guy turned up at the hotel with clay mannequins he'd made of me and Naas Botha. When one of the players saw the Naas doll he snapped off its head. That's how hyped up we were and what we felt about the Springboks – Naas in particular.

He was the prime example of South African arrogance. He and Uli Schmidt even videotaped one of our training sessions. They sat in the grandstand taping our moves in broad daylight. I was disappointed in him. He'd been a hero of mine in 1981 for the way he played in New Zealand. But now he was such a superstar in South Africa he acted like he could do no wrong. Even his wife is famous – she's competed for South Africa at the Barcelona Olympics in the long-jump.

South African arrogance worked in the All Blacks' favour. They refused to see that their isolation might have hurt them and almost stubbornly insisted on doing things the old way. This became noticeable during the test. Basically, they were too slow and too concerned with set-pieces, the scrum in particular. Forwards and backs rarely combined and they kicked too much good ball away.

ULI SCHMIDT

'Our team was pushed together, but our guys were not a team, they didn't like each other so much.

For 10 years we had no international competition so for 10 years our rivals were other South Africans.

I'd spent five years in the military, for example, fighting a border war for my country. But among the team there wasn't the same *esprit de corps.*

Then there was the politics. The tour was on-again, off-again . . . all this talk about not playing the anthem . . . about changing the name of the Springboks . . . we were pushed into a black suburb to train . . . We were confused. I said at the time, 'We're not ready for this.''

PIETER MULLER

'It was my first test and I didn't really know what to expect. Now, having played a lot more international rugby, I see John Williams' coaching methods were very old-fashioned, maybe 12 years behind the times.

Our training was predictable. We never did any grids, no skill work, just forwards and backs splitting up and doing the basics.

We were so nervous before the test. From my point of view, as a player you usually have a slight feeling in the back of your mind you're going to win. But we never had that feeling against the All Blacks.'

ULI SCHMIDT

'Rely on Naas – that was our game plan. We didn't practise a lot of moves. Whenever you play with Naas, that's it. He decides everything. You give the ball to Naas, he kicks it down-field, we get a penalty – and Naas will kick it over.'

The weather for the test was ideal. I woke about 7.30am and saw it was another perfect South African winter's day. Ideal for the All Blacks' style of rugby.

The atmosphere at Ellis Park was just unbelievable. The Australian team were already there, spying on the Boks before their test the next week. They made no bones about it, they really wanted us to win. "Best of luck Sean, best of luck All Blacks . . ." was their general attitude as we walked from the bus to the dressing rooms.

Running onto the ground we received the loudest roar I've ever heard from an opposing crowd. The cheer we got was phenomenal.

As we lined up for the anthems, you could see the crowd was in a frenzy. It was unlike any other test match I've played in . . . the noise, the emotion . . . you had guards wrestling with people who were running onto the field carrying banned South African flags . . . When we heard the South African anthem I realised it wasn't meant to be played but at that stage of a test those things don't bother you. The game is all you're focused on.

PIETER MULLER

'The goose bumps you felt as they played the anthems was something you can't really explain. I think maybe it was because we were so emotional that it took us so long to get into the game.

The All Blacks intimidated us. At every line-out or scrum they'd 'brush' past you. We let them. I was 21, inexperienced . . . it was a real experience.

We played Australia a week later. I think Australia was the more technical side, the All Blacks were the more physical. On the Sunday after the All Black test I could hardly walk – I was just so sore, the game had been so hard.'

The Springboks went at us like mad dogs in the opening half-hour . . .

They were good in the scrums early on, very good. I wasn't too surprised – our scrummaging had been below par all tour in South Africa.

But gradually we hauled ourselves back and once we got in front we controlled most of the test.

Naas and I were not getting on. We clashed in the first minute when I had a go at him. He got the ball on the 10-metre line and put in a big up-and-under.

As he was going down I gave him a nudge and he chased after me yelling insults. He called me a "dirty animal".

About 20 minutes later I tackled him heavily and he continued abusing me. It was all water off a duck's back to me and I knew he was rattled, so I kept baiting him. Every time he was talking to the referee, I'd interrupt.

"Come on Naas, let's get on with it." He couldn't stand it.

I thought Sandy McNeill, the ref, handled the test pretty well. There had been a lot of publicity about how the South Africans lifted their jumpers in the line-outs, and he was under a lot of pressure to keep this in check.

WAHL BARTMANN

> ‘People ask why we didn't change tactics when Sean kept running at Naas. But it was up to Naas to change the tactics. He was the captain, he called the shots, he was the law.
>
> It wasn't your job to question.’

I was pretty happy with my game. I had a few good runs. I thought the team hung together brilliantly. The score flattered South Africa, but a year's intense rugby caught up with us in the end. We were clearly the best team in the line-out and the loose and the backs put together some brilliant moves. At 27-10, however, the altitude, the heat and the travelling all hit us. Muller's try should never have been allowed – du Preez knocked on during the move – and Gerber's try was scored when the game was over bar the shouting. Some moaners weren't satisfied with the narrow victory. A three-point margin? It didn't matter. We had the victory, that's what counted.

It was a fantastic feeling in our dressing room afterwards. Laurie and Earle and Thorbs were grinning away and everyone felt the whole tour a success. Even our security guards were over the moon we'd won.

I had a picture taken of me holding a Springbok jersey; it really felt like we'd scalped them.

While we were getting changed Laurie told Zinny he owed his place in the team to me.

He said, "You played great football today Zinzan – but you were lucky you got the chance. You owe it to Sean that you're here. He said you could do this, you could do that, but I had doubts if you'd do the hard work. But Sean was right, you did."

It made me feel great that my judgement had paid off, but, more importantly, I was so happy for Zinny. Finally, he had shown his amazing talent at test level. His try was proof of his confidence. That's all he needs – confidence. New Zealand saw what the Auckland team had known for ages.

At the press conference, Naas was his usual arrogant self. He didn't praise us, he just bagged Sandy McNeill.

"The referee was disgusting," he said. "During the game he was not very nice to me at all." I was sick of him by now so I said, "Well you weren't very nice to him either, Naas. Let's drop it."

The local journos looked shocked. You just didn't question Naas Botha's opinion. And never in public.

There were about a thousand people at the after-match function, which was back at the hotel. We were meant to be there at 7.30pm but we arrived about 7.45pm. We needn't have worried about being late. As soon as we got there we were told, "The Springboks haven't arrived yet."

Fine, we said, we'll have a team session until they do. Come and fetch us when the Boks arrive. Then everyone said a few words and we gave our gifts to the management.

I told Laurie how much the team had enjoyed working with him and the other selectors. Then Laurie said how wonderful the team was, how he had his doubts at the beginning of the year but now he actually rated Aucklanders – "you're not such a bad bunch of blokes". It was a good evening, everyone was having lots of laughs . . . the test victory feeling better and better by the minute.

At 8.30pm we said, "Right, let's go mix and mingle." Time dragged on, and the Springboks were nowhere in sight. The officials were furious. We were meant to have speeches but without their players nothing could begin.

At 10pm they still hadn't arrived. I couldn't believe it, I'd never seen the host team not front before. Lion Lager, their sponsors, were spitting. There was talk of the Springboks getting revenge on them for putting their money into black rugby and coloured rugby instead of the team fund, which wouldn't surprise me.

Finally, at about 10pm, Naas and his boys walked in with no sorrys, no explanations, no nothing. He said, "It's been 10 years since we've had an international game. We had a lot of initiations to perform." I said, "Yeah, great, nice to see you," walked off and never spoke to him again.

Later I found out about the Springbok "initiations" . . . apparently, after the test, all the new caps take their pants off. Then they lie down on the floor and the rest of the team belts them across the buttocks with a belt . . .

It was a late night. After what seemed only a few minutes we were up again, going home.

I was pretty drained. I'd been All Black captain for five months and the victory felt so sweet. But my strongest emotion, as usual after a big victory, was utter relief. I remember packing that Sunday, aching and hung-over, and my overwhelming thought was, "Thank God it's over."

CHAPTER SEVEN

Last Action Hero

"I doubt whether [hooker] is the ideal position to be a captain . . ."
– Andy Dalton, *The Geriatrics*

AFTER FIVE MONTHS AS All Black captain I believed I'd come a long way, both as a person and as a leader.

Basically I had two challenges in 1992: to be a good influence within the team, and improve the public image of the All Blacks. Both were very different demands; both were equally important.

Within the team I got feedback on how I was doing by asking people. I'd say to JK, "Am I saying too much, or what?" And he'd tell me to my face.

I talked to the younger guys too, guys like Ant Strachan and Arran Pene. I was constantly making sure I treated the young guys as equals, not like some ogre. I made sure they knew I was just another player in the team, I didn't get special treatment, I had to put in the hard work just like them.

I suppose I played as well as I had on any previous tour. But even though I was made Player of the Year I don't view the tour in terms of my individual performances. As you get older you appreciate the games the team wins more. It's only when you're younger that your own performance matters so much.

Frankly, I find it hard talking about myself because I don't like people who talk about themselves that much. The "How great thou art", the "I, I, I" sort. Some players aren't scared to tell you how well they played, but I can't recall any games that stand out. Obviously, I knew my overall form was good. I thought I still had work to do in terms of decision-making on the field, I knew that.

ROBIN BROOKE

> 'Everyone liked Fitzy. But he got respect because of how he plays, not what he said.
>
> In his team talks, there was never any 'Do it this way' sort of line. It was usually a 'get-on-with-the-job' approach. He didn't say a helluva lot, but he might ask one of the players to speak instead, like Foxy.
>
> In training, he'd call a halt and clear it with Laurie if he wasn't happy with something. He wasn't afraid to ask questions of the coach – a lot of other players would've gone blindly along.'

GRANT FOX

> 'I don't know if Sean will admit it but in 1992 he got his 'number one hooker' rating back. It hurt him to lose it at the World Cup. We've all got egos, we all want to be number one.
>
> What made it easy for us to accept Fitzy as captain was his form. It's always easy to follow someone who leads the way, but his form was better than just good. I don't ever think he's played better rugby, or put his body on the line more often.
>
> And his public speaking was so good the guys thought he had a double.'

With so many new guys it wasn't too difficult to get their respect. I possibly found it a bit harder with senior players like Stevie and Loey, because we'd been together for so long and they saw me as one of the lads still. I tried to be sensitive to their situation. Probably, if one of them had been made captain I'd have felt the same way . . .

But even old mates couldn't get preferential treatment.

If I had something to say to them I'd be direct and I'd say it in front of everyone. One time in Africa I had Loey on for the way he spoke to Jamie Joseph at training. He exploded, saying I was acting like a "typical Aucklander". This went on for ages, and we were getting nowhere. On one level it really annoyed me because, as a captain, I'd tried to erase any tension between the guys. But I also knew that Loey's irritability was a sign that he was ready for the test; it wasn't personal with Jamie.

After the flak we got in 1991 for our off-field behaviour I had a very definite image of the do's and don'ts I wanted in the team. A definite don't was to show off. If I saw someone like Ant Strachan – a naturally cocky guy – being a "showgun" I'd say, "Strawny, I don't like that . . ." And Ant would look all innocent and say, "What? Me?" So I'd say it again: "Strawny, you *know* what I mean."

Nothing changed overnight but gradually players understood they had to be more responsible for themselves. I couldn't teach them everything. A player like Ian Jones, for instance, discovered he was now the senior lock. Where Gary Whetton used to be dominant and all Ian had to worry about was his job, now he needed to look after the younger guys.

Jonesy realised he hadn't played that well in Australia and he got nailed a bit, in meetings and privately, about his contribution. He took it on the chin, thought about what we'd said and in Africa he pulled it all together.

He captained the side against Orange Free State and in an explosive game he kept control and played outstandingly. Superb.

ROBIN BROOKE

'After the first test loss against Australia we had a team session and Fitzy spoke very calmly, very sensibly. He didn't bag anyone, just told us all to take a good long look at ourselves over the next few days.

Later that night, Sean got around to all of the players individually for a few words. That's his style, he's done it a few times since.'

EARLE KIRTON

'You could hear a pin drop when he spoke to the team. He was playing so well, his work rate was tremendous, everyone had total respect for him.

We knew he had words with players if they stepped out of line but he never told us. And we didn't want to know. But you'd see it in them at training the next day. They'd have picked up their act.

He had to have that input too, it was crucial to our success. Players have a different feeling for their captain than us grey-haired old coaches . . .'

JOHN KIRWAN

'Getting the team together and saying 'do this', or 'do that' is not Sean's style. When he spoke to us as a group he'd speak for as long as he thought necessary. If he didn't have much to say, he'd wouldn't drag things out. You'd be surprised how rare that is. Some captains speak on and on because they think they have to.

Sean achieved a lot of his authority through chats with individuals on a one-to-one basis.'

"Captaincy has done many things for Fitzy but it hasn't improved his golf." — Grant Fox

I COULD TELL IT was a happy tour off the field because of the lack of whingeing. Guys who weren't playing well, or who got dropped, didn't let their personal situation affect the team. Out of 30 players who went away, I knew of only two who grumbled and moaned . . .

It was excellent. Ours was a happy team, probably one of the happiest teams I've been away with. And I'm not just saying that because I was captain.

Take Zinzan Brooke and Arran Pene. Before the tour they didn't know each other from a bar of soap. In the early days they were a bit wary, like two dogs sniffing each other out because they were both competing for the same place . . . by the end of the tour they were best of mates.

I was also influenced by what happened with the 1991 team and my first overseas tour, to France in 1986. There were lots of lessons from them.

The '86 tour of France was the height of the Cavaliers – David Kirk tension. I saw a lot of it because I roomed with a Cavalier, Cowboy Shaw. Cowboy and Kirky were at each other hammer and tongs for weeks. Once the two of them stayed up all night arguing about Kirky's decision not to go with the Cavaliers. Cowboy wasn't alone. A lot of the Cavaliers were really sour on Kirk.

Things got pretty heated at times, although deep down I think Cowboy respected him. Kirk's an obstinate little bugger. He'd argue about which brand of light bulb is the best if he thought he'd get a good debate.

But sometimes it was malicious. We had a champagne breakfast the morning after the Nantes test and a few of the emotions that had been bottled up for months finally surfaced. Maybe it was the loss, too much booze, but a few of them got stuck into Kirky verbally. They were each drinking a bottle of champagne and challenging him, "Come on Kirky, drink up like a *real man*."

There was never any trouble like that in 1992.

The biggest progress I made was in learning to trust my instincts.

After the Aussie leg of the tour I went to Laurie and said, "We've got a problem with a couple of the older guys. They're not happy at not getting any games."

A thing was developing about a "Wednesday team" and a "Saturday team". The major grizzles came from two of the most experienced All Blacks, Terry Wright and Steve McDowell. For years they'd been first-choice All Blacks, but on this tour they were on the outer.

Laurie didn't have much sympathy. He said to Steve, "Richard came away as the number-two loosehead prop, but he's trained his bloody guts off. Now he's number one. What have you done to get your position back?"

In a lot of ways I felt really sorry for Stevie. He's a big mate, we've shared a lot of great experiences. I think he's one of the great All Black props. His record proves this. If he has a weakness it's that he's not self-critical enough. Everyone had told him how good he was for so long that he couldn't believe it when he wasn't in the test team any more.

Laurie would tell him, "Steve, at every scrum you've got to push. At every training you've got to push yourself as hard as you can. Keep the pressure on all the time." Laurie obviously thought Loey was more consistent at this area of the game, because he displaced Steve as the number one loosehead on tour.

Steve's great company and so it wasn't surprising the young guys would want to spend time with him off the field. I was a little concerned: Stevie's done everything in rugby, he has his own touring style, he knows his limits and they're not those of most people. I didn't think these young guys on their first tour were in a position to be too individualistic. I could see Steve latching onto a couple of them, taking them out for a few drinks when an early night would've been a smarter option. I didn't want to interfere – these are grown men – but the more I watched the more I knew it's not what I wanted in the All Blacks.

I went up to Marc Ellis, one of the young guys, and I said to him, "What's the problem? Do you feel as though there's an A Team and a B Team?" He said, "Yeah, there is."

"Have you got a problem with it?"

"No – but I want to be in the A Team."

"Is there a bit of ill feeling in the B Team then?"

Marc said there was. "Only because we want to be in the A team. I feel when I've played well enough I'll be there. So do most of the guys . . ."

I said, "That's a good attitude. When you *are* playing well enough I hope you'll get there too." But I wasn't really comfortable with this "A team, B team" talk, so I went to Laurie and told him, "I think you're going to have to have a bit of a meeting with the team and get a couple of things straight . . . I don't want any divisions. What would you say to the three selectors and myself just having a day of interviews with the players?"

So that's what we did.

In the first few days in Johannesburg we spoke to every player individually. It was quite formal – they'd come into the team room and Laurie, Earle, Thorbs and I would talk to them about everything. Laurie said to each one, "Right so-and-so, we're here to sum up how we think the tour's going for you so far, check the goals that you should be setting yourself and discuss how we think you're playing . . ."

The interviews took three days to complete. All the guys said they really appreciated Laurie telling them what he thought of them. And they couldn't believe it when he finished each talk by saying, "Now I want you to tell me straight out: how do you think *I'm* going?"

In the interviews the only two people who said there was an "A team" and a "B team" were Stevie and Terry. Laurie was straight-up with them. I admired Laurie for being honest, even though it wasn't what they wanted to hear. At least they knew where he stood.

Laurie said to Terry, "You've been injured throughout the tour and it's affected your form and confidence." Obviously I felt sympathy for Terry. He had a fantastic career. But his lack of size counted against him in the end. For years he defied the odds. He'd bounce back from everything like an indiarubber man. He was more suited to an open style of game where there was room to use his pace.

But with the new rules in 1992, our style changed. Our wings needed to be bigger and stronger, able to bash up the middle and create ruck situations. Terry couldn't do that. On the other hand, JK and Inga complemented each other perfectly.

JOHN KIRWAN

'I'd say there were three main reasons for Sean's success. First, he thought a lot about the job and how he could best relate to people so that they'd perform.

Secondly, he wasn't insecure: he was prepared to listen to different points of view and he'd go with the best one – whether it was his idea or not.

Finally, he was a good learner. He'd obviously picked up a lot watching the different All Black captains over the years. And he was intelligent enough to use only the good things . . .'

EARLE KIRTON

'In retrospect, Sean could've been captain earlier in his career, such was the success he made of it.

I called him 'OFV' – Old Fashioned Values. He set himself such high standards in terms of personal discipline that everyone was impressed.

He didn't go down the back of the bus, he didn't mix with the Auckland boys, he gave up a lot of fun he could've had. I applauded the gradual way he went about things. It's a lonely cause being a captain like that and he did it for the sake of the team.

I then realised how much character the lad had.'

Captaincy can be quite lonely. That was a surprise, probably the hardest part of the job for me. There *has* to be a certain amount of aloofness from the rest of the team, you can't get too chummy. One of the things that makes the guys get really close is because we room together. It's the fastest way of forming friendships. Being a captain means you're isolated. You room alone. In the morning you wake up and go to breakfast by yourself. This was pretty hard for me because I like people, I like company. When I was just a player you'd get into a rhythm with your team-mate, go for a run, keep up to date with all the gossip.

But everyone was pretty good to me. They kept me informed. I knew that Gary Whetton used to find it pretty hard being left out of things when he became captain, and on tour I understood why.

A captain has more time to think. He sits up the front of the bus by the coach, he's got more outside pressures on his plate, he can't let his hair down so easily . . . I had fun, but not like other years. There's a time and place to act the goat, and one of those places isn't as All Black captain. My real satisfaction came in watching the team develop into a very good side.

EARLE KIRTON

> 'He was his own man. He talked with us and we confided in each other but he didn't want to be seen as a management lackey, a political piece. He kept his distance too.'

> *"I always found the team talk difficult, not so much to do, but to believe in."* – Graham Mourie, *Captain*

AFTER I RETURNED HOME I got lots of requests to give talks to various sports teams on motivation. But I turned them down, because I didn't know the individuals involved. Motivation is about knowing the people, not having a few magic words to say.

I probably would have found captaincy a lot harder without Laurie. He was immensely supportive. There is a clear line between us though. He kept his promise to remain that little bit distant from the team, and that included me. As a rule, he won't drink for the sake of drinking. He's no stick-in-the-mud – he knows how to celebrate – but he's extremely disciplined. He'd rather go out by himself. I admire that, and it doesn't affect us at all. We've got a common goal because we both want the All Blacks to be successful.

Laurie was the undisputed number one but Earle Kirton and Peter Thorburn played important back-up roles.

Thorbs joined us late in Australia after coaching the Colts to victory in Brisbane. He spent a lot of time with the "B team" and played a big role in turning them around after the disaster against Sydney.

Aucklanders aren't meant to like Wellingtonians, but Earle and I had got on well since he coached me at the trials a couple of years before. He's a good fall-back for Laurie, too. They're complete opposites in personality – Earle is more relaxed, Laurie's more intense.

The management had a firm hand, but they treated us like adults. They liked a drink or two as well. Earle was the main advocate of us getting away from the team session system.

Sessions are good occasionally, but you don't need them after every game.

Earle stressed that touring must be enjoyable. He warned us about getting too intense about rugby. It's an easy trap to fall into.

LAURIE MAINS

'The coaches didn't spend a lot of time socialising with him. The relationship in that respect was quite professional. Our style of communication is a lot of one-liners; short, to-the-point discussions. No prevarication.

We didn't have beers together; I like Sean as a person, but I'll have plenty of time to know him socially when we're both retired.'

EARLE KIRTON

'It's part of our being fair to the team. We made it our policy not to get too close to any player, not even Sean. We were well aware of what resulted in the past when that happened.'

One of the best things Laurie did was to get rid of the system of three old guys in the back seat of the bus. In the past the All Blacks sat in the bus in a very hierarchical way. Not this team.

LAURIE MAINS

'Before we left I was determined to avoid any cliques. In the team room I noticed all the players sat together in groups with their provincial team-mates: Auckland here, North Harbour there . . .

So I told them straight. I said, 'If I see any clique developing in this team, any clique at all, then I'm going to send a player home. I'll walk in and choose someone – and they're off the tour. I'll be the first All Black coach to send a player home for being in a clique. But I'll do it.' '

EARLE KIRTON

'I was watching the players. And you had individuals easing away from their team-mates while Laurie was speaking. No one said a word. You could've heard a pin drop.

It was essential he laid down the law. I wasn't prepared to lose money from my practice, to go away for weeks and put up with the sort of off-field behaviour that developed in 1991.'

LAURIE MAINS

'It wasn't as if they didn't believe me – they believed me all right . . .'

Laurie stressed to the guys, "You've got to be careful what you do. You can't just go out and get drunk and fall asleep in the gutter, because the next thing you know, you'll be on the front page of the *New Zealand Herald*."

After the South African test, Robin got a bit carried away at the function and Zinny took him aside and told him to sort out his act.

He didn't, so in the middle of the function Thorbs took him home and put him to bed. He'd dropped a couple of glasses or thrown something at somebody, and that's just not acceptable in this team.

There weren't many discipline problems. Certainly nothing to set the headlines on fire. Cooksley had a talking to at one stage, but it was the classic case of a young guy following bad habits.

After a test the reserves usually have a pretty quiet night because they haven't played. So they go to bed early and get ready for the game on Tuesday. But after the first test in Sydney I saw Cooksley in the bar at about one o'clock. A few minutes later I saw him walking down the road with one of the older guys.

I was surprised: I knew they both wanted to be test players. If it had been me, I would've retired early and been up for a run first thing. The older player had been on several tours and he knew the score. Still, that was *his* problem. Whether he knew it or not this player was influencing Cookie. That was *our* problem. So we had a word with Cooksley and told him to pull his head in. "If you haven't played, Mark," we said, "then you don't go out."

He took it well. And later in the tour, after he played well in Africa, he saw me in the bar and said with a huge grin, "I suppose *you're* going to bed at 8 o'clock tonight, aren't you Sean?"

I was the reserve that day.

JOHN KIRWAN

> 'Sean brought a smile back to rugby. Literally. Ever since he's been captain, if you watch him closely in TV interviews you'll see how he smiles at hard questions, he smiles whether the team's won or lost . . . he shows emotion.
>
> It's great PR, but it's also a very smart thing to do. That grin, that laugh, buys him time to think of the right answer – instead of blurting out the first thing that comes into his head.'

NEIL GRAY

> 'Right from the start the ground rules were laid down to the team – no scowly, unattractive postures in public. Always endeavour to smile. In Sean we had the ideal man to represent this new image.'

From the moment I became captain, it's been a passion with me to change preconceived ideas about what many people think the All Blacks were, and are, like. I know some see an All Black and automatically think: dumb, thick thugs.

I was determined any All Black side I led would not be thought of like that.

I found it was the little things which counted for a lot. Soon after I got back from South Africa I was at a function where I saw some people who had some connection with Auckland rugby.

It would have been easy enough to ignore them, or just nod

hello, but I found out their names and went across to them, shook his hand, gave her a kiss and chatted for a couple of minutes. I wasn't putting on an act – they had seen me and it would have been unbelievably rude of me to have ignored them.

RIC SALIZZO

'Only when you look back do you see clues or signs that were always there. Sean always had an excellent sense for what makes good public relations, but he wasn't seen as future captaincy material, so no one noticed.

I remember the time the All Blacks visited Ireland in 1989. Sean got off the plane, saw the cameras and after he'd taken his first step on Irish soil he turned around and said to the media, 'It's good to be home.'

I mean those sort of comments look so easy, but they're not. They are the sort of comments which get picked up by people. And the Irish absolutely loved it. Even then, he knew what made great PR. It's an instinctive thing.'

ANDY HADEN

'The All Black captaincy hinges a lot on the public perception of honesty. Honesty and success – combined – give a Buck Shelford seal of approval for a captain.

Whilst Fitzpatrick's All Blacks didn't win immediately, he got back quite a bit of the Shelford mana because it was seen that he was clearly trying to put things right. I liken him very much to Ian Kirkpatrick; Kirkpatrick knew what the job represented and in his heart of hearts how it should be done. Fitzpatrick also knows what the job requires. The public saw that too.'

Captaincy quietened me down. It had its drawbacks. I became a lot more intense, I didn't relax as much as I ought to have. But when you're put into as many different situations as an All Black captain is, with no safety net, you either make an idiot of yourself or you do OK. Every time I was successful in public my confidence grew. I got more of a buzz in, say, meeting de Klerk and handling myself live on South African TV than just being one of the boys on another tour.

Murray Mexted said to me after the Irish test that he was really impressed with my style on TV.

He said that as a viewer he thought it was great that instead of saying the usual cliches I admitted we hadn't played well and we'd need to put in a lot of work.

PETER FITZSIMONS

'After the game in South Australia where I'd been sent off I found them a far more affable crowd. Sean had a word with me after the game, gave me a smile and said, 'You've been up to it again, haven't you?'

It was human of him. An old-style All Black captain would've probably snarled something like, 'You ____, you buggered it up . . .' ’

NICK FARR-JONES

‘They *were* different. On the whole I found the All Blacks very approachable, a lot more so than before. I got on particularly well with a lot of guys when I was over there captaining the World XV. In Australia we didn't see a lot of them, and the only real occasion we sat down together to chew the fat was after the final test, but relations between the sides were good throughout.

At the dinner I probably said only 20 words to Sean all night. But that was because he was sitting next to my wife Angie, and they must have spent about three hours talking about their respective daughters. Seriously. Here we were, the last night of the tour, and Sean and Angie are swapping notes on our kids.’

PAUL SISSONS

‘After the Irish test at Carisbrook, Sean brought a bunch of little Downs Syndrome kids into the dressing room. These little kids were just absolutely in awe, they talked to the All Blacks and shared a Pepsi with them. Then as they were leaving Sean gave one of them the socks he'd worn that day. This little kid was absolutely over the moon with these socks, all sweaty and filthy . . .

Meanwhile, all the journalists are standing outside the door busting their guts to get in and talk to the All Blacks. The message was: 'Wait. We're talking to the kids.' That was Sean's influence.’

"Ever since they made Fitzpatrick captain of the All Blacks, he's really changed. Really changed." – Peter Fatialofa

I ALWAYS SAID I wanted to be there when my first child was born. I dreaded the idea of being away on tour. When Bronnie fell pregnant, of course it was due right in the middle of the All Black tour. I was in a dilemma – I just *had* to be at the birth, but I was captain and I worried if I should leave the team.

There was a precedent for an All Black coming home for a birth, but that player wasn't the All Black captain.

I felt uncertain about what I should do, so I took advice. I spoke to Gary Whetton who said he thought it was fine if I came home. I raised the matter with Neil Gray during the Irish series and he was behind the idea. When, finally, I asked Laurie he agreed too. Neil thought it was a great way of showing the All Blacks in a new light.

We planned my exit like clockwork. I'd be away for four days and miss just the one game – the midweeker in Cairns, which I wouldn't have played in anyway. So after the Queensland game I was rushed to the airport, jumped straight on a plane and within three hours, while the guys were probably still celebrating victory in Brisbane, I was at home.

If it was a choice between rugby or the birth, I'd definitely have taken the birth of the baby. That Sunday evening, however, it felt very odd. It was fantastic to be with Bronnie again, but it was really strange leaving a tour with unfinished business to do.

The next day Bronnie checked into hospital. Coincidentally, John Drake was there too – his wife had given birth to their first baby the day before. Drakey was very much the expert at fatherhood now and he showed me around the delivery suite like Dr Kildaire. I was as nervous as hell. Nothing I'd ever experienced in rugby was as nerve-wracking as birth.

The baby was born after midnight on the Tuesday morning. I found the whole experience amazing, the best feeling I've ever known. Words can't describe how fantastic it was.

After the grandparents visited, they moved Bronnie and our brand new perfect little girl to another ward to get some rest. I was emotionally exhilarated but drained. I went home.

It was nearly 4am. The city was fast asleep. I remember getting a can of beer from the fridge and having a celebratory drink by myself.

I was over the moon: I was a father.

Bronnie and the baby came home that day. Lion Nathan brought in a guy from their PR company to handle all the media. It was a marvellous gesture, it removed all the pressure from me. One picture was taken, one press statement released.Then we had our privacy again.

Some time later, AJ and Joe came around. I remember trying to change a nappy but I was hopeless; Joe ended up having to do it.

The next day, with greatly mixed feelings I flew out to rejoin the team. Bronnie and the baby were both well, and Bronnie told me to finish the job and beat the Aussies. When I met up with the guys in Brisbane, Loey's first question was, "How's Grizzelda?" They'd heard we hadn't decided on a name yet.

For the rest of the tour my little daughter was Grizzelda.

Bronnie and I were more traditional and actually called her Grace Eva, which just happens to be both of our grandmothers' names.

An interesting little PS to the birth – which shows the human side of international rugby – occurred on the field before the second test. I was psyched up, totally focused on the job, knowing this was the game we had to win or the series was history.

And as we were tossing the coin to decide ends, Nick Farr-Jones shakes my hand and says, "How's Bronwyn? How's the baby? Good on you, mate . . ."

Peter Bush

'90, and a great team's unbeaten run of 50 games is about to end.

Peter Bush

ttling away during the 1991 World Cup – one of the biggest disappointments of my career.

Colorsport

In need of a miracle.

JK says the selectors took a punt on making me captain – he was right. Third test vs World XV, 1992.

Colorsport

Top players are either born with a competitive streak – or they get one real fast.

A bit of leakage . . .

Sean Fitzpatrick collection

Touring has given me many life-long friendships. With (clockwise from above) JK, Foxy, Doc, Stevie and Gary, AJ and Bullet.

Sean Fitzpatrick collection

Sean Fitzpatrick collection

My size was a problem early on – I was always much bigger than the other boys.

After the 1986 All Black tour of France, I stayed on to play club rugby . . . Bronnie joined me for our first white Christmas.

BOOK II

Olympix

What It Takes

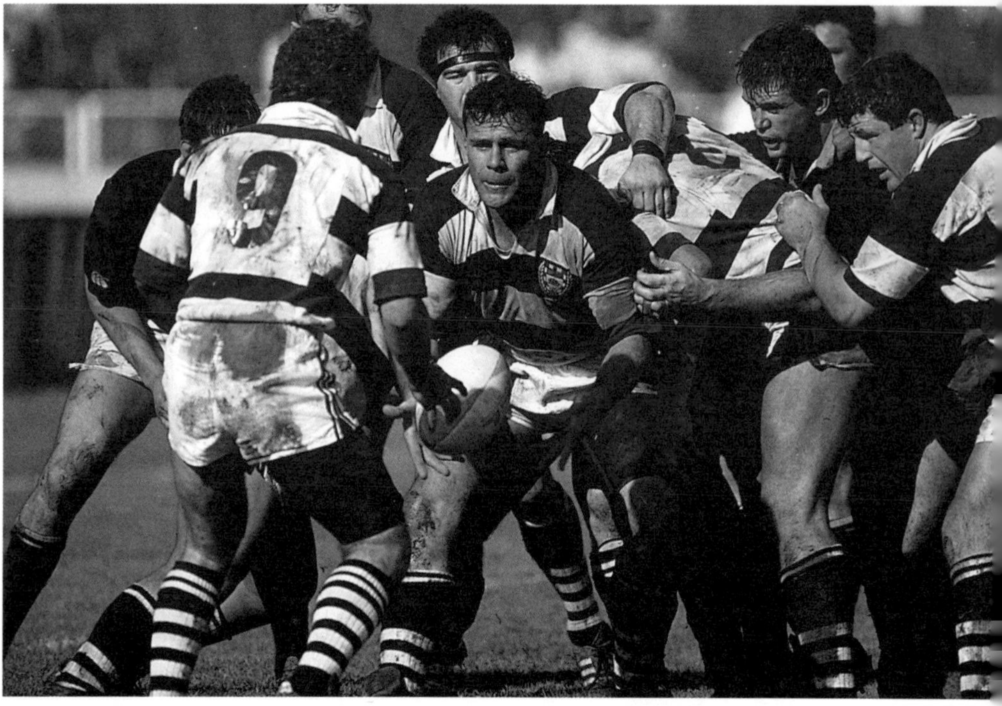

The 'A' Team in total control – protected by the forwards, AJ gives halfback Jason Hewett an armchair ride.

BELOW: Geedub and I enjoy another Ranfurly Shield triumph – the symbol of Auckland's dominance over the rest of New Zealand.

CHAPTER EIGHT

The Dream

"Gemini (22 May – 21 June) is a positive, masculine sign, and is the most youthful of all the signs of the Zodiac. Versatile but superficial, excellent at communicating but often inconsistent, Gemini combines rationalising with restlessness . . ."

JK AND I WERE standing on Manly beach. It was the morning of the Bledisloe Cup test in Sydney. The beach was right in front of our hotel, and we were killing time watching people strolling along, swimming, larking about.

It really struck us how much fun people seemed to be having. As usual, we could feel the tension and pressure that comes with the build-up to a big game. We both agreed: "Wouldn't it be great to have 'normal lives', and not worry about letting New Zealand down today . . ."

The more we thought about swapping places, however, the more we realised these people were probably thinking how great life must be in *our* shoes.

It's the same old story: the grass always looks greener some place else. As JK said, "Let's not be in a hurry to give this up, Fitzy.

Most of these people would give their right arm to play in the test this afternoon. Enjoy it all. Remember, we're a long time retired."

> *FITZPATRICK Brian Bernard James*
> *b. 5.3.1931, Opotiki*
> *Second five-eighth*
> *Represented NZ: 1951, 53, 54; 22 matches – 3 tests, 15 points – 5 tries*
> *" . . . strongly built, standing 5'10" and weighing 13st 8lb, Fitzpatrick was a punishing tackler and a powerful runner . . ."*
>
> – From *The Encyclopedia of New Zealand Rugby*

I dreamed of being an All Black as a kid but I never thought I'd be good enough. As for being the captain, that wasn't a possibility. Ever.

People look back at my career and say you played for a strong rep team, a strong club team, you played for a good school, your father was an All Black – it's no wonder you made it too.

Nothing could be further from the truth. I was just another rugby player until I wore the All Black jersey for the first time. I wasn't a boy wonder like JK or Foxy.

Looking back, I realise my background was ideal. I played for two strong teams at school and club level. This gave me a solid grounding in the basics. There were a few painful obstacles to overcome along the way, too, which were probably character-building.

Perhaps most important, I was never put under any pressure from Dad, or anyone in the family, to succeed. I progressed at my own rate of ability and determination.

If I'd been hopeless at sport it wouldn't have made a scrap of difference to Dad. As long as I was happy, that's what mattered. It's been the same with my whole career. If I'd thrown it in at any time, like after the 1991 World Cup, he'd have been right behind me. I think because Dad was an All Black he knows what it's all about. Perhaps other fathers, other parents, get carried away because they don't.

For me, All Blacks were the ultimate heroes. I can still vividly remember the centenary at College Rifles. Grant Batty *the All Black* was invited. It was amazing to *see* an All Black. I can sense it when it happens to me now, especially from little kids . . . to be honest, it makes me feel good. You feel you're somehow keeping the All Black dream, the magic, alive.

Dad never made an issue about his having been an All Black to us as kids. It was only other people who even mentioned it. As I've got older I've learned more about his career. He was obviously a pretty good player, but he retired very young. He was 20 when he first got picked and I think his last game for the All Blacks was when he was 23 or 24. He never played a test in New Zealand, but he toured twice with the All Blacks, to Australia in 1951 and the UK in '53-54.

His old team-mates, guys like Kevin Skinner, have since told me how good he was, that he was a hard tackler, how he used to cut people in half when he hit them . . . but Dad never talked about himself to the family.

I know he's as proud as punch to have been an All Black though; he still wears his All Black tie to big games.

And I never let him forget that he was in the last All Black team to lose to Wales. I give him heaps about *that*.

LOUISE FITZPATRICK

> 'The children were never really in awe of Brian being an All Black because he never mentioned it. You had to drag stuff from him. I suppose that's where Sean gets his modesty from.'

BRIAN FITZPATRICK

> 'Why is it that if you get one good sportsman in the family more often than not it comes out again in another generation?
>
> I've often wondered why that was with Sean and me. Mark was a good sportsman too, a good club player, but he got badly concussed and was told never to play again. Both the girls played tennis and were good players.
>
> I never made a big deal about my days in the All Blacks but I'm certain it helped Sean that I was around for his formative years. I'd be mowing the lawn and he'd be mucking around, kicking the rugby ball in the yard. If I saw him doing it wrong I'd stop and show him the proper way . . . then I'd get back to the lawn.'

Even though Dad never pushed me to play, I think it was inevitable I took up rugby. Mark usually had a ball handy and when Dad coached Mark's team, College Rifles, I was its mascot. I remember I played my first game when I was four; I wasn't supposed to play until I was a year older. From the beginning I loved it.

I can remember, just, going to watch Auckland play at Eden Park with Mum and Dad. I was probably eight or nine. We sat on the terraces. In 1975 I saw the All Blacks live for the first time in the "rain test" against Scotland; we were underneath the broadcasting boxes trying to keep dry. What an amazing game – for freak weather conditions only the Llanelli game in 1989, with its gale, equals it. Around that time my sister Anna brought home Bryan Williams and Andy Haden's autographs. I was so excited I stuck them on my wall.

As I progressed through the grades Dad was always there in support. He never commented too much, he never said "do this" or "do that". Only if I did something wrong would he have a go at me.

Later, when he saw I had some ability, I think he was pretty keen for me to achieve something in rugby. One time we were going to some trials and he said to me, "Wear some shin pads, they'll make your legs look bigger." I didn't have them, so he got an old newspaper and stuffed it down my socks. I was a big guy already so I must have looked huge.

BRIAN FITZPATRICK

> 'I didn't coach Sean at College Rifles. The future politician, Jim Anderton, was his coach then. I was happy he played rugby: I think it's a game suited to the New Zealand nature. Certainly it fits Sean's; it's a contact sport, which teaches courage, and it's a team sport, which develops social skills.
>
> New Zealanders are a people of innovators from a farming and agricultural background. Rugby's our game. I don't know if any other sport, or activity, would have developed 'the New Zealander' in us as much as rugby. I think it suits Sean particularly.
>
> Mind you, in the beginning, Sean wasn't a very good rugby player. Keen – but he was a bit too rotund.'

My size had a lot to do with things.

I was a big kid at school, and got a hard time because of it. I still feel sympathetic to anyone who gets rubbished for what they look like. I never do it.

There were lots of little humiliations. In form one our art teacher got three of us to stand on desks at the front of the class. The rest of the boys had to draw our figures. When she looked at me she said, "Sean, there is no gap between your legs. You're too easy to draw – you're just round. Hold this cricket bat: it makes your shape more interesting."

My constant memory of this period is of always trying to lose weight. At weigh-ins at College Rifles, when I was eight or nine years old, I ran around the carpark in rugby jerseys; I was trying to sweat off enough pounds to get under the weight limit to play in the same team as my friends. That was a pretty harrowing time for me. And the sweat-it-off tactics never worked.

Once, in the second form, I played Roller Mills right through to the final trial, but at the weigh-in for the final you had to be under 8 stone – and I was 10 stone. So I got drop-kicked out of the team. For a young kid that sort of experience is devastating.

MARK FITZPATRICK

> 'As a boy, Sean was a podgy barrel. He was called Sean the Prawn for a long time. My daughter Lucy, who's three-and-a-half, still calls him Prawny.'

BRIAN FITZPATRICK

> 'In form one he was quite a tubby number and in a race, I think it was the mile, he surprised us all by leading the field in the final lap. But then he stopped 20 yards short because he mistook the finish line and the other runners overtook him.
>
> It was the end of his bloody world. He was in tears . . .'

At secondary school life wasn't any easier. I wasn't always popular – once, some boys flushed my head down the loo. Not a great memory. I always felt very sensitive about my size. I was never in the same rugby teams as my friends because I was always too big. Maybe that's why I enjoyed cricket so much. Size didn't count in cricket, only your ability. I was good at cricket, playing in the First XI in the fourth form.

I never thought of myself as a top athlete at school. In my time I won the discus and the shot-put but I wasn't anything special. Especially not at rugby.

I had some success – I was captain of the Intermediate First XV – but I was always dogged by inferiority. This was due to my size and the fact that I never played in the same teams as my mates. I was always too big for their teams.

In form three, I weighed over 10½ stone which meant I should have played open-grade rugby. But I was only 12 years old, which was too young, so I was granted a special dispensation to play in another weight-restricted team. This team, 3D, had the worst players in the school.

It wasn't good rugby, and it didn't do much for my confidence.

My team-mates were all older boys. It was very physical and I took a few knocks.

I did get encouragement from our Fijian coach, Guy Davis. Once or twice he said to the other guys, "Look at Fitzpatrick. He knows how to do it," which made me feel I wasn't completely hopeless.

Because I was stuck with all the seventh formers who hadn't made it in rugby, I was never seen as a future star. Even in form five I was only in the 2nd XV. I wouldn't break into the 1st XV until the resident hooker left school.

Sacred Heart has always been one of Auckland's top rugby schools, and they've produced their fair share of All Blacks over the years.

Kieran "Colt" Crowley was the huge rugby star when I was at Sacred Heart, though I never played in the First XV with him. He finished in 1979 and I only played my first year in 1980. Kieran was a school hero, a great player. He kicked goals from half-way, and saved the day a few times. *And* he was a good cricketer too.

Colt has a dry sense of humour. There was a bit of a funny time between us when I came into the All Blacks because of the Cavalier thing. But everyone then was stand-offish. I suppose at school we didn't know each other very well because he was older.

Once I finally made it, I spent two years in the First XV. The first season I was a hooker, but the next year I played prop where my size was of more advantage to the team.

Sacred Heart had a strong forward pack. Also playing was Mata'afa Keenan, the future Western Samoan lock. Mata'afa was a character and he and I had many laughs at University later on. Back then, I had no ambitions beyond 1st XV level. I'd already gone further than I ever imagined I could.

BRIAN FITZPATRICK

'I don't think you can overestimate how important it is to play competitive sport for a good school. I was lucky; I went to Gisborne High School which was then one of the classic rugby schools in New Zealand.

It was there I learned about leadership. I was captain of the First XV, a prefect, the school's swimming and tennis champion . . . I learned how to win at sport, to be part of a team – to be a leader through experience, I suppose.

Sean was in the Sacred Heart First XV for two years. I was co-coach, but I looked purely after the backs. Like now, I'd seldom suggest anything to him. If he came to me I'd help him but very seldom would I suggest anything first.

And when he did come he'd nearly always ask, 'Dad, how bad was I?'

Brother Brian Sklenars, who coached Sacred Heart, actually wanted Sean as captain but I was dead against it – he wasn't that good a speaker. I didn't think he could cope off the field.'

BERNIE McCAHILL

'*Everyone* knew who Sean Fitzpatrick was in school-boy rugby. He was one of the feared men. You knew who Grant Fox was too, Frano Botica, Timo Tagaloa, Michael Jones . . . the star players were all well-known. Sean had a big reputation.

I was a first-five for St Peter's. In one game we played Sacred Heart on a day that was pouring with rain, the field covered in water. I can still picture Sean bursting out of a ruck, our halfback hanging onto him like a monkey – and him running straight for me . . .'

I was really competitive in those days. I hated losing. I had a real pride in playing for Sacred Heart, especially since I was boarding there. My memories of this time are pretty loose, not specific at all. I don't think a lot about old rugby games. What's done is done. My individual achievements don't stand out because I probably never dwelled on them. The next game was all that mattered. Some guys I know can tell you the exact date of every moment in their careers; I'm the exact opposite.

BRIAN FITZPATRICK

'Sean's first break came when he was picked for Auckland and the North Island Under 16s. He couldn't believe it. After that he never missed out on anything. He was in the Under 17s, the Under 18s for Auckland and the North Island.

Sacred Heart was a very good side in the toughest school competition in New Zealand, so he got lots of top rugby at an early age. Great for his career.'

ANNA VOSS

‘Everyone thought Sean was so strong and tough but to me he was still my baby brother. I'll never forget the first time I started calling him Seany. He was at school and playing rugby for Sacred Heart and I was yelling out, ‘Go Seany, Seany's got the ball, go Seany.’ And he stopped on the sideline and said, ‘Don't call me Seany. It's so embarrassing.’

Everybody calls him Seany now.’

ANDREW HARVEY

‘He didn't really develop muscles until he was 17 or 18. Before that he was all fat, a real porky, a Billy Bunter. He had curly hair – I think it was an afro – and he looked round. But he was tough.

And competitive.

I was halfback for St Kentigern's the day we played Sacred Heart. Because we're great mates Sean and I had lunch together and then I drove him to the game in my car.

No one could believe opponents would turn up together. And then we ended up having the only fight on the field. Fight's not the correct word. When Sean was bailed up, his hand was around my jersey collar and he was getting ready to punch my lights out.

Typical Fitzy. I was his mate but he was ready to bang me one. He's always been aggressive on the field. At touch rugby he was lethal.’

MARK GREATBATCH

‘I'd been at Sacred Heart in the third form and knew Sean from then. Actually he stuck in my mind more as a cricketer than a rugby player. He used to smack a million runs and bowled a bit. I bowled leggies and kept wickets.

By 1981 I was at Auckland Grammar and we were opponents in First XV rugby. I was a lock, he was a prop. I found schoolboy rugby a very high-pressure sport. First XV games were our test matches, the ultimate stuff.

Sean always had a touch of arrogance about him, even then. Now that we've both made it in sport I see it was a sign that he had what it takes to be successful. He wouldn't have got where he is today without it.

Our big crunch game that year was watched by about 3000 people, a huge crowd for a school game. That day, Fitzy showed me his competitive streak. Getting up from a ruck he rested the old sprigs onto my hand and gave a bit of a twist; rather painful if I remember rightly . . .

In the scrums he had a fair bit to say too. In fact he wasn't short of a word anywhere on the field.’

In terms of enjoyment, First XV rugby – without a shadow of a doubt – was the greatest of my life. I trained very hard, and I played hard. I never scored many tries; actually, I can't even remember if I scored one. But I loved running with the ball any chance I got.

I made a few rep teams for Auckland and the North Island but that didn't convince me I had a bright career lined up. I wasn't particularly upset at being a reserve for the North Island, for instance. I accepted the other guy, Tony Flay, was better.

In 1981 I was chosen as Auckland's secondary schoolboy Player of the Year. I couldn't believe it. It was a total shock. The guy who presented the award to me was a pimply-faced little guy who smoked a lot. He was in his first year out of school and was tipped as having a big future. His name was Grant Fox.

I still wasn't entirely over the consequences of my early doubts about my size. I'm probably still not, though I don't think about it. Somewhere, deep down, I've got those doubts. It's probably a good thing in its own way. It helps keep me on edge.

Quite a few of the players from my era made it in higher grades of rugby. Frano Botica, Mark Brooke-Cowden and Ron Williams became All Blacks. Ian Wood, the centre, was almost there too . . . Mark Greatbatch could have been a very good forward but he switched to cricket . . .

JOHN HART

'Fitzpatrick was a schoolboy star.

He was well known among club coaches as a very strong young man. No doubt pedigree helps.

There was certainly more prestige about secondary school rugby in those days than now. To do well at Sacred Heart was a sign that he had a degree of class.'

A lot of factors have shaped my career. My on-field experiences are only part of the story. Success in rugby depends on so many things.

Probably the most important influences are those you have no control over: family and upbringing. They were crucial to my development as a rugby player. You can have all the skill in the world but if you don't know how to relate to people, or don't have an inner set of standards that you live by, then the chances of making it to the top are probably a lot more difficult.

My family was very supportive. They are strong, confident people. But the person everyone talks about, even though he died when I was only four, is my grandfather, Jock.

LOUISE FITZPATRICK

'My father, Jock O'Loghlen, was from an Irish background and my mother was part Dalmatian – a Soljak.

Dad was in the customs game. He owned a successful trucking business and freight forwarding company

Dad loved people, loved parties, just like Sean.

My mother was a lot younger – she was 19 when she married Dad. He was 40. When Sean was born, Dad was in his seventies.'

BRIAN FITZPATRICK

'Jock occupies a huge chunk of this family's history. He was such a character – some of it obviously rubbed off on his grandchildren.

Everyone wanted to know Jock. He had the gift of the gab, real blarney. He was an expert at smoothing ruffled feathers. People in trouble sought him out. He was known as 'Mr Fixit.'

Sean loved going for walks with him. He was only a toddler, but he loved Jock's world. It was full of interesting characters.'

LOUISE FITZPATRICK

'Dad came from nothing. He was an only child. His mother owned a boarding house in Newmarket, and he went off to work when very young.

In those days it was hard for Catholics; a lot of big companies didn't employ Catholics then.

But he overcame the prejudices against him through hard work and the sheer force of his personality.

Dad was the first president of the Lions Clubs in New Zealand. In fact he was president of the Auckland Club, the Lions, and the Avondale Racing Club in the same year.'

BRIAN FITZPATRICK

'I'm more Irish than the lot of them. My father was born in Ireland, my grandmother was Irish. My father was in forestry, away a lot, and I didn't see much of him; my mother died when I was very young, so I was brought up by her brother, Tom, and his wife, Chrissy. According to Louise, they spoilt me rotten.

I was born in Opotiki and raised in Gisborne. At 17 I joined the BNZ because I didn't really know what I wanted to do. The bank sent me to Head Office in Wellington. That's where I played for the University rugby club. I spent some time with Shell, but after I married Louise we lived in Auckland. Rugby was less important by now. Providing for the family mattered. I worked for Jock for a few years.

O'Loghlen's was the chief baggage handler for the New Zealand Shipping Line, one of the biggest in the country.

I ran the cartage department. I was in charge of 20 trucks and about 50 people. Ninety per cent of our work came from clearing everything through customs. We delivered everywhere in New

Zealand, and had some pretty big clients: Tasman Pulp & Paper, DB, Whakatane Board Mills, motor companies like Shorters . . .

There were no containers in those days so you had to be prepared for anything, you learned to think ahead. You made sure you carried a case of beer in your truck, in case of 'emergencies'. And you always carried a bottle of Scotch – premium – for the same reason.

The waterfront was a unique world, with its own morality. It taught me a lot about life. Sean has never asked me much about our family, but if he ever needed advice or seemed unsure of something, I'd do my best to tell him what I could. I suppose a lot of that is shaped by my time on the waterfront.

Later, I went into business for myself shipping particle board around the country. I suppose I needed independence. It's a desire all the children seem to share.'

BROTHER RICHARD DUNLEAVY

'I spent several years teaching at Sacred Heart, where Sean went to school.

As a teacher, you get to see the dynamism of families and I think it's very interesting what life has given Sean from his. The key is definitely Brian and Louise. They are marvellous parents.

You have the Dalmatian side from Louise – intellectual and pretty tough. Brian has the Irish charm, the ability to work hard and a sense of independence. He married the boss's daughter of a very successful firm and left it to set up his own business. And he built that up.

Brian is a person who works physically hard, with his hands, he's not ashamed of it, he doesn't look for the easy way out.

Louise too has that incredible Slavic grit and determination to get things done, never be beaten. She was the first woman President of the PTA at Sacred Heart.

These are some of the extremely important elements which have made and shaped Sean, made him the person you see today.'

The weather: partly cloudy and cool with scattered showers.

- *Pope John XXIII dies at 6.49am (New Zealand time), aged 81.*
- *Napier is "two inches from disastrous flooding" after the Tutaekuri River nearly bursts a stopbank.*
- *The Auckland Harbour Bridge Authority seeks investment in the Harbour Bridge.*
- *Arthur Nathan's "special of the week" on TV sets is £8 deposit and £3/6/9 weekly.*

- *Advance tickets go on sale for West Side Story, the most-hyped film of the year. (The winner of Auckland's Natalie Wood look-a-like contest will appear at the film's gala showing.)*
- *A new Chrysler Valiant (6-seater, 6 cylinders, 3.7 litre, 145 bhp) costs £1,298.*
- *Hollywood announces that Dennis the Menace, the famous comic strip character, will be turned into a television series.*
- *United States President John Kennedy warns a group of Australian visitors "to prepare for difficult days in the South-East Asian and Pacific areas".*
- *Dennis Young (33), of Canterbury, plays his 17th test as All Black hooker three days earlier. New Zealand defeat England 9-6, courtesy of a late 65-yard Don Clarke goal from a mark.*
- *Young, described by one writer as "tiny", is 5' 7¾" (1.78m) tall, and weighs 13st 10lb (88kg) [after 17 tests, Sean, by comparison, was 26 years old, stood 1.83m (6' 1") and weighed 105kg (16st 7lb)]*

– *The Auckland Star* (4/6/63)

My date of birth is 4 June, 1963. According to Mum, I was born around 7 pm on a Tuesday.

LOUISE FITZPATRICK

'Sean was the baby, several years younger than his brother and sisters.

While he was growing up we had an open-home policy for all the children's friends. There were children here all the time.

When they were small, we always seemed to be doing things with them. Brian coached rugby and athletics and I helped build the kindergarten, helped with Plunket. Just normal family things.

I think I can say without fear of contradiction we never had any problems with our kids.

Certainly there were a few 'majors' – battles over long hair, the suitability of one or two of the girls' boyfriends, a few car accidents, the occasional time when they drank a bit too much . . . but nothing that every New Zealand home doesn't share at some time. Honestly, they were all great kids.

In Sean's case, the age gap was the big thing. Because Sean was so much younger than the rest of his brothers and sisters, he always tried incredibly hard at what he did to stand out.'

LOUISE FITZPATRICK

'He was quite a modest child. I remember he was very good with money. Where all the others spent, he saved.'

JULIE McDIARMID

'As a child, Dad used to stress to you to always 'give your best' at anything you did. He was a stickler for manners, too. He'd be the first to say, 'Good morning' to everyone. The importance of manners is something we've all inherited. You can see it in Sean when he does TV interviews. He is naturally polite, nothing is forced.'

LOUISE FITZPATRICK

'The family spent every Christmas holidays up north. We had a beach house there and Sean loved it. There were parties, people coming and going the whole time . . . he was in his element.'

My upbringing was pretty strict in terms of manners. The magic words were "please" and "thank you". You were taught to be grateful for what you were given. You couldn't leave the dining table until you had eaten everything.

I still remember times when, with my mouth full of food, I'd ask to go to the toilet. Then I'd spit out everything I didn't like – usually spinach.

As kids we went to the Bay of Islands frequently. We'd go camping, do a lot of sailing and fishing, boating . . . the usual things kids do. Mark's mates often used to beat me up. I was tied up and left in the garage or staked out on the front lawn quite a few times. Then they'd go and leave me. The reason was for being a smart little so-and-so, they said. Sometimes they didn't bother with a reason.

I didn't have any James Dean rebellion years, I was never in trouble with the cops or anything like that. It's fair to say I lived for sport, not study. I've been back to Sacred Heart to give talks since, and the headmaster says he could spend half an hour extolling my sporting achievements, and about 30 seconds on my academic record . . .

I loved the outdoors. I think it was bred into me. We used to go camping at school a lot, and at the family bach in Russell we'd spend most of the holidays playing in the bush or down at the beach.

My best friend then was a guy called Andrew Harvey, and he still is. The Fitzpatrick and Harvey families spent a lot of time together up north, and our ties run deep.

Though he played the game to 1st XV level, Andrew is one of the many non-rugby people I know. He's a photographer and we were best man at each other's weddings. Some people seem surprised that I don't spend all my time socialising with rugby players, but Bronnie and I have always had a wide variety of friends. The last thing I want is my life to be totally dominated by rugby, rugby, rugby. At our wedding, for instance, we had about 120 guests; only 20 would have been connected to rugby.

As a teenager I was in my element around water. I'd muck around in a P-class dinghy all the time. Today I grab any chance I can to go fishing, or diving, or water-skiing. I love *doing* things. The only things I don't like, physically, are long car journeys. When I was young I used to get sick a lot, and car sickness is something I've never entirely beaten. Gary used to joke I'd never make it down the back of the bus because I couldn't handle it.

I spent a lot of time around older people as a kid, a pattern that's been repeated throughout my life. I was part of older rugby teams, I went to parties with older people, I hung around with Mark's mates a lot, an age gap of five years.

When Mark got a beach buggy one of his friends taught me to drive. I was about 12, still learning the basics, when I crashed the beach buggy right over Mum and Dad's letterbox and through the brick wall. Dad went off his head. It didn't stop my enthusiasm; Mark and I would go to squash with Dad every Sunday and while he played, we'd take turns driving around the car park, perfecting our style. Driving was something I can always remember doing: I drove Dad back from the Bay of Islands when I was 14 – no one thought anything of it.

I've always been fascinated by cars. That's why I loved the chance to drive in the celebrity car series in Wellington a couple of years ago. Driving is in my blood.

Mum and Dad always treated us as adults. For example, they had a common-sense attitude to drink. They never tried to hide it. I'm a great believer that because we saw alcohol while we were young, usually at Mum and Dad's parties, we've treated it sensibly since. It wasn't a taboo you felt you had to break. On holidays up north, for instance, I was allowed to go to the pub with Dad when I was a year or two under age.

Sure, you make the odd mistake with booze. I think all kids go through a stage of seeing how much they can drink in one go. One fatal night Mum and Dad went out and we opened up the liquor cabinet. We drank it dry and got completely sozzled. We were ill for the next three or four days. Lesson learned.

MARK FITZPATRICK

'Sean has always mixed with older people, so he's learned things a lot more quickly than probably most people the same age. There's five years' difference between us, but we've always been close. He tells me a lot about his career, things that probably no one else has any idea about.'

BRIAN FITZPATRICK

'As a very small boy Sean loved watching the building of the Hyatt. He was fascinated as it slowly developed shape.

When I was in the particle board business I'd often take Mark and Sean down with me to work on a Saturday morning. We'd start about 6am and finish at 8.30am.

Then we'd all change and go and have breakfast at the Royal Hotel. They loved it.'

LOUISE FITZPATRICK

'When Sean was at secondary school we decided to send him to Sacred Heart as a weekly boarder. There was no one else living at home then and he was doing so much sport that we hardly ever saw him anyway. And he wasn't doing enough study.

Sacred Heart was wonderful: it gave Sean a rounded education. It wasn't elitist. He mixed with Maoris, Islanders, Europeans . . . he saw a lot of different cultures.'

BROTHER RICHARD DUNLEAVY

'A Sacred Heart old boy once told me that the social mix at the school was one of the best preparations for life he could have. He said a danger of going to, say, an establishment school like King's College was that it tends to foster an elite. At Sacred Heart grocers' and bus drivers' sons mix with the sons of lawyers and doctors . . . it would have been an ideal background for Sean.'

ANDREW HARVEY

'Sean and I have been best friends since we were kids.

His humour is one of the stand-out things about him. He doesn't take life too seriously, he loves a laugh. So after leaving school it didn't take long before Sean and I decided we needed our independence. We moved into a flat overlooking the Orakei Basin. We lived on a diet of pies, burgers, cigarettes, and beer.

Some nights when the mood was there – which was pretty common – we would crank up the stereo, make sure the fridge was well-stocked, and, from our balcony, hit golf balls into the Orakei Basin.'

I've given up now but through my teenage years I was a pretty serious smoker: a 20-a-day man. I had my first cigarette when I was 10 or 11. It began the classic way: sneaking down the back, having a smoke in the bushes. I liked it, and when I was flatting with Andrew I smoked all the time. I'd have one each day when I first woke up, another on the way to work . . . I gave up eventually because I knew it wasn't doing anything for my fitness. I still appreciate the odd cigar, though, especially to celebrate a test win.

Strangely enough, the more I progressed in the game, the less I watched rugby. If it was a choice of going to Eden Park or going skiing, I'd go skiing every time. During the 1981 Springbok tour I didn't stay in Auckland to watch the test but went skiing instead. I played sport for fun back then and rugby was only part of life.

For most of my life I'd been more interested in sport than schoolwork. Now I was even more interested in life than sport. The University Rugby Club was the perfect environment to mix sport with pleasure.

"I think our team was full of born optimists.
We fancied our chances with the girls."

– Grant Dickson, University team-mate

AS A SACRED HEART old boy, the obvious club to play for after leaving school was Marist. But the Fitzpatrick-University connection was a solid one. Dad and Mark were University men, and Anna was flatting with two University players, David Kirk and John McDermott.

I immediately liked Varsity. You could tell at a glance it was just a good fun club where everyone obviously put a lot of emphasis on having a really good time.

Varsity was a players' club, it had no officials – which is probably a weakness. Every Saturday night a team was rostered on the bar; I'm sure the club never made any money from bar-takings but we appreciated the subsidised drinks . . .

Our team was a good one. It came second in the championship and I made a lot of good friends. I was 18 and most of the side were 20 or 21, so I was mixing with older players as usual. I was still a tighthead prop. That season I made the Auckland third-grade rep team; I was captain. I knew I was a handy player but didn't think I was that flash. There were so many other good players around.

BRIAN FITZPATRICK

'The first time I saw Sean's real captaincy potential was at the funeral of Auckland's third-grade coach.

He spoke bloody well . . . emotionally, tenderly even . . . straight from the heart.'

At the end of 1982, when I was 19, Graham Henry, the University seniors' coach, said to me, "If you want to go any further in rugby you'll have to change from prop to hooker." He thought I'd be more effective operating in the middle of the front row, and as University was well equipped with top props, and I was eager to do anything to play in the senior team, I agreed.

That's the story of how I became hooker.

JOHN DRAKE

'I'd seen Sean play for Auckland Secondary Schools. Very impressive. When he came to Varsity it was just a matter of time before he got in the seniors.

We had a great forward pack, so that made it easier for Sean. He joined a well-oiled machine. But we weren't choir-boys. Any bad habits he's tarred with now he probably picked up from us. We used to fool around a lot. And probably if we hadn't fooled around we would have won more championships.'

BRYCE BEVIN

'University rugby means you can be an individual and do what you want. In the team which Sean joined, self-reliance was the big thing. You were always expected to make your own way in life.

University kept you honest. You can never drop your guard. You've got to give as much as you get or you're history. It's not a slapstick sort of humour. It's not nasty but it gets personal. And you've got to be able to handle it.

Most of the guys were about three or four years older than Sean. I think at first he lacked a little confidence.'

RICHARD FRY

'I really understood how special the University culture was when I switched unions and played club rugby in Counties. At after-matches, the talk switched from girls, to cows with bloat.'

ANDY HADEN

'He wasn't typical of University players of that time. He had much less arrogance about him than the McDermotts, the Collinsons, the Drakes and Frys . . .'

GRANT DICKSON

'That first year of senior rugby he had a lot of baby fat on him. And he already had a reputation: his family's name. The Fitzpatricks were open, popular, extroverted people who made it easy for him. Everyone loved BBJ and Sean's brother Mark.

Fitzy was a junior in the team. We definitely didn't go to him for his philosophy on the game.'

RICHARD FRY

'We all used to crack up the way Sean would disappear away with the fairies during games. I remember at one line-out everyone was standing around, waiting for him to throw the ball in. But Sean was staring at the sky. An overhead plane had caught his eye.'

I was 19 in my first year in senior club rugby so I was eligible for the New Zealand Colts. When I got picked, I thought I was the absolute bee's knees. After making the Colts' "test" team against Australia, it was the greatest feeling I'd ever known.

Although there were some future stars in the ranks – Foxy, JK, Paul Henderson, Ian Wood – I don't think it was a great team. But there's more to life as a Colt than just the rugby. When you're with a group of guys who are 19 or 20 and away on tour, often for the first time . . . well, it's a wonder any rugby gets played at all.

Colts rugby is a great experience for city guys like me because it's an introduction to the no-holds-barred rugby you get from tough farming teams like Taranaki and King Country. It gets pretty physical. You learn to stand up for yourself.

I suppose selection for the Colts the next year was a sign I might go further in the game. I was captain of that team – more a reflection on the lack of suitable alternatives than on any outstanding leadership qualities I had. My form wasn't a problem, but I doubted I could do the job. I didn't back myself with public speaking.

LOUISE FITZPATRICK

'We went to watch him lead the Colts against Wanganui. I suppose we were all nervous about his public speaking. I know I was dreading it. And he was doing well, he was saying all the right things until he thanked the local officials for taking the Colts for a ride on the Whanganui *harbour*.

I couldn't help it, I was so embarrassed, I remember going 'aarrghhh . . .' out loud.'

After my second season in the Colts, I realised I could compete at top-level rugby and that, at my best, I could dominate. I wasn't always consistent, but I was getting experience of, and a taste for, top rugby. I went on a Barbarians tour of Australia in 1985, and toured Europe with the New Zealand Universities later on that year.

What I remember most about this period is something Colin Meads said to me after a Colts trial: "The way you played today, Sean, I felt like picking you for the All Blacks." I thought I'd had a reasonable game but Pinetree's remark blew me away.

Little did I realise how much I'd appreciate his comment over the next two years. These seasons were the black hole of my career.

CHAPTER NINE

You Can't Always Get what you Want

(but sometimes, you get what you need)

> *"Nobody is born the best. You have to practise and train to become the best."*
> – Cus D'Amato

NOBODY GOES LOOKING FOR the school of hard knocks as a way of finding out if you've got "it", the heart and willpower to overcome setbacks. As I know very well, fate hunts you down and, when it's found you, you have to cope, or go under.

In 1984, within the space of a few months, I went from one extreme to another. Early in the season I made my Auckland debut and was given the Colts captaincy. By the end I felt I was on the rugby scrapheap.

They say you show your true colours when your character is tested. I had a long time to show mine: getting back from the outer took me the next two difficult years.

If I look at the big picture I'm sure the consequences were positive. But at the time they either demoralised me, or fed the doubts that were never that far away – that I wasn't really good enough.

I had a dream start with Auckland. Possibly too easy.

I'd played one season in club rugby – my first season as a hooker. Then John Hart phoned me out of the blue and asked me if I wanted to come on Auckland's world tour. He said the players who succeeded would be the basis of his Auckland team in the future.

JOHN HART

'It's well known that in 1984 I took an Auckland team on a learning tour overseas. Sean was one of the young players picked.

I didn't know a great deal about him, personally. I probably knew his father better. As a kid I remember watching Brian Fitzpatrick play at Eden Park. In Sean's case, I was more aware of the pedigree than the individual. But on that tour I was growing the person, not the player. I wanted to see how players like him handled the intensity, the exposure, the pressure.'

When I went away with Auckland I was still getting used to the demands required from a hooker. For example, while I was getting good reviews for my around-the-field game, it was always a bit of a joke with the Varsity seniors how badly I threw in the ball.

Precision line-out throwing is so crucial. With scrums basically a restarting mechanism, the modern game revolves around winning ball from the line-out. I didn't see the warning signs until I was overseas. A lot of players have great memories about that tour but for me they're mixed.

That tour I came to hate training. Because I was a real hit-or-miss thrower, I found perfectionists like Glenn Rich and Andy Haden and Gary Whetton – all senior guys – treated me like dirt if I didn't get it spot on. The first time.

Haden was really hard on me. If I threw in poorly he didn't give me any slack; he used to stop training and say, "No, that's not right." Then he'd make a big deal by drawing a sketch of what he wanted on the ground. He did this in front of the whole team. I felt so small.

Rich was typical of an older player who made no allowances for the fact that you were a rookie. His attitude, which was quite common, was that if you were in the side you were expected to do the job. Inexperience didn't cut any ice with him. I didn't like it but it taught me how to handle myself against an older player, not to lose my self-confidence.

That's easier said than done. After my second game I could hear Rich and some of the guys bagging me, saying basically, "Fitzpatrick can't throw the ball, he's hopeless . . ."

When you hear that your self-confidence does suffer. Worse, I didn't get picked for any more games that tour. I was supposed to play in the last game, against the Grizzlies in San Diego, but at training I blew it.

Hart said, "We'll have line-out practice now." I was nervous and threw the first ball in off-target. So was the next one, and the third one. Andy Haden just stopped the practice, and said to me, "Get out of here." Hart didn't stop him. I had to go. Abo played instead.

JOHN HART

> 'He was a pathetic thrower-in of the ball. It was the first time he'd come into contact with 'professional people' who don't tolerate sloppiness.
>
> It's a lock's job to win the ball and it's damn near impossible to do well if your hooker can't throw the ball in straight.
>
> He did come under pressure from some players. Whether he handled it the right way is another matter. But that's how you learn.'

It was clear I had to master the art of throwing-in correctly, because I got the big swerve from the Auckland squad for the rest of the season.

This really got me down, so I asked the Marist hooker, Kevin Boyle, for help. I rated Boyle from club rugby, I liked his attitude. And he knew how to throw in the ball.

Boyle was wary, because even though I was a lot younger, I was a rival. It took a while for him to reply but then he rang back and agreed to give me a hand. He spent a couple of times a week with me working on my throwing in. I also spent a fair bit of time throwing a ball against the side of goal-posts to perfect my aim.

When I got better, more confident I could control the ball, I rang Andy Haden and asked him if he'd help me. And Haden went down to the Domain after work to help me too. I don't know why he came, we weren't friends or anything, but he must have seen I had some potential. He is good like that.

And after Haden I switched to Bronnie.

BRONWYN FITZPATRICK

> 'This went on for ages. In the middle of summer, for example, instead of sun-bathing or going to the beach, Sean would insist on using me [as a jumper] to practice his throw-ins. In the end I developed a very reasonable two-handed take, if I do say so myself.
>
> Sean's throwing in still needed more work.'

In 1985, despite my extra work, Harty still wouldn't pick me for Auckland. I had the occasional sign that not everyone had forgotten me; I toured with the New Zealand Barbarians and the New Zealand University sides, and did okay.

However, everything came back to Auckland. Auckland was my goal. This was the era when they absolutely dominated provincial rugby. You didn't need to be a genius to see that guys in the Auckland team stood a great chance of becoming All Blacks.

I wanted to be an All Black too – I didn't know if I'd be good enough, but that's what I wanted. University had two: Foxy made the All Blacks in 1984 and Kirky was already half-back.

At one stage I considered changing back to prop. I said to Drakey, "I'm so desperate to play rep rugby, I'm going to try propping." I thought I was still good enough to be a prop. I didn't know much about a new guy who'd arrived from the Bay of Plenty called McDowell.

JOHN DRAKE

'Who knows? Sean might have got a place in the Auckland side as a prop, but it all depends who his hooker was. If he had a big hooker he could have been OK. But I never really saw him as a prop. And I could see no point in him trying to be one. He was paranoid about his throwing in and wondered if he'd ever be able to do it right.

One thing I know: Sean would never have made the All Blacks as a prop.'

JOHN HART

'There was no way he was going to get into the Auckland team at that time. Maybe his expectations were too high – in my view I think he came back from the Auckland tour and his feet left the ground for a while.'

Things looked really bleak for me when Hika Reid moved to Auckland. Abo was firmly in the number one spot, you had one All Black, Mills, as a reserve and another one, Hika, also in town. It would be an understatement to say I was pretty unhappy.

PETER FATIALOFA

'Fitzy and I were reserves together. He was just like a time bomb waiting to explode, and once he got his chance he took it. It was just a matter of him breaking in. Everyone knew how good he was, but he had to sit back for those two years.'

JOHN HART

'Sean was a guy I never got close to. I don't think many people have. I never felt he gave easily. He wouldn't talk about weakness; it seemed to discuss weakness was a weakness in itself for him.

I had the philosophy that I tried to show people the way but people had to be themselves. I only heard later that he'd got Boyle to help him, for example.'

DAVID KIRK

'Sean was not particularly patient, and I wouldn't expect

him to be, not with that sort of ability. But I think his apprenticeship was important for him. In terms of explosiveness, robustness and ball skills he was already the best hooker in Auckland.

Putting it bluntly, it was only a question of time before Sean overtook Abercrombie. He was the better player. He was a better hooker than Dalton, too.

But he wasn't the best in terms of knowledge, experience, and basic skills like throwing in.

That's why he wasn't in the Auckland team.'

JOHN HART

'Ultimately, he came to me. I told him two things: 'You're still not throwing in the ball well enough, you're too inconsistent. And I'm sick and tired of watching you play for Varsity and giving away penalties with your over-aggressive play.'

I think he got knocked back by this. In 1985 he was a better player than Abercrombie but not as professional.

If I'd put Sean in the team in 1985 he would never have been a great player. Good, but not great. I use him as an example in speeches.

But after Sean got his chance with the All Blacks I had to face facts. Iain Abercrombie was holding onto his place by the skin of his teeth then. He was calling on all his experience, commitment, skill.

Iain's a very special person to me and these decisions are the worst: dropping someone you respect, who's given tremendously, for someone who's better.

But you can't not make the choice. And that's why I picked Sean in 1986.'

"Luck exists all right. The best you can do is put yourself in a position where luck can come your way. If it's there you get it." – Peter Sterling

IN 1986 THE FIRST-choice All Blacks toured South Africa as the Cavaliers, got banned for a couple of tests as punishment, and a whole bunch of new guys were chosen as All Blacks.

Incredibly, I was one of them.

It was the fulfilment of a boyhood dream and yet almost straight away I started getting thoughts like, 'Am I good enough to be here?' creeping into my head. I'd achieved what I always wanted . . . but I was really apprehensive about whether I could perform.

I was so inexperienced. I couldn't even make the Auckland A side – Iain Abercrombie had the position sewn up – and now I was suddenly in the All Black test squad. I knew a lot of people didn't think I should be there.

Some people have said I got a lucky break. I can't deny I was fortunate to be around that year. Once the Cavaliers were banned, the door opened for a new All Black hooker. Hika Reid and Andy Dalton were ruled out, and Bruce Hemara was the favourite. Some people were tipping Abo who was playing well for Auckland. I wasn't in the reckoning. Until I got an All Black trial.

My selection raised eyebrows but there was logic to it; BJ Lochore, the All Black coach that year, had coached the Colts in 1984.

Ironically, opposing me in the trials was Abo, the man keeping me out of the Auckland team.

IAIN ABERCROMBIE

'That season I had a bad back injury and was taking a lot of painkillers. I knew Sean was being watched closely by the selectors – Brian Lochore clearly had eyes for him. In the trial I had a bloody good game, our team won by 20 points.

I spoke to Fitzy afterwards. Even though my back was pretty sore – I could hardly walk – I was quietly confident of making the All Blacks. After all I was the incumbent Auckland hooker, he was my reserve, so I wasn't being presumptuous. If I'd played badly, I'd have accepted that, but some people who I respected complimented me on my performance.'

"Unfortunately, Blenheim [the trial venue] turned on a shocker of a day, reducing the event to an essentially forward struggle . . ." – 1986 *New Zealand Rugby Annual*

I THOUGHT I PLAYED pretty well. It was a dreadful day, hard for anyone to shine.

IAIN ABERCROMBIE

'The test team was being announced while we were flying back to Auckland. At a stopover in Wellington airport, however, Don Cameron, the *New Zealand Herald's* rugby writer, came up to me and said he'd heard the side, and was sorry to hear I wasn't in it. Bruce Hemara was the hooker and Sean was the reserve.

I was shell-shocked. I couldn't believe it. I thought I'd done enough to get the reserve spot, even to have got in in front of Hemara.

Of course I congratulated Sean and tried to act magnanimous and happy for him, but I was thinking, 'How the hell did he get there?'

It still rankles, it always will. I can't talk about it to anyone without feeling some bitterness, even now.

You look back and get horrible thoughts: Brian Lochore obviously had high regard for him after the Colts . . . I had no problems with Sean as a player, I just didn't think he had served his apprenticeship or earned his place.

Sean said, 'Your back's not right.' He made it sound like my back injury was the reason I didn't get picked, but he was just being decent.

I could see he was elated.

I never learned why I didn't get picked but I'm not the sort of guy to ask. I knew I could never change things so I never found out.'

HIKA REID

'I rated Bruce Hemara highly.

Bruce was the fiercest player I ever played against. His problem was he didn't have enough pounds on his body. When I played him I could always mow him down in the scrums. His heart was huge but he just wasn't big enough.'

When the All Black team assembled, I felt very much like many of the young All Blacks would do in 1992. Everything was so new, you were very quiet, no one stepped out of line.

There were other similarities. The selection of the side was against a background of controversy and huge public interest. Then it was politics; in 1992 the interest was in a new panel, new players and the dropping of several star names.

The test was being played at Lancaster Park, in Christchurch. A memorable ground for me: on it I made my debut, captained the All Blacks for the first time, and played my 50th test against the Lions.

It's usually forgotten that I was picked as a reserve for the Baby Blacks.

But at our first training session it was pretty obvious that something was up with Hemara. He was a small hooker, and after a few scrums I could tell he was feeling his ribs. It turned out he had a ripped cartilage, which is damn painful.

I was in the opposition forwards putting down live scrums against the test pack. People have no idea how full-on practices get, especially between forwards. For Auckland there were never any easy training sessions – with the All Blacks, there was *definitely* no holding back. Even though this was my first time with the All Blacks, I wasn't making any allowances for Bruce. I didn't know his injury was a bad one.

Eventually, we had to stop scrumaging. Bruce's ribs were completely stuffed. So he stepped out of the session and I trained with the test team for the rest of it, hooking between Kevin Boroevich and Brian McGrattan.

Later, I went to see how Bruce was feeling. He was in the physio's room. He had needles all through his ribs, getting treatment.

And then Brian Lochore came and told me that I was playing on Saturday. I felt sorry for Bruce because he'd waited a long time to get his opportunity and now he'd lost it.

KEVIN BOROEVICH

'Sean's attitude was exactly right. You want guys in the All Blacks who desperately want to get to the top. There's no such thing as holding back because Bruce was injured: if you find a weak link you go for it. At test level there's no love lost between players going for the same position.'

Bruce was a nice guy. He took his disappointment really well, wished me the best of luck. Then he left and the selectors called Abo into the squad.

Abo was pretty good when he joined the team. That was pretty hard for him. And because of some muck-up he didn't get to keep his All Black jersey and the Rugby Union gave me another one for him. That was awkward – I had to bring his All Black jersey to Auckland training later, and give it to him.

IAIN ABERCROMBIE

'It was good to know I was the next in line but it was a bit empty all the same. I'd had the disappointment of not making the original side and when I heard my name this time there was no celebration.

At that stage my back was really sore, too, and I probably couldn't have played. Having said that, during the test I was hoping Sean would injure himself and come off – like any good reserve does.

I was super-critical of Sean to justify myself, but he played really well. During the test, Sean's throwing in was a real strength. It was so good we dicked them in the line-outs.

It shows you what a good player he was. With no proven experience to speak of he went straight into a test and played to that calibre straight away.'

DAVID KIRK

'His inexperience wasn't an issue because the whole team was inexperienced. Once you go below a certain level of experience it ceases to become an issue, it's irrelevant.'

The reality of test match rugby is that it is a slog. Though we won the first line-out – they threw it to the back and Mike Brewer got a two-handed take – every scrum was just a disaster. I was under such pressure, I could hardly breathe.

They were just so much heavier than us. Gutsy as our guys were, the front row was getting smashed the whole time. Their tighthead prop, Garuet, was putting pressure on me. They were just too big and too heavy. We were so light in the forwards. They just killed us, they applied so much pressure on our ball. Every scrum was an absolute nightmare to be in.

Sometimes we were pushed back so far they walked right over the top of us. In one respect the French were unusual – this was probably the cleanest team I ever played against. They didn't kick us at all.

But right from early on, even though we were struggling, we believed we could win. I can't explain why we felt it so strongly, but we did. I remember Coops making a big tackle within the first 10 minutes which was pretty inspirational stuff. And Kirky kept pretty good control throughout. Everyone else was quiet, just doing their jobs. Boro said quite a bit in the forwards, but me, I said nothing. I didn't have any extra breath to waste on words . . . most of the time was spent running on adrenalin. It was a very unusual game, everything was just helter-skelter.

KEVIN BOROEVICH

> 'Our locks had a lot of heart, but they were beanpoles. We kept sliding backwards. It was a case of good big guys shoving the good little guys aside. We could do nothing but keep trying our best.'

I think I played okay. Made it around the field pretty well. I got back a few times and helped out. In the last five or 10 minutes I kept thinking, 'How long to go, how long to go?' Then it was over. The game actually finished on a scrum. We'd won, 18-9. After that it was just immense relief: 'Thank God that's over.'

In the changing room I wasn't sure what to do. I was exhausted and wanted to lie down but part of me wondered, 'Should an All Black lie on the ground?' We didn't know the protocol. It was all so new. Did you swap your jersey for a French one? No one wanted to give up theirs . . . For once the rugby administrators got it right and gave us two jerseys, so we kept our test one and swapped the spare.

At the function I immediately sought out Dad, who'd flown down especially to watch me. His face said it all.

> *" . . . there is no sport like rugby for exposing character."*
>
> – Graham Mourie

I ALWAYS KNEW THE Cavaliers would come back once their ban was finished. I wasn't sure how that would affect me. After the one-off test against France, the All Blacks hosted a tour from Australia. I was selected for my second international, but unfortunately, we lost by one point. The critics said I played well, but they'd also written the team off before we beat France. I certainly wasn't relying on *their* judgement. Actually, I was worried the selectors might bring back Hemara if his ribs had healed.

It was a Sunday morning, and I was at Mum and Dad's having breakfast when the second test team was announced about 10 o'clock. We were glued to the radio when we heard, "Here is the All Black team. There are 10 changes. Dropped are the whole forward pack . . ." Mum started crying. I thought, 'I hope I get into the reserves.' And when I made the reserves I was just thrilled. At least I wasn't complete history.

Hika was back.

HIKA REID

'He played well in his debut but I didn't believe Fitzy deserved the number one spot. He might've been a worthy All Black but he wasn't the number one hooker in my book.'

DAVID KIRK

'In 1986 there were several decisions – including Sean's non-selection – that were bad. In that series the selectors confused inexperience with ability. They didn't get it right when they named the team to go to France later that year, either.'

HIKA REID

'Sean and I had a real rivalry, far more so than anything I had with Dalton. I always felt I was a better player than Dalton, but he had the captaincy to keep him in the team.

Whenever I played Sean I went out to intimidate him, more so with him than any other hooker.'

When we assembled for our first meeting with the "Cavalier All Blacks", things were different right away. This wasn't the "all-for-one" friendly atmosphere of the Baby Blacks – these were "real" All Blacks, guys like Gary Knight and Mark Shaw. Legends.

Hika was good to me. He said, "I'm bloody surprised to be picked ahead of you."

The revamped All Blacks just won the second test, so I knew I wouldn't play in the decider at Eden Park. It was probably a good thing. The team were badly beaten in the third test and we lost the Bledisloe Cup.

Off-field it wasn't a particularly happy team.

The return of the Cavaliers brought seniority and hierarchy into the set-up. What was left of the Baby Blacks had its place, and that was the bottom. It wasn't so much a "them and us" situation as one of, "OK, the A team's back, you youngsters do what we say."

We were legitimate All Blacks to them, but junior ones. There was a very rigid structure you had to conform to. Young guys were meant to be seen and not heard. Later I think Lochore realised he should have kept the young team, but apparently Meads, his fellow selector, wanted Cavaliers. The result was a compromise which didn't work.

The Baby Blacks would have died for each other. After their time in Africa, the Cavaliers were close too. In between was Kirky. He bore the brunt of their hostility.

The Cavaliers had this team song which they seemed to launch into at the drop of a hat. The rest of us had to sit there and listen. In the team meeting before the second test, Jock Hobbs said, "Right, let's show these young pricks we're still the best." That summed up their attitude.

During this period, I still learned a lot by watching.

Take preparation. I realised even legends have their own idiosyncracies. Gary "Axle" Knight would stroll into the dressing room, take off his tie, lie down on the bench and go to sleep. The first time I saw him do this I thought somebody'd better wake him – there was only 10 minutes before the test started. Eventually Axle got up, dressed, and made the game right on time.

I was only a reserve, but I loved the All Black set-up. Even after the disastrous third test I swapped jerseys with the Australian reserve hooker, Mark McBain. Back in our changing room I packed away my souvenir discreetly.

At the end of 1986 I was chosen in the All Black party to tour France. After being involved in all the tests at home, either playing or as a reserve, I'd have been shattered to miss out. But I wasn't happy until I heard my name. I feared they might still take Hemara and Hika.

The team assembled in Auckland. As pretty much a new boy I kept a low profile. This was in the era of anti-South Africa feeling and I remember one night climbing along the roof of the 'Poe' – it must have been about 10 o'clock – because protesters were outside, booing the inclusion of Cavaliers in the side.

One of the Cavaliers, Mark Shaw was my room-mate. A character. After training every day Cowboy had a ritual where he'd drink four or five cans of beer – he'd invite a few of the guys back to the room to share them with him. I'd sit in the corner, saying nothing, while they'd polish off their five cans.

Cowboy called Auckland guys "movie stars". He was a big one for knowing your place. I remember there was a call to do some practice line-outs on a slight hill. I said I thought it was better to do them in the car park, where it's flat. Cowboy looked at me and said, "We've done them *here* for five years, you bloody movie star." I never said another word. All I could think was 'God, I've upset Cowboy – and I'm rooming with him.'

When we got to France the guys had to state their ambitions for the tour. Hika said he'd been sitting in the wings so long as Andy Dalton's reserve that now was his big chance to kick-start his career again.

I sat there thinking, 'Fair enough, good on you, you deserve it.' What I said was, "I'm happy to be here and I'm going to try to put a bit of pressure on Hika for his spot."

I was lucky to be chosen in the first game because we played really well that day. We killed them in the scrum. Lochore was impressed.

In the second game the All Blacks struggled; Hika had a few fights and that didn't go down too well with BJ. At Toulon, in the third match of the tour, I played one of my best games for the All Blacks. Straight afterwards Hika came up to me and said, "You played really well, I've never seen a hooker play so well." And then at the team session, in front of Lochore and everyone, Hika said publicly, "Sean, well played, you are really putting the pressure on me." I didn't know what to say, I felt a bit embarrassed.

Hika bent over backwards to be fair to me, which was a surprise. I'd heard that he bad-mouthed players in the past, but I think what mattered to Hika was respect: and Hika respected me as a player. Whenever I played against him he always tried to stick it into me, have a go at me whenever he could . . . I took it as a compliment.

That French tour made me as an All Black with the older guys: the Cavalier All Blacks. The more they saw of me, the more Stevie and co realised I was probably the better hooker. And it boosted my confidence to know this because I knew they were all so loyal to Hika. The guys used to say Hika played exceptionally in Africa, that his form there was utterly superb.

GRANT FOX

> 'Hika's form for the Cavaliers was outstanding, but he wasn't as good a scrummager as Sean, nor as big and powerful. In France we were only just starting to see Seany's true value to the side . . . his power and strength was awesome.
>
> If Hika thought Sean was going away as his junior on that tour he didn't read Sean right. Sean doesn't care about reputations. He's ambitious . . . and that ambition's what any great All Black needs to have.'

When they named the All Black side for the first test and I made it, I was rapt. It was my first test selection purely on merit. There were no Baby Blacks/Cavaliers politics . . . it was all about who was the best hooker.

As I ran onto the park before that first test I pictured the scene back in New Zealand. I knew all my mates would be sitting at home watching the TV, and I remembered the times we sat up till 3 am, a lump in our throats as the band played *God Defend New Zealand* . . .

I could remember us cheering on the All Blacks with a few beers – and now, at Toulouse, here I was: listening to the national anthem, doing the haka, performing all the things All Blacks did . . . part of the whole spectacle.

After that game I felt like a genuine, fully-fledged test All Black. Even better, the team won.

CHAPTER TEN

Up Front

"Rugby is a man's game . . . A player must be hard because he is expected to play against hard men and he must make contact with hardness . . . Rugby is a game for a man with a stout heart. A faint heart cannot be accommodated."

– Danie Craven

MICHAEL JORDAN, THE GREAT American basketballer, has a saying that I identify with very closely: "If you're not going to compete, then I'll dominate you."

In my career there have been games where I've struggled. Games where I've survived – but only just. I've faced opponents who were so fierce and determined to win that playing well against them wasn't good enough. You had to be *better*. If you weren't, you got crushed.

That's happened to me once or twice earlier in my career. Now my competitive streak just won't allow it.

I think I'm pretty relaxed as a person, maybe even to the point of laziness, but my philosophy in taking on any activity is clear: I like to win at everything. If I try something new and I can't do it straight away, then I just won't bother. I hate mediocrity.

I'm at my most competitive when playing for the All Blacks. I can honestly say I have never been intimidated as an All Black. The moment that happens, you've just taken the first step to getting beaten.

I'm the rule, not an exception. All Blacks are competitive by instinct. People like Foxy and AJ are born with competition in their blood. Even in retirement they're still as competitive as they were as All Blacks. If I play golf with Foxy it's like the final round in the British Open. When I go fishing I have to catch more fish than AJ. It's natural for us all.

Touring was an endless series of unofficial "world championships".

All Blacks compete in everything from telling the best joke, skiing the roughest bits on a mountain, driving a golf ball the furthest, eating the most Big Macs . . . Whatever the "championship", it's saying one thing: "I'm the best."

Zinny Brooke is probably the ultimate competitor. Look at his form in the UK last year: on paper he was a "spare parts" man in the loose forwards, yet he forced his way into the test team, on merit, as an openside flanker.

Competition is a valuable form of motivation. Top players need a wide variety of ways to stay mentally fresh. This doesn't happen only at the end of your career, either. The season by which my whole All Black career gets measured is 1987. In the public's mind, I've never been allowed to drop below that level of form. But after we won the World Cup and Bledisloe Cup back-to-back I felt myself going stale. Run-of-the-mill pedestrian rugby didn't have the same appeal.

To motivate myself for the rest of the season I used the media. I'd read the *Herald* every Monday morning and if my name wasn't mentioned in the sports pages I felt annoyed. No news was bad news. So I used this as an incentive to play harder next week. When I saw my name in print I knew it had worked.

My best games are the ones where somebody else is competing as hard as they can against me. I'm talking about players like Tom Lawton or Phil Kearns. Their determination raises my standards too.

I'm not very good at festival or friendly games of rugby. There's no competition in them. I need the rivalry to spark me. It's also an age thing. When I was younger I treated every game as a test match. *Every* game. It gave me an edge.

So many of the All Blacks in the 1980s shared this intensity. I can remember heaps of times at training when we almost got into fights with teams that had come along to *help* us.

When I play against a new opponent, they always know who I am. Some are dominated immediately by playing against an All Black, but quite a few will test me out. It might happen at training when a new hooker joins the squad and we practise against each other. I've even had First XV hookers try it on when we scrummage against them in PR games. The newcomer wants to see if my image is true, or if it's over-hyped. I never allow anyone to have any doubts; I have a reputation to protect and live up to. Sometimes my reputation presents a target for up-and-comers to have me on.

I remember playing against Counties for the New Zealand Universities as a youngster. Andy Dalton was their hooker. I "tried it on him" in a couple of scrums and when he'd had enough of this upstart showing him no respect he went at me hammer and tongs. I had no complaints; that's the way it was.

A few years later, when Andy was coach of Counties, their hooker tried to knock my head off on a couple of occasions. I told Andy afterwards that he'd found a bit of a wild man. Andy laughed. "Sean," he said, "now that you're the All Black hooker everyone's going to do that for the rest of your career. It comes with the territory."

PHIL KEARNS

> 'Success in rugby is all about getting on top of your opposition, and I think it's especially true in positions like hooker. At hooker you've really got to dominate your opposite number or you'll come out second best.'

JOHN DRAKE

> 'Hookers are often pugnacious and aggressive people but I don't think that attitude's unique to the position. There were guys like Andy Earl and Kevin Boroevich who had these fantastic attitudes too. But maybe Sean stood out because for an Aucklander it was pretty rare.
>
> I remember one club game against North Shore. They had a former All Black, Brad Johnstone, in their front row. I used to push him back, which he hated, so any time he got the chance he'd whack me and stomp on me. Sean must have been very young and impressionable because we rolled them back one day and then Sean went right over the top of Brad. Brad couldn't believe this lack of respect, but Sean wasn't scared. I think he loved taking on the big names to see if they were as tough as their reputations made out.'

I was fortunate; I think you need to be born with the attitude that demands you won't give in. I doubt you can "learn" it if there's nothing there to start with. Certainly, you can develop it. I've played with a lot of competitive players whose influence has been enormous. I also try to take note of the attitude of top performers in other sports.

That's why I admire Michael Jordan so much. His style, his attitude towards competition and winning, his training ethic – they're all first-rate.

In his book he says he never takes it easy in practices. If he does, how can he expect to turn it on in big games? I've never complained about training, either. It's something I have to do. It's not always easy – who wants to get up in the middle of winter and go to Eden Park at 6am for training three days a week? – but I know it's essential to get the pay-off.

I almost get more fun from taking part in training at club level than with Auckland and the All Blacks. Sometimes it's more honest. The average club player is incredibly dedicated, tries hard all the time, he just hasn't got the skills. Too many skilful players at rep level, even, sadly, the All Blacks, lack the heart or won't consistently give 100 per cent.

If you compare me to a player like Inga Tuigamala, we're very different. I have the attitude that I'm prepared to go through the pain barrier every time. Inga won't. In something like the Beep test Inga sets his pain threshold. Once the pain starts, he hates it. He reaches his target, then he stops. I believe that when the pain starts, that's when the gain comes. So I fight through the pain even though my body's crying out to quit.

The payback is clear: because I don't give up until I've got nothing left, I have confidence that even in the toughest game I will last out. I don't "hope" I'll survive the last 10 minutes. I know I will, because I've trained to do so.

Andy Haden demanded the best of the players around him. There was no such thing as an easy Auckland training session with him there. Nothing was ever formally explained but without a doubt Haden's attitude rubbed off on me.

Haden wanted to be the best line-out jumper all the time, so he insisted the hooker who threw him the ball was the best too. If you couldn't meet his standards, then you had to go – he'd get someone who was of use to him.

Every player has that part of their game they want to excel at. It might be tackling, taking the high ball, reaching the loose ball first . . . in Haden's case, he really prided himself on his jumping. I can remember sitting next to him after our last Shield game of 1986. He said, "I can retire a happy man now," because he'd cleaned out his rival in the line-out. Again. That was the private battle within the game he had to win. Every time.

I didn't view it like this back then, but a rugged learning experience early on in my career had a huge bearing on my subsequent approach to rugby.

I first played against Tommy Lawton, the Queensland hooker, for the New Zealand Colts against the Australian Colts in 1983. Tom was already very big, very mean, a bit older than me. His nickname, very appropriately, was "Crusher". He was already a Wallaby and he was all menace. When I came up against him at test level three years later he was probably at the top of his game. I was in a test pack that wasn't as strong as his. He murdered me.

In the front row things were a disaster right from the first scrum.

Lawton went over the top of me as soon as he could. At the same time he told me to "___ off little boy, or I'll crush you today". It set the pattern for the game: physical and mental intimidation.

I said nothing, just gave it my best. It wasn't good enough. Tommy controlled the scrums and all the time kept snarling in my ear, "___ off, little boy," "___ off, little boy." I said nothing.

Late in the game he underlined his total superiority. In a succession of scrums, the Wallabies just pushed us back as though this was a training session. Each time Tom walked over the top of me, asking things like, "Are you still here, boy?"

I'd been apprehensive before the game. Our scrum was inferior to the French in the Baby Blacks' test, and Australia had a better scrum than the French.

But this was worse than I'd imagined.

Tom and I didn't share any beers or anything like that afterwards, so I never got to find out if there was a really nice guy lurking beneath the monster I'd played. I'm not sure if it was deliberate but it was yet another sign of how he called the shots between us.

Tommy Lawton won a huge psychological battle over me that day.

A year later, after the World Cup, we took on Australia in Sydney. On the tour of France, in the trials and in the World Cup I'd systematically evaluated my game against all the game's great hookers: Reid, Deans, Dalton, Dubroca. I believed I'd done well. But lurking in the back of my mind was how I'd go against Tommy. I didn't believe I could think of myself as a true world champion if we lost, or he played better than me.

I was really keyed up for the game.

From a front rower's point of view, this test was just so satisfactory. It was the first time the All Blacks dominated the Aussies up-front – and I got my revenge on Lawton. Our scrum was rock solid, and we controlled the Aussies as completely as they controlled us the year before. Drakey played superbly in what turned out to be his final test. I can still remember how shocked they were to be back-pedalling in the scrum. They hadn't been shoved around for years. Even when they led we drained their power with a series of rolling mauls and big scrums. Tommy Lawton, to my immense satisfaction, was struggling with the pace of the game.

That afternoon I scored two tries, and afterwards everyone was praising me. I could see Tommy was put out, which I didn't mind in the least. All he said, in a really sarcastic tone, was something like, "See you stumbled two tries on the wing today. Well done." I said nothing.

Tommy and I had further battles over the years, in All Black-Wallaby tests and for Auckland against Queensland. They were always games I prepared for meticulously. I think the honours between us were pretty even, but we both knew that if either one was off their game just a bit, the other would go for the jugular.

We never really got close off the field. When you're arch-rivals, I don't think you can. We said the odd word here and there but it was never very chummy. The respect was always present. Always.

Tommy's biggest weakness was his lack of speed. Phil Kearns, who replaced him in the Australian team, is a lot more mobile.

When the All Blacks toured Australia in 1992 I kept telling the guys about how good Lawton was, even though he was now at the tail-end of his career. I'm not sure if they really believed me.

Typically, in the match against Queensland, Tommy was at me the whole game. It was a real battle. And then in the last four scrums, as if to confirm everything I'd told the guys, Tommy forgot about me and switched the attack to Olo Brown. And Olo just couldn't believe it. Technically, Olo is such a good player that he ties most front rows up in knots. But here was this giant hooker treating him like a schoolboy.

After this game Tommy spoke to me.

He came into our changing room and said, "It's been great to play against you over the years, mate. But this was probably the last time. I've enjoyed the battles. Best of luck."

I said, "Good on you, Tom. You've been a great opponent, too." What I was actually thinking was, 'Thank God you'll not be playing any more.'

I can see that Tommy treated me in a similar way to how I've treated Phil Kearns. Whereas Tommy started to respect me only as he got older, it took me a while before I respected Kearns.

When I saw the Aussies had dropped Tommy I was so happy I didn't care who his replacement was. But I wasn't about to show Kearns any favours just because he was young.

KEVIN BOROEVICH

'In rucks, as players got up, Fitzy always made sure he stood on you. It was niggly stuff, an example of typical Auckland arrogance. But it upset players, who often retaliated – right in front of the ref of course. Bang. Another three points to Auckland. It's a skill on its own to upset the opposition like that. And Fitzy was a master.'

PHIL KEARNS

'I played my first test for Australia against the All Blacks in 1990. Sean then was obviously the best in the world, but I didn't know much about him. Tommy Lawton had been axed, and our reserve hooker, a guy called Mark McBain, wasn't one for going over the top and giving advice to guys like me who'd just taken his position . . .

So there was no one who told me, 'This bloke's really good, but watch out for him, he's a tough bastard.' All they said was, 'Go out and do your best.'

It was a pretty big step going from second-grade rugby in Sydney to a test. On the field I soon found Sean whispering in my ear, saying things like, 'Get off the field, little boy, you don't deserve to be here, leave it to the men . . .', 'grow up, little boy' – and all this sort of stuff . . .

I don't know how I reacted to it really. It definitely didn't worry me too much.

I was surprised – I'd never really come up against anything like that before.'

"The hooker is the brains in the middle of the scrum."

– Uli Schmidt

WHAT DO YOU NEED to be a good hooker?

I rate a hooker by four criteria. One: their scrummaging ability. Two: their line-out throwing skills. Three: their defence. Fourth: their general play.

I probably rate defence a lot more highly than other people but I think it's a facet of play which gets overlooked.

Without doubt the best hooker for functions one and two was Tommy Lawton. He is the best hooker I've faced. I think Phil Kearns is probably the best all-round hooker today. Then I'd rate a group of Frenchmen: Dominique Bouet, Daniel Dubroca and Phillipe Dintrans. Bouet wasn't as good as the others overall, but he was a fantastic scrummager.

I found Scotland's Colin Deans a journeyman. I was quite surprised: at the time he was considered the best in the world but I found him nothing out of the ordinary.

Uli Schmidt, the South African, was apparently a one-man band against the Cavaliers in 1986. By the time I played him I think he was past his best. I'd love to have taken him on at his peak. His performance for Transvaal against Auckland in the 1993 Super 10 final was an indication of how good he was.

I don't rate England's Brian Moore at all, which is no surprise. He's a "9-to-5" sort of player, nothing special. He's said some really stupid things about me publicly and I don't respect him as a person or a player. He's from the old-fashioned school of hookers, but it's his mouth which is the most obvious feature of his game.

I'd be a liar to say I get on with opponents. Things have been a bit strained between me and many of the world's top hookers at times because we're all trying to out-do the others. As they retire, or fade from the scene, the intensity seems to go too. I think once I've hung up my boots I'll probably enjoy meeting a lot of these players over a beer or two.

I've never thought much about other New Zealand hookers. I've never had any reason to go looking for the good things they do because we're rivals, they've wanted my place in the team. I watch other hookers all the time, especially on video. I note what they do well, how they run their lines, the way they take up position before a scrum. I *learn* about them; I'm not awed by them. I never store it away and think, "So-and-so's a better thrower in than me . . . he's faster than me . . . he's stronger than me . . ." If I did that, I'd be giving them a mental advantage. I'd concede that some part of their game was better than mine.

I respect them all, but I don't dwell on their talent. When I play them I'm only concerned with exploiting the weaknesses I've seen. Every player has a weakness. I know mine, but I'll never talk about them until I'm retired, if then.

Probably I found Kevin Boyle, of Marist, the most difficult New Zealand hooker to deal with. Hika Reid and Bruce Hemara were always competitive. I never played much against Andy Dalton but he was obviously a class player.

There were two guys who reserved for me in the All Blacks until 1993. North Harbour's Graham Dowd was a converted prop who got better and better with experience. Warren Gatland, too, was a good player but he never really got the breaks. Currently I've got Norm Hewitt breathing down my neck for a place in the team. Not far behind him comes young Slade McFarland of North Harbour. It's great, I love the challenge.

Everything comes back to that: the challenge. Those hookers who accept my challenge and give 100 per cent back are the ones I really respect. My criteria for what makes a good hooker is different to the public's. They judge too much on the externals.

That's why titles like "the best hooker in the world" mean nothing from people who don't know anything about rugby.

People confuse my general game – the tries, the runs – with my ability as a hooker. As far as I am concerned, my reputation as a hooker depends on those things which aren't spectacular at all.

As a player, you do get influenced by reputations though. I remember how tense I was before the World Cup quarter-final against Scotland in 1987. In their team was Colin Deans who was meant to be the best hooker in the world. But judging on his performance, I feel he was overrated. That's typical of the British press. They often hype their players. Will Carling's a perfect example.

I couldn't believe it when Deans was chosen in the best World Cup team at the end of that tournament.

HIKA REID

'Fitzy was able to make such an impact because he was talented *and* had an attitude. A lot of other hookers had one or the other but not both.

Iain Abercrombie was a good player, but he was never a

warrior. John Buchan was another average player. But Fitzy . . . I always knew he was there.

Usually I'd ignore the other hooker and set to work on the tighthead. But I couldn't do that with him, especially if he had a good tighthead beside him. The biggest compliment I can pay Fitzy is this: with him I knew it was always going to be a real hard battle up-front.'

ULI SCHMIDT

'Fitzpatrick and I are similar players. We don't want to just take the ball and run with our heads down. If Phil Kearns gets the ball he will run back to his forwards, but Fitzpatrick and I will probably run or pass or kick . . .

I think he's the ideal hooker. A good scrummager – though I don't rate him as one of the greats – he has no weaknesses, not even a little.'

Hookers are probably the most competitive individuals in a rugby team. I think that's why I like the position so much.

When I first appeared in senior rugby the job definition of a hooker was simple: Win the ball. Block in the line-outs. Try to get the tighthead.

But when I played hooker with University, Drakey wouldn't let me go for a tighthead. He'd say, "Just push." So I'd push in one scrum and then at the next scrum I'd say, "I'll go for tighthead now, OK Drakey?" and he'd say, "No, Sean. Shut up and bloody push." This happened game after game until I understood what he was getting at.

JOHN DRAKE

'To hook as Sean does you've got to be technically good but you've got to have the right physique too. If you haven't got that . . . well, you can't put round things into square holes. Sean has the ideal physique. Sean's a big guy, very strong, and that's helped the All Blacks. A lot of props who have played in the All Blacks at the same time as Sean wouldn't have the reputations they do today without him, they wouldn't have looked quite as good without such a big hooker like him pushing beside them.'

I owe Drakey so much for what he taught me about front-row play. He was my mentor. When I first got into the Auckland team, he was the one who always kept an eye on me. It would have been harder without him; how much harder I wouldn't like to think. And when Stevie came along he made things perfect. I was very lucky to have played with those two props. Hika Reid said once, "Anyone can play well with props like that." At the time I thought it was just sour grapes, but Hika was probably right.

The scrum is the most important part of rugby because, unlike line-outs, it's the one set play where you can guarantee you'll get the ball. If you have a solid scrum it gives you a whole range of attacking options.

The front row is like a war zone. It's a world of its own. A lot of private games go on in there which few appreciate. It's badly misunderstood by many people in rugby – especially referees, coaches, backs. That's why there are so many jokes about it. In Australia they say you choose props by sending your team running through the bush. The first guys to hit the trees become props.

There's a story told of how South Africa selected its hooker for the test against us in 1992. There were so many possible candidates they decided to use an intelligence test.

The selectors called the first guy into the room.

"What's 12 minus six?" "Tuesday," was the reply.

They called another guy in. "What's 13 minus six?" "Wednesday," was his answer.

Then they called in Uli Schmidt. Uli's a doctor so they had big hopes for him. They made the question a bit harder. "What's 42 minus 12 multiplied by 56?"

"One thousand, six hundred and eighty," said Uli without batting an eyelid.

The selectors were astonished. "That's exactly right." Then one asked, "All the other players were hopeless. How come you knew the answer?"

"That's easy," said Uli. "I just took Wednesday away from Tuesday."

"Put out of your mind any idea that the powerhouse chaps can be without a brain amongst them."

– Fred Allen, *On Rugby*

LIFE IN THE FRONT row is a very physical, extremely psychological experience.

It starts with how you form. The All Blacks always have real urgency to form a scrum first: it's a way of showing the opposition you're on the ball, you're ready.

Dad always said to give your opposition front row the "killer look". Richard Loe's excellent at it: an "I-haven't-smiled-for-a-week" look. Steve McDowell possessed a real mean stare.

Olo will call when it's time to go in because, as tighthead, he's the first guy to make contact.

The impact in the first scrum often sets the course of the game. Watch any test and if you focus on the front rows you'll get a good indication of which side is mentally better prepared. You can do 100 scrums at training but they can't duplicate the feeling of that first hit: aggressive, low, driving through as hard as you can.

A good hard scrum early on unsettles them and gives you the advantage.

It's like the opening round in a boxing match. You want the upper hand as soon as possible. That's why scrum machines are so unrealistic. They can't duplicate your opponent's aggression. Against a machine you can work on technique and timing. But unlike people, machines don't move around and sniff out a weakness. In a game, every scrum is a battle – you don't win every time. Think of how often a team is hard on defence on its own line and yet it upsets the attacking side's scrum. It's because everyone is so desperate, they're all working as one to prevent a try.

When a front rower gets "popped" it looks spectacular but your team loses the advantage. You've got nothing to push against, only their stomachs. It's a much better tactic to keep them down, with their backs buckled . . . then you control everything.

Control. The best scrums always have it. Often I won't strike on the opposition put-in because a successful eight-man shove pushes them back and back and back. Even if they get the ball, it's often of poor quality and puts their whole team on the defensive. So you've "won" that scrum anyway. And it's an exhilarating feeling to have another pack scuttling backwards. It demoralises them and you know they've conceded you the advantage.

HIKA REID

'The thing I've come to realise since taking up coaching is that you look for the best combinations, or potential best, first.

If you've got 13 guys from Auckland, like the All Blacks had for so long, your job is basically done.

It's especially true with front rows. And Sean was part of a combination. No matter how hard I wanted to see it differently, I understood why they picked him.

It was a case of history repeating itself. I couldn't break the mould with Dalton, Knight and Ashworth – the "Geriatrics" – either. If I ever wrote a book about my career I'd call it *Bad Timing.*'

PETER FATIALOFA

'Fitzy, Stevie and I believed in each other. There was a couple of times we got pushed back, but that was only because one of us wasn't thinking, or concentrating. And the others would say, 'Come on, we're better than this,' and smash them.

When you have someone as big as Fitzy as your hooker he applies a lot of pressure to the other hooker, or the other tighthead prop, which makes it really uncomfortable for them. Then you've got Stevie mowing in on one guy, or Fitzy and Stevie together focusing on one guy. I felt sorry for that guy.

I'd say, 'Fitzy, move over to the left and help Stevie, I can do this end on my own.' But that's the difference between any other front row and ours. Usually, if you leave another guy by himself he'll end up getting screwed. At 128kg, I could do it.'

A lot's been said of Auckland's power-scrum. During the '80s and early '90s, we cleaned up a lot of sides in big games through our scrum domination. We weren't that physically large – in fact often opposing packs were taller and heavier. But our technique was superb. Stevie, Peter Fats and I could spot a flaw in an opponent almost straight away and we could "take" most scrums when we wanted to. When Olo took over from Fats, things carried on as smoothly as ever. They were different sorts of players, but the ease in which we adapted showed the ability of individuals to play a number of different games.

I think the one game which showed how much everybody feared our out-and-out domination was the Canterbury Shield challenge in 1990. Buchan, their hooker, got sent off and the game turned into an absolute joke. Hiding behind the law they said they didn't have a spare hooker and we had to use tap-kicks instead of scrums. It was totally unsatisfactory: the crowd hated it, the Auckland players hated it and what should have been a great end to the season was a farce. History shows we won 33-30. I've had harder games of touch rugby.

In the mid '80s, Auckland's front row was the biggest debating point at referees' conferences. Refs couldn't understand why we were so much better than other teams. Apparently, they discussed us at length. Their solution? To be so good we must be cheating.

On Auckland's ball the scrum was always solid, but on the opposition put-in we'd always upset the scrums. Many scrums collapsed. Refs, who didn't have a clue what was happening, assumed Auckland was being disruptive. That was nonsense. We just put an incredible amount of pressure on and most teams couldn't hold us up.

Other teams deliberately dropped the scrum. They took the easy way out. If you're on attack a collapsed scrum is the last thing you want because you won't get the ball. But refs didn't understand what goes on and they pinged us more often than was fair. It got really frustrating.

Even at test level refs are too often in the dark about front-row play. Ray Megson penalised the All Blacks against Australia at a crucial moment in the 1991 Sydney test for pulling down a scrum. We didn't pull it down at all, the thing just caved in. But his ignorance gave Australia a penalty at a critical stage. They scored from it.

In this year's trial at Napier, Dave Bishop, the number one referee in the country, penalised us when he didn't have a clue what was going on. Nothing's changed.

JOHN ALLAN

'I made my test debut in 1990 against the All Blacks. Scotland had a great front row too: I played between two "greats", David Sole and Ian Milne.

I was really apprehensive before the game; I knew I had to be physically and mentally ready or I'd get wasted.

I can still remember that first scrum. It was one of the hardest scrums I've ever been in for impact.

I've played against them all individually and they weren't as powerful. Their secret was that they complemented each other. They bent the scrum the wrong way – this used to suit McDowell – which buckled the opposition.

You need a lot of strength to do that, and all three have to be on the same wavelength. Two won't achieve it.

Technically, in the 1991 World Cup, they were still the best.

In the game against Scotland Fitzpatrick was in so much control he would direct play with just a word. He'd give the call and they would do it to perfection.

Normally a call needs to be screamed and shouted to get everyone focused, but they knew each other so well they just did their job with no fuss.

Interestingly, when Fitzpatrick's All Blacks played against us in Natal a year later, he was screaming at his forwards; that's when I knew they weren't as cohesive.'

We played 33 tests together, a world record for front rowers. But when people ask, "Why were you and McDowell and Loe so good?" the truth is I don't know if we *were* that good. We never really dominated another team at scrum time. Personally, I think the best All Black front row was the 1987 unit because Drakey was there.

John Drake summed up everything I believe the modern front-rower needs. He was a born competitor. You can see it in him today, in his approach to squash, to business – he has to win. That attitude, plus his technical ability and strength, was so important to the All Black scrum.

Stevie and Richard were both fine players too. I think the secret of our longevity was that we complemented each other. And after so much time together you learn to think as one. I've no idea how many scrums we've taken part in over the years, whether at training or in a game. They must run into the thousands. It's hardly a surprise that we developed a combination; it would have been almost impossible not to.

They had very different styles. Stevie was shorter but had a distinctive, technical style. He made his name with his runs around the field, the way he'd hit into rucks. His ball skills were excellent. I think it helped me that he'd been a hooker for a while; he understood my needs. Players much bigger than he was couldn't budge him. Stevie's form was crucial for me: if their tighthead lowers the scrum, it prevents me getting a clear view of the ball. With Stevie, I always got plenty of time to strike.

Richard was big and snarly, very physical, very difficult to move in a scrum. Loey is an "old-school" All Black. He gets on with it. If he's hurt, you'll never know. He just laughs at you, even if you know inside he must be screaming. A fantastic man to have in a tough situation. And, given his reputation, other teams are scared of him. He just has to frown and the opposition tense. Instead of thinking about their game, they concentrate on him which works in our favour.

The All Black front row in 1992 was almost as good as the 1987 team's. We were up against very good opponents in the Australian trio of McKenzie, Kearns and Daly. I believe honours were even after that series: we'd earned each others' respect.

Test rugby's probably not as physically demanding as even when Drakey was playing. The game's quicker now, aerobically faster. In terms of strength it's not as demanding. There aren't as many scrums, perhaps only 10 or 15 a game. In years gone by there might have been 60 or 70 scrums. Obviously a lot more emphasis was placed on power.

Olo Brown is probably the ideal modern prop. Tight forwards have to get in and do the hard work in terms of getting a drive on and securing the ball quickly for the team. Players like Stevie who make a lot of big runs aren't seen as that essential by selectors; they'd rather have a guy like Olo or Craig Dowd who's going to get in there and make sure that the Joe Stanleys of the world are given the ball. A guy like Mark Allen's come a long way recently.

"Sean is probably one of the greatest referees the game has ever seen." – Phil Kearns

RUGBY IS A PSYCHOLOGICAL game as much as a physical one. Talking to the opposition is a big part of it.

In the front row there's always a bit of verbal – par for the course. It's for your team's benefit and it distracts opponents.

You might tell your loosehead, "That was a good scrum, we drilled them then. Next time we'll go higher . . ."

The opposition hear all this too and if they're struggling it puts them off. If they're scrummaging well, it sows doubt in them – they often make unnecessary adjustments. It's bluff, or double bluff. I couldn't put an exact figure on it but I estimate probably 90 per cent of talk in the front row is nonsense; it's all psychological.

HIKA REID

'Fitzy uses his mouth to intimidate whereas I use my body. As a result, we had a lot of battles. I remember in one Shield challenge Fitzy was mouthing off so I just punched him. He never complained – that was the way things were between us.

There are a lot of private battles going on in a game. It's an unwritten law of rugby. I never did it to hurt him but private contests motivated me to play better. I'm sure he would agree.'

JOHN DRAKE

'You've got to talk to your own players constantly about what's going on in the scrums.

If you're having a hard time, you have to tell your hooker. You can't tell him after the game. Likewise, you've got to manipulate the opposition if you think there's a little problem there. You've got to try to exploit it.

In that way, Sean and I complemented each other.'

GRANT DICKSON

'Seany started chipping off Drakey when they played at Varsity. That's where he learned it from. Drakey was more trouble than he was worth with refs.

It wasn't solely Drakey's fault. Varsity was a real bad *team* for chipping refs. If Sean had played for a club like Otahuhu I don't think he'd have picked up some of the bad habits he did.'

Quite a few refs have said to me, "Since you were made captain it's been much easier to referee you." I think when I wasn't captain I was a lot more difficult for them. Today I'm just a shadow of the talker I was. My peak was 1990 – I was probably at the height of my sledging ability that year.

Too many refs lack confidence or don't have the ability to handle the pressure of top-level rugby. I can't stand that, especially if it's an important game with a lot at stake. A bad official makes it hard on everyone and it frustrates the players.

If I think the ref's a good official then I don't give him much needle. If you get someone like Dave Bishop, or even Keith Lawrence, I'll have a laugh with them, give them a bit of a hard time. Paddy O'Brien's another referee who impresses me. There are one or two high-ranking names that, frankly, I find a joke. They see rugby as a series of rules instead of a game which needs to be controlled by common sense. Obviously, that type and I don't get on. There are so many complex rules in rugby. To blow up for each one would result in virtually no rugby being played. Good refs aren't whistle-happy, they judge each infringement by its impact on the game.

With me it's all a bit of fun. I just like trying to put one across refs, it's in my nature. Bishop knows that and he'll give back as good as he gets. But it's nothing too big, just little things . . . I might question the odd decision they made.

It's effective because it gets the opposition really going. It drives them nuts. They forget about the game and get obsessed with the ref and me.

Referees often say to me, "Look, you, just shut up. I can make my own decisions, I don't need you to tell me what to do." When that happens and I know they're serious I'm very apologetic. "Sorry ref."

PHIL KEARNS

> 'In the 1990 series against New Zealand I got the nick-name 'Lightning', because the ball never struck the same place twice when I was throwing in. Sean latched on to it and took every chance to remind me.
>
> At every line-out I'd hear Sean, 'Now come on Lightning, get this one in straight, come on Lightning.'
>
> He never shut up. So when I scored my try in Wellington I told him how happy I felt. I had something to say back to him, finally. It's been reported I invited him to a barbecue. That's not quite what I said.'

There are times in rugby when you go too far. I once shot my mouth off at North Auckland hooker Mike Barry, the brother of Liam, and John Hart tore shreds off me afterwards. "Totally unnecessary," he said. He was right. I'd overstepped the mark.

It's when players overstep the mark physically that rugby gets a bad name – and can become dangerous.

I'm always wary of the dirty players, and the dirty players are known within the game. I remember a certain prop forward who had a bad reputation and players like him, you kept a wary eye out for.

No one has ever punched me out, although an Argentinian prop one time kept on sticking his tongue down my ear.

Dirty play takes many forms. The deliberate late tackle. The punch or swinging boot from somewhere in the maul. A kick in the head after a collapsed scrum. Stomping. The stiff-arm.

They're obvious. Sometimes, the issue is not so clear; even for players it's a fine line between what's acceptable and what is dirty play. For example, players always try to push the rules to the limit, and if they're warned to stop, but keep on infringing, they'll get a whack. They know it, you know it, refs know it. It's gamesmanship.

Some games you ignore it, but turning the other cheek can also have the wrong effect too: your opponent thinks you're weak and takes liberties for the rest of the game. You've got to judge the situation as you see it, but if the ref won't help . . .

Players have an unwritten, but universally understood, code about what will be tolerated. It's actions like biting, or the intentional use of a boot on an exposed head, which fall into the not acceptable category. A bit of a biff . . . depends.

BUCK SHELFORD

'Around '89, Sean started chipping and niggling. It usually happened if the All Blacks were under pressure. He started to talk back to refs, stand on players' hands and legs, take guys out after the whistle. And that part of his game stayed with him until the end of 1991.

I noticed that when he became All Black captain these things disappeared. He understood that a captain has to lead: at his level of football you don't need to niggle guys by sprigging them.'

RICHARD FRY

'Fitzy was just aggressive to everyone, even mates like me. I discovered this playing for Counties against Auckland.

During the game I ended up on the wrong side of the ruck. Next thing I feel this huge whack on my leg. It was really painful, it caused a real bad haematoma. I didn't know who did it, then I heard Fitzy's voice.

'Frybee,' he said, 'I had to reach *way* across to get you . . .'

That's rugby. That's not dirty play. Fitzy's not dirty. He'd never kick you in the head, or eye-gouge you or grab your balls. But he's hard.'

JOHN DRAKE

'Sean's an absolutely hopeless puncher. Without us to protect him he wouldn't have lasted 10 seconds in a fight . . .'

PHIL KEARNS

'At Eden Park in 1990 I thought Sean went in with a couple of cheap shots. I remember he dug his knees into Willie's [Ofahengaue] back a fair way after the whistle had blown. I told him to piss off and he mouthed back, but that was it. He's always been an aggressive player in that way, but a couple of times he's gone over the top.

At the same time, if he's copped a belt, he's copped it sweet.'

On tour you'll always come up against some hotheads but, as a rule, I don't believe one country is dirtier than another. Scotland get away with a lot more than most would suspect. Australia is probably the cleanest team: they usually play good hard rugby. They wouldn't get too worried about us, either.

The exception is France.

In France you're never off guard. You're always watching your "privates" and the back of your head. And if you're OK, you look out for your team-mate, put a hand over his head if his arms are caught in a ruck. If you don't the French will take advantage. They will grab your testicles, eye-gouge you, kick you . . . It's always there and it's rarely personal: it's par for the course. You sometimes wonder if they're expected to do it as part of their reputation. Which doesn't make it any easier to deal with.

On my first tour there, in 1986, the rugby was really dirty. I'll never forget the second test. I was already carrying 18 stitches on my scalp from when Carminati and I bashed heads in the first test. For a week my head was so tender. Sleeping was hopeless.

I probably shouldn't have played in the second test at Nantes, but I was young, Hika was breathing down my neck and I didn't want to give him a chance to reclaim his test spot. So I turned out. Big mistake. The All Blacks were walked all over that day. I know. Early in the game the scrum collapsed and, as I lay there, a French player came through with his boot and positioned it on top of my head.

Then, quite deliberately, he ripped his foot right down the back of my scalp. I needed 28 stitches to close the wound. To make matters worse, in every scrum afterwards, Condom, their lock, kept whacking my head, trying to aggravate the wound.

There was one Frenchman I grew to respect, even enjoy meeting. We always clashed when we met, but there was an underlying respect between us. His name was Pascal Ondarts, the loosehead prop.

Ondarts is a Basque and like all people from that region has immense pride. He's no oil painting, Pascal: his nose looks like the letter 'S' and he has eyebrows which are almost falling off his face. He's not a tall man . . . but he's very strong. Technically he's a wonderful scrummager. And he believes that you do whatever you have to do to help your team win.

Whatever you have to do. We had some dust-ups.

PASCAL ONDARTS

> 'When we play the Blacks we are maybe more aggressive because, unlike other teams, the Blacks are always winners. We put more intensity into beating them than any other team. After the game, everything's perfect. Sean and I have swapped blazers, a great honour for me.
>
> On the field Sean was a vicious opponent. He wasn't afraid to take the game to me, and I would never turn away from a fight. So we had a lot of fights. But Sean is a great player, certainly the most French Black I ever met.
>
> That is why it was such an honour to swap blazers with him.'

One incident I deeply regret.

In my early club career, playing for University against Grammar, I got sent off. Back then every game between the two clubs was just a real ding-dong battle. We knew the Grammar boys really well socially, a lot of them were mates, but when it came to this fixture all friendships were suspended.

The day I walked early, the game was even worse than usual. John McDermott and Kevin Ramsey were belting the hell out of each other at every chance; there'd be Drakey and somebody else fighting; and Gary and AJ trying to pull Grant Dickson's leg off. One of their guys had been sent off in the first 10 minutes and throughout the game I'd been giving the referee heaps of flak.

Then their halfback passed the ball and as I tackled him, I kneed him in the back. The ref sent me off. I felt terrible.

BRYCE BEVIN

> 'I felt really sorry for Sean. Those games had their own strange kind of 'rules' – there was always lots of niggle in them from start to finish, but not real fighting. I think he slid into Grammar's halfback on his knees, gave him a push with his knee. It wasn't anything drastic, but the ref sent Seany off as an example to the rest of us.'

JULIE McDIARMID

> 'He was terribly sad. For days he wasn't eating properly. His whole world had fallen down around him, he was so ashamed.'

I've been dealt to a few times.

Steve Smith, the Irish hooker, hit me in Wellington and knocked out three teeth. I was trying to be the peacemaker, holding off one of their locks who was wrestling one of our guys. Smith didn't it see it that way and hit me from behind. It was a good punch. A bloody good punch. I wasn't bitter; we had a laugh about it later. (Contrary to popular myth, Earle Kirton, who is a dentist, *didn't* fix my teeth. He'd charge me too much.)

In Wales in 1989 one of their props was really annoying McDowell. Stevie gave him a warning but this bloke wouldn't see sense. So when the ref wasn't watching, Steve whacked him. It was a terrific sock. Trouble was, his aim was off. "You've just hit me, mate," I told him. And I had a great big cut in my face – I've still got the scar. The rest of the All Blacks thought it was hilarious. "About time somebody got you, Caveman. You've stood on us all these years . . ."

One of the most unusual incidents occurred at Ellis Park in 1992. I got hit by a Springbok but never saw who did it. It was a solid blow, I needed stitches afterwards.

Later that night, at the after-match, Uli Schmidt swaggered up to me. "I see you've hurt yourself, Sean. Just so you know, that was for the punch you gave me four months ago in Wellington in the World XV series."

I said, "Oh, so it was you who hit me, Uli?"

He said, "No, I got one of the locks to do it for me."

I didn't mind too much. We'd won. And I knew I'd play him again.

There's an old All Black saying: "Never get mad, get even."

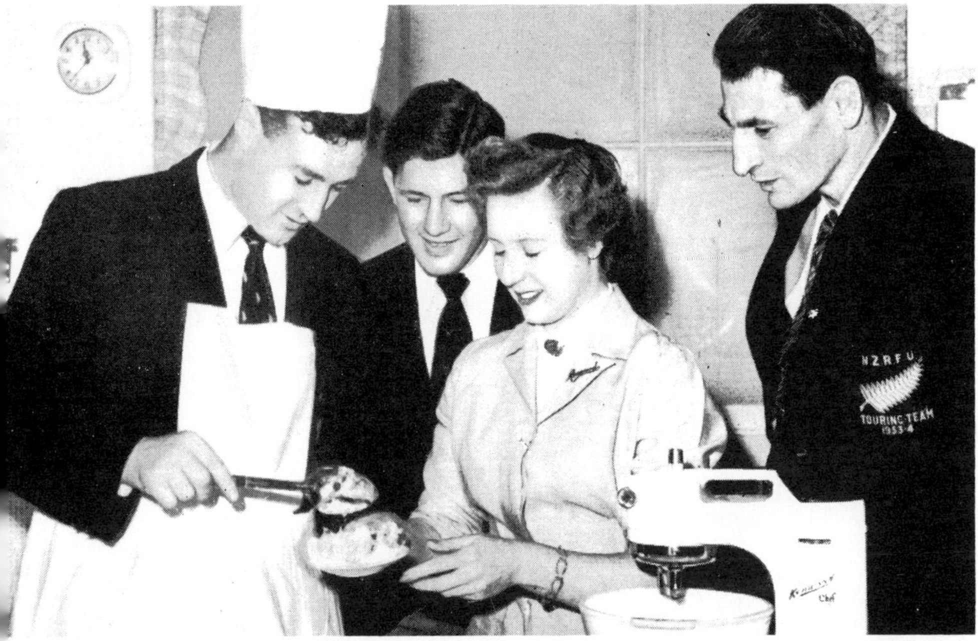

Sport and General, London

Dad reminds me, rugby tours were very different 40 years ago. Here he is in the UK with All ck team-mates Kevin Skinner and "Tiny" White.

Sean Fitzpatrick collection

recent years I've learned to scuba dive – unfortunately for this poor lobster.

Olympix

Defence: the part of a hooker's game which is too often overlooked.

Olympix

ree with Michael Jordan's philosophy: "If you don't compete, then I'll dominate you."

The person who knows me better than anyone – my wife Bronnie, the mainstay of my life for t past decade.

BOOK III

Olympix

Only a Game?

CHAPTER ELEVEN

Dressed for a Funeral

"History never repeats, I tell myself, before I go to sleep . . ."

– Split Enz

I COULDN'T SLEEP.

It was sometime near dawn and I'd switched to countdown mode. The final test against the Lions, the biggest game of my life, was just hours away. The tension hung over me like a big, dark cloud. Once more I took some deep breaths and tried to clear my mind. But I was too alert.

Usually I find sleep comes easily, even before the biggest internationals. But this time the pressure was smothering. I was fighting to stay calm, relax, switch off. I wasn't having too much success.

Whenever we play an Auckland test it's customary for the All Blacks to stay at the Poenamo Hotel on the North Shore, the perfect environment for the team. The staff know us, look after our needs . . . we're ensured of privacy, quiet, comfort and, best of all, lots of support.

But not even the familiar surroundings of "the Poe" could reassure me now.

The bottom line, if things went badly, was that this test would probably signal my final All Black appearance. The thought utterly depressed me: I wasn't ready to say goodbye to the black jersey yet. I didn't want to become "Sean Fitzpatrick, former All Black".

Less than a year after defeating the Springboks in Johannesburg, I was fighting for career survival. As I lay restlessly turning in bed, I was in no doubt that my future depended upon the outcome of just one match.

Pressure? Tell me about it.

I HADN'T THE SLIGHTEST inkling of what lay ahead as I went for my first pre-season runs in January. I've wondered since, had I known of the future pressures and worries, if I'd have retired then. I think it's a possibility. But I was eager and excited in early 1993. It was a good summer, I was feeling in the best of spirits, really enjoying life.

I eased my way into fitness. There was no need to go overboard. The All Blacks had an incredibly demanding year lined up – an unprecedented seven tests in less than two months. There was a Lions series; the Bledisloe Cup a fortnight later; and then, in the last weekend of July, Manu Samoa at Eden Park, a virtual "home test" for them in the largest Polynesian city in the world. Finally, there was an All Black tour to the UK.

On the domestic front things were just as hectic. Auckland was after the first-division crown; the Ranfurly Shield was on the line for the eighth consecutive season; there was also a new competition, the Super 10, beginning in April and May.

As I blocked out the year's fixtures on the planner board in my office, I realised nearly every weekend was taken up with rugby.

My first game, a friendly match in Westport, was scheduled for February. My last game, if form and fitness got me through, would be in Cardiff in the first week in December. A total of *forty-four* weeks devoted to playing, training, or some other involvement in rugby. Add another month of pre-season running to that and you had 11 months of the year gone.

GRANT FOX

> 'The first three weeks of any season are usually the worst. That's when you endure the worst pain, the pain of getting fit. I never looked at it in terms of 10 or 11 months; I broke the season down into segments.
>
> If it got hard motivation-wise I'd do one of two things: picture we were playing Australia, it was 18-all and we were down to the last 10 minutes. You needed every ounce of fitness then . . .
>
> Or else I'd phone a mate. Quite a few times I'd ring Fitzy and say, 'Mate, I'll meet you at the Domain at 10 o'clock. Let's go for a run.''

ANT STRACHAN

'The first year for the ABs was, in hindsight, easy. This time it was different. I probably didn't realise it but even in that first game [at Westport] the pressure was on. You become a bit of a public name, you're in the paper, on TV – whether it's a President's game, a Baabaas game, people automatically expect you to be the man because you're an All Black.

In my case I was carrying a couple of niggling injuries. I'd busted a finger playing indoor netball and it hadn't properly healed. But I played the game as a favour for Sturge and, while I played okay, it wasn't the perfect start. And then Earle had a bit of a chat to me after a Super 10 game. Looking back, I think that's where my season started going downhill. You start looking for ghosts that aren't there instead of jumping in and playing by instinct.

That's what the pressure's like in every game once you're an All Black. And I think the worst pressure is what you put on yourself. How you handle it comes down to the individual.'

After the gains made in Australia and South Africa, the All Blacks had a strong base to build upon. There was only one problem: the selectors were in a no-win situation. They had two requirements to meet – two *contradictory* requirements.

The New Zealand public makes no bones that it expects World Cup glory in 1995. They also demand a successful All Black team every time it steps out on the park. The two aims, while desirable, are not complementary. You can stack a team with older, "one-series" guys you know will do the job and get the short-term result . . . but the nagging doubt remains: can they sustain form till '95? We'd held on to some players too long at the last World Cup. Alternatively, the Aussie way of blooding youth at the cost of test defeat is not possible with the All Blacks.

This paradox is unique to New Zealand. No other nation stacks on the pressure to win *every time* like this country. The way the public went berko when we dropped two provincial games in France in 1990 was enough proof of their intolerance.

Often Laurie would phone me and we'd have a chat. It wasn't face-to-face stuff: that happens in test week, or on tour. But he kept me involved, included me where appropriate, asked me what I thought or could contribute in any way?

I gave frank, unbiased comments about who I thought was best suited to play our tactics months before the trial teams were picked. As always, the final decision was his.

To speak so openly requires total trust in Laurie – and puts a lot of responsibility onto me. I agonise over what I say to make sure personal feelings don't cloud my judgement. I think I was successful on tour – the other players would've been the first to resent signs of favouritism, or misguided loyalty. And Laurie would have lost faith in me long ago if he considered my views consistently off-beam.

Inga was a crowd favourite, for example, but he was also one of the laziest players I've ever known. He always had an excuse for ducking training, or missing that tackle. Your respect diminishes for that sort of player. I told Laurie what I thought; how Laurie handled it was up to him. He is the coach.

JAMIE JOSEPH

> 'Everyone knows the captain talks with the coach. But it's not an issue.
>
> I know one or two guys wonder when they play against Fitzy in [national championship] games if they should get stuck in to him, in case he'll tell Laurie. That's not my attitude at all and I doubt if it's Fitzy's. I've got heaps of respect for the guy, and he knows it. I think he respects me, too.
>
> Whenever Auckland play Otago I don't hold back just because I'm playing against the All Black captain. I'm sure Fitzy wouldn't want it any other way.'

Laurie's approach is smart: he is dependent upon me to be his eyes and ears on the field. No coach can ever totally know who's putting in the grunt, or who's fading out of a game, just by watching from the sidelines.

Only players know the true effort other players give. Only if you're involved can you tell which player puts his body on the line and who flinches from that commitment. Up close you'll see who shifts away from making the hard runs or putting in the big tackles. It's easy to be Joe Expert and pick the glamour boys from the sideline – but a crowd pleaser isn't always a "smart" player, one who can sum up a game with one brief look. There are a lot of players, even All Blacks, who are "dumb" in their choice of options.

It's not only my input he relies on. Laurie talks frequently with a handful of trusted rugby friends. He will act on their advice, even if it's not what he wants to hear. I know of choices he's made with extreme reluctance. It's a brave thing to do. It's also ego-free. The essential factor is: if he deems a tough decision is necessary for the *team's* sake, Laurie will make it.

Contrary to the wisdom of popular opinion, I know the selectors have solid reasoning behind every decision they make. They are practical men. They are ambitious to do well for the All Blacks, the country, themselves.

In preparing for 1993, the selectors' eyes were open wide.

Five of the seven tests were against Northern Hemisphere teams. That meant devising new tactics to deal with "British-style" rugby. We anticipated, correctly, the magic of rugby's new attacking laws wouldn't be seen by them during this series.

The Five Nations tournament was our proof.

British coaches had obviously studied the laws and deliberately gone against the spirit of them. Their teams mass-produced the same defensive tactics.

As a style it's unquestionably effective. And dead boring. If we made a mistake in our planning it was underestimating how deeply entrenched this conservative approach was in the Lions' thinking.

Very few of our future critics seemed concerned about the Lions. If you believed the early talk, you'd have thought the All Blacks only needed to turn up for a test and the game was in the bag. Before they got here, the Lions were dismissed as easy-beats.

Everyone was writing them off far too easily. The critics said they were too old, too slow, too inflexible. What got overlooked were their very obvious strengths: their set pieces, their management and experience. Over half of them had played in New Zealand at some stage of their careers. Englishmen dominated the selection – and England had been the best Five Nations team for quite a while.

I knew the series would be close. New Zealanders were expecting a 3-0 whitewash; as far back as February in an interview on the subject, I predicted a 2-1 result was far more probable.

> *"It is almost universally accepted in New Zealand that the Lions will be on a hiding to nothing when they meet Sean Fitzpatrick's men."* – *Rugby World & Post*

BY THE TIME THE Lions tour kicked off, the season already felt incredibly long. Auckland narrowly, and unluckily, lost the Super 10 final; we completed a tough couple of trials in difficult conditions; there were All Black fitness tests on several occasions.

By the first week of June I was still to play my first game of club rugby.

Most of the guys were in form. One or two weren't firing like Laurie wished, but he was confident that with time and a few training runs together, the team would gel as it had in Africa.

Match number seven, in Christchurch, was the first test – and my 50th international for New Zealand. Seven years earlier I'd made my All Black debut at Lancaster Park. The media played up this coincidence for all it was worth. I gave interview after interview about the "significance" of such a milestone.

Good media relations were a priority. We knew our displays would be scrutinised a lot more closely by the public and critics. Laurie stressed: "Beware of 'second year syndrome'."

The council's decision to create the position of press officer was much-needed. Ric Salizzo got the job. His role was to take the heat off Laurie, Neil and me. He knew the journos and, most importantly, because he'd made several videos with JK and helped out in Africa, he was trusted by the guys.

But public support and a satisfied press would only come with the results.

After the patchy early tour form of the Lions results were certainly expected by New Zealanders. The All Blacks started the series as red-hot favourites – the last thing we wanted. It only added to the pressure associated with any test.

The Lions were a strange mix of skill and inconsistency. They had dropped a game, to Otago. Laurie warned us not to place any significance on that defeat. If anything, we knew it would only rev them up.

Not surprisingly, our team was the same which had beaten South Africa except for two forced changes – Eroni came in for JK, who had only just got back from Italy, and Craig Dowd made his test debut at loosehead prop because Loey was suspended.

The team trained well, but after 10 months apart we didn't have that split-second understanding. Even so, I remember saying to Foxy that I felt reasonably happy. You sense when a team is switched "on" or not. There was nervousness, but the desire to do well was certainly there.

Laurie added a bit of edge to the build-up by singling out three players in the team session and, in front of the guys, warned them they needed to produce a big match.

JAMIE JOSEPH

> 'Every player is different. Laurie's done it to quite a few of us at different stages. But he only does it to those who can handle it.
>
> Guys like Buncey, one of those who copped it, are hard nuts. They've been around a while, they're tough campaigners.'

A fallacy exists that All Blacks have a lot of time to prepare for a test. In a home series it's a myth. That's why touring is so vital to build up a pattern. Touring gives you time to develop and experiment.

For the Lions series, the routine was standard – squeeze as much as possible into a very tight schedule. We assembled on Tuesday and had a hard workout that afternoon. That left us just two full-scale practices, on Wednesday and Thursday, to develop our game options. Most of this was taken up performing drills until they worked smoothly. Laurie doesn't believe in a "give-it-your-all" session on the day before a test, so on Friday we visited the ground, had a light run and a few line-outs; soaked up the atmosphere.

BRONWYN FITZPATRICK

> 'People don't realise how demanding home tests are. They seem to think Sean just turns up on the day of the game. The reality is for a Saturday test he's gone first thing on a Tuesday

morning and not home until Sunday afternoon when he's always absolutely shattered from the demands of the game.

Win, lose, or draw it's always the same. But when you tell people this, they have blank looks on their faces. You know they're thinking something like, 'It's not as if he's going to France . . .''

There was a lot else going on that week in Christchurch. The first version of the All Black Club was launched live on *Holmes*; we were outfitted with gear; we had to fulfil several sponsorship and media requirements – we confirmed our part in TV3's Telethon, for example; the team discussed several issues relating to All Black Promotions, the company by which the All Black team makes money. These activities all took time.

The argument that such non-rugby activities distracted us was nonsense. Physically you can't train for more than a couple of hours a day or else you leave your form on the training paddock. That leaves a lot of spare time on your hands, so it's good to have different things to do.

Sponsor's functions don't drain the All Blacks. For the modern player, they're a totally accepted feature of the rugby environment. The key, as it is for every successful rugby team, lies in getting the time between rugby and non-rugby properly balanced.

For example, on most occasions you want to train in the morning, so you can have an afternoon off to, say, play golf. Or you'll study a rugby video on the opposition *before* you train, not afterwards. That way you can work on the bad habits in your game, or implement the tactics to use against the opposition, having just seen what's needed.

ANT STRACHAN

'Laurie was the key man in the All Blacks; the other coaches were all spare parts men, to coin a phrase. He's been a dominant figure in my career from the days when I was a scarfie in Dunedin. I certainly don't have many criticisms.

To describe his style I'd say he's a dominant person, he likes to be dominant, likes players to know he's in charge.

His job certainly puts him in the hot seat.

Before that test he knew better than anyone how hard it would be for the team to come together after so many months apart. We'd been playing a smorgasbord of all types of rugby and it takes time to build the team pattern again. Three days was not enough.'

The $64,000 question was, how much impact would All Black history have on our performance?

Everyone knows the All Blacks are slow out of the blocks. We rarely do well first-up at home. One hundred years of stuttering starts is evidence enough. In 1992, we'd struggled against the World XV and Ireland in both first tests.

We were determined not to repeat this habit. But as the build-up intensified, we became tense and uptight.

Consequently, struggle is exactly what we did.

We began well; Buncey scored early, and Foxy matched Gavin Hastings kick for kick. JT tackled superbly at the back but we blew our lead and the last nine minutes, when we trailed by three points, were desperately hard as we fought to save the game.

Thanks to Foxy's last minute penalty, we won 20-18. The team was very subdued after such a lacklustre display. We'd been hesitant, made too many unforced errors, incurred stupid penalties, dropped the ball.

GRANT FOX

> ‘I never looked at the scoreboard. I never thought, 'This kick could win us the game.' Instead, I said to myself: 'You've kicked this thousands of times before in training . . . it's just another kick. There's no big deal.'
>
> After the game – sure, that's when I thought about the significance. As I said to Laurie, 'I owed you that for last year.'’

Our dressing room was unusually sombre for a test victory. I got changed slowly, and thought about all the things I could have done better. I'm not a person who puts great store in individual achievements. While I was extremely proud to have played 50 tests for my country, I was more relieved to have got the win. I was concerned too – it's not acceptable to use our history as slow-starters as a valid excuse for repeating mistakes. The bottom line was that we'd under-performed. The Lions had too. I wasn't kidding when I told the press the series was very much alive.

Critics rarely consider how disappointed the players get when our plans go astray. Apart from any other emotion, it's really frustrating.

Who wants to leave your family for four or five days, flog your guts out in training, worry like mad every night that you're going to make a fool out of yourself in front of 50,000 people and everyone at home watching on TV . . . to do all that and then play like a turkey?

The Lions produced much superior rugby to anything they'd shown in previous tour games. They mauled well, tackled strongly, and – full credit to them – they slowed the game down to a Dad's Army pace which suited them. We let them do it.

This test also revealed the Lions' clinical, cynical, approach to rugby.

In the old days, Lions teams were renowned for their great backs and hopeless tight five. This bunch were the complete opposite: you never saw their backs because they were so forward-obsessed. They'd go into rucks and maul with only four guys and then collapse it on the ground. We weren't controlling the ball or delivering it fast enough, which gave them time to plug their extra forwards into the backline. Instead of seven All Black backs against seven Lions, we had nine, sometimes 10 red jerseys to deal with.

The Lions got away with murder. Michael Jones was penalised three times for holding onto the ball in a ruck, but video conclusively showed two of those penalties were undeserved. Yet when Dean Richards did the same thing at the end of the game the Lions cried injustice.

When they had the ball, there was never any real intention to run it – they didn't have the loosies fast enough to get out wide. They just kicked.

EARLE KIRTON

'You have to applaud the Lions: they'd obviously watched a lot of videos of us and were very well organised, especially on defence. We made it easier for them than we should have. We wanted to go straight down the middle, take it in and then move it wide in second phase. They knew we did and they were successful in stopping us.'

PETER THORBURN

'Under the new rules there's not a lot you can do if the opposition is blatantly negative.

In the '60s and '70s there was no such thing as a pile-up or maul or rolling maul. Then you had rucks which kept the momentum going.

But the British developed an obsession with mauls, and once the ball's on the ground you're not driving any more. The whole point of driving is to put your opposition on the back-foot.

But like British sides do, these Lions negated our driving game. They stood flat in the backs.'

Over the next few days, as the test was analysed, the Lions escaped most of the criticism. Instead, it was the All Blacks who wore much of the flak for not running the ball more, and the Lions' claims of a "moral victory" were given a lot of air. They ripped into the referee for his decision to award Frank Bunce his try, and then award us the late penalty.

This annoyed me because too many people appeared to overlook which team actually won the game. I admitted we hadn't played well and were lucky to walk away with the victory – but in test rugby, every win's a good win. As I said at the after-match function, when acknowledging Foxy's 1000th point for the All Blacks which he brought up during the game, it was the *last* three I particularly liked.

If I harboured any doubts that the media would go easy on us this year, they vanished after Christchurch. The honeymoon, most definitely, was over.

"The All Blacks always go to their matches suitably dressed for a funeral, but this time they went on their own." – John Reason, *Sunday Telegraph*

FOUR DAYS BEFORE THE second test, Hawke's Bay heavily defeated the midweek Lions. At the time I didn't place a great deal of importance on the result. Though pleased for the Bay players, I didn't think the loss would have much effect on the test – this was only the Lions' second-stringers, after all, a very ordinary outfit.

But this was the game when the Hawke's Bay hooker and All Black reserve, Norm Hewitt, played like Superman. He scored a try, picked up a tighthead and made some fantastic runs. The crowd loved it. Norm, deservedly so, got a lot of attention for his performance.

I took Norm's form as a personal challenge. It made me extra determined to deliver a blinder in Wellington.

ANT STRACHAN

'To actually see your name *not* in an All Black team is devastating. When I was dropped [after the first test] I was very disappointed. I wasn't bitter: I wasn't playing well, I'd seen the writing on the wall a bit before that . . . but when it actually happens . . .

When guys get dropped from the All Blacks you know team closeness can only go so far. Sure, you have sympathy but when guys get tipped in and out you can't let it affect you too much – or you'll be the next to go.'

Going into the Wellington test I think we'd subconsciously relaxed. By playing badly and still winning, the guys were lulled into a false sense of security. All Black teams are masters at playing below par and still winning. Allow us another chance and we'll grab it with both hands. No one would admit it, but we probably thought we'd automatically pick up our game. The selectors clearly had doubts: they made a few changes to the team, and Laurie cracked the whip at training.

It's not as if we lacked incentives, either: a win at Athletic Park would give us the series and for those successful players almost certainly book them a trip to the UK.

Nine times out of 10 we would have raised our game and won the second test . . . but this was occasion number 10, and we paid the price for our sloppiness.

There were no excuses to offer; as history shows we were on the wrong end of a record defeat. And as we would have to watch in graphic detail, TV captured every error, very clearly.

And yet . . . we could hardly have prepared better. There was real urgency in our manoeuvres. The changes in the line-up ensured no one was complacent. Laurie and Earle spelled out very clearly what we needed to do. Everyone knew their function. Motivation was excellent.

Individually we just didn't come to the party.

The result showed the unreliability in comparing test matches with tour form. The Lions had dropped two further games since the first test yet those defeats counted for zip at Athletic Park.

In the second test the Lions played with the pride and intensity of men with everything to win and nothing to lose. If they'd gone down they knew their tour was a shambles. For them, the second test was backs-to-the-wall stuff. We knew this . . . and yet our intensity failed to combat their desperation.

Their tactics weren't pretty: per usual they stacked their backline and shut us out, and Rob Andrew kicked all day. When we got the ball we made mistakes which they scored from. They played the percentages and succeeded. I admired them for their courage in forcing the series to a decider at Eden Park. It wasn't gala rugby they played, no matter how much the British press crowed.

For the All Blacks the loss was devastating. Another learning experience, we agreed – but I was getting sick and tired of how long we were taking to learn. In two consecutive tests we'd prepared with thoughtfulness and deliberation – and then turned in two lousy efforts. It was as mystifying as it was painful to accept. As soon as the final whistle blew I got off the park. I was really upset; I didn't leave the hotel that night.

I had good cause to lie low. I had turned in an absolute shocker. I don't think I could have played more badly if I'd purposely set out to. This was my poorest display in an All Black jersey. Ever. Unfortunately, it didn't occur in up-country Argentina or in the back-blocks of Ireland. This was in full view of everyone. The whole world got to see my non-game.

My mistakes were most noticeable in the worst place: the scoreboard. I gave away two penalties which Gavin kicked. And then midway through the second half, with the game on a knife-edge, I knocked on. For once they spread the pill wide, and Rory Underwood scored in the corner.

Game, set and match, the Lions.

With the crowd going wild, and the Lions all mobbing each other like they'd won Lotto, I trudged behind the goal posts to prepare for the conversion. It was one of my loneliest rugby moments. There are times in life everyone wants to curl up, roll over and hide from a mistake. This was one of them.

It seemed I couldn't do anything right. The ref and I weren't getting on at all – I felt I only had to run into a ruck or a maul and I'd get a blast from his whistle and a telling off. Now an elementary handling mistake had helped lose us the game.

None of the team was firing, either. We never left second gear all day. Our Achilles heel was the line-out. What ball we won we weren't using well, and too often we were getting cleaned out on our throw.

As more than a few people were quick to point out later, which player has the biggest influence on line-out calls and where the ball's thrown? Which player could have varied the throws? Which player threw in a couple of times off-target?

The critics had no problem identifying the culprit and sticking the knife in. The culprit was me.

PETER THORBURN

> ‘There were plenty of options, but the experienced people relied on Fitzy and Foxy to make all the decisions. But if Fitzy's at the bottom of a ruck, how can he make the correct decision? And if Foxy's view is obstructed by something on the blindside, how can he make the best call?
>
> It's got to be a team thing. And too many people weren't talking.’

We expected criticism in spades after the result. We got it. But the situation developed way out of reasonable proportion. This wasn't criticism – this was out and out character assassination. I'd never known a situation like it – I assume the World Cup loss was treated much the same.

In the papers, on TV, on talk-back radio . . . everywhere we turned we were slammed. Everyone had something to say, or offer a theory on what went wrong: there were not enough Waikato players in the side; there were too many Aucklanders; we were distracted by the launch of the All Black Club; Laurie was a bad coach . . . it went on and on. Endlessly. It would have been funny if it wasn't so serious.

Personally, I felt it was open season on me. I hated it. I suppose I'd been lucky in my career. Until this point I'd never really been blamed, as an individual, for a poor game. The reaction I got after this test made up for lost time. There was absolutely no doubt in Joe Public's mind that I was a liability. Some critics believed I'd done my dash, I was washed up, over the hill . . . Norm Hewitt was the form horse. Norm, they said, was younger, faster, meaner. He offered the All Blacks more options.

I thought back to all the praise lavished on me before my 50th test. That was only two weeks before – a lifetime ago. Suddenly, I was the worst player in the world. The public were in no doubt at all: I had to go.

CHAPTER TWELVE

Eden Park

"In fields and stadiums everywhere
The name New Zealand is one to fear
And our hearts swell with patriotic pride.
But when our All Blacks finally lose
We'll drown our tears in Kiwi booze
And curse them all for letting down the side."

– from *Mud In Your Eye*

THERE IS SOME DEEP part of me which refuses to give in when things go wrong. I just can't let things beat me. I have to see if I can overcome the obstacle, or answer the challenge head-on.

Flying back to Auckland the day after the game, I was completely downcast. I promised myself that if I was chosen for the next test, I would do everything I could to make amends. My worry was that I wouldn't get the chance, that I'd be flicked.

I was in no mood to listen to the talk-back analysis of the game but through my friends and family I got the basic idea of what was being said. I was surprised at the intensity of ill-feeling out there. I know journos in particular think players are too thin-skinned, that we can't take criticism, but how many people in this country –

except, maybe, the Prime Minister – get bagged like Laurie and I did that week?

JOHN KIRWAN

‘I think this was probably the first time Sean had really got bad publicity. Unfortunately, I know what it's like. I was the boy wonder for so long that when people turned against me, they turned with a vengeance.

For most of his career, Sean's been 'hidden'. He was just another player. Once he became captain, everyone looked at him twice as closely as before. He was now public property. In 1992, people were tolerant. They were prepared to give him, and the team, some time. And Seany played brilliantly.

Against the Lions, the public would only accept victory. When Sean didn't play that well in just one game – and the team lost as well – that's when the knives came out. It was a big shock for him.’

"You're going to wake up in the morning and not be able to go anywhere without people staring at you, you're going to have most of your meals interrupted . . . you'll say something off the top of your head and your mistakes will be recorded for future generations to snicker at." – Debra Winger, American actress, on the price of celebrity

TOO MUCH OF WHAT was said or written was sheer drivel and inspired by the media. It's happened since, and the consequences are huge – I know better than most how influential the media is. They're the single biggest source of the public's ill-informed views.

There were repercussions between the press and the All Black team as a result of their unbalanced reaction to our loss. For quite a while relations were strained. We never returned to the bad old days of snubbing them – but a definite tension existed between us.

I'll be frank: much of the progress that we'd achieved with the journos in 1992 was put at risk.

It was an unfortunate situation. At the heart of the issue was trust: we felt they'd broken it by not reporting fairly, or with accuracy. We didn't want to muzzle them – we just wanted a fair deal. At times the reporting was so bad you wondered if the journos had any idea of the game they were commenting on.

In their defence, journos merely reflect the psyche of the country. New Zealanders do not lose quietly.

Journos say it's their job to criticise. I accept that – if it's not mindless. I think constructive criticism is something different from a remark like, "Fitzpatrick had a shocking game" that isn't backed up by any evidence. Equally, if I read I've played brilliantly just because of a try I've scored or a barging run that catches people's attention,

I'm not impressed. What I *should* be judged on, my work in the scrum or the accuracy of my throwing in, is usually overlooked. When the media went to town after the second test, they didn't know half of what they were stating. I'd played badly all right – but they didn't know why.

GRANT FOX

> 'I don't think our media are fair, to be honest.
>
> I know players say to them 'if you haven't been there, you don't understand' but it's perfectly true.
>
> Now that I've retired, to some degree I can be a little more objective. Where my attitude has changed is this: even if the media don't write or say what I like, or agree with, at least they care. The day we're not talked about – even if it's criticism – is the day we as a country don't care about rugby.'

RICHARD BECHT

> 'I've been a journalist for 21 years – 15 years in newspapers, six in TV with TVNZ.
>
> At Network News, where I am now, we've been perceived by the NZRFU as being negative to rugby. What is overlooked is that News is completely stand-alone from [TVNZ's] Sports department.
>
> Partly as a result of TVNZ's news coverage of the Lions series, which apparently hadn't gone down too well with the NZRFU, we were asked to a meeting between members of the council, Laurie Mains, Colin Meads and Ric Salizzo to sort out some common ground. The inference from the councillors is that news should help to promote rugby. We said, that's not our job. Our job is to tell stories. We are guided by journalistic ethics in how we tell them, not other considerations.'

I think too many journalists don't understand the intricacies of the game. In most cases they haven't played it for years. Anyone from the media who's played top-level rugby – if only to provincial level – is someone the team will respect. Until it's proven otherwise.

But if a journo doesn't have the background, he has a hell of a lot of work to do. That's why the trend to use former rugby players as commentators is a good one. Players take them more seriously. They've paid their dues.

This approach works well in cricket. When New Zealand lost a test to Pakistan a few years back, I remember former captain Jeff Crowe, who was commentating on TV at the time, called them "gutless". I'd guess that when Jeff made that remark the team would have known he was right. But if a commentator like Peter Williams had said they were gutless, the reaction might have been, "How would *he* know?"

The Aussie league commentators seem to have found that happy knack between entertaining viewers and conveying in-depth knowledge of their sport. Guys like Graeme Hughes and Peter "Jacko" Jackson are a pleasure to listen to. In New Zealand rugby, at least in my time, I don't think we've ever had a decent TV or radio commentator. Individually they're nice enough guys but they lack the flair and depth of rugby to be anything above pedestrian.

The newspaper guys are cut from the same cloth.

I don't think it's asking too much that a journalist knows his rugby inside-out. If you're a brain surgeon you can't get by with a basic knowledge of medicine. If you're a mechanic you've got to know more than just how to change spark plugs. But your typical rugby journalist gets the job at an early age and then holds onto it for life. The players try to accommodate their needs but probably we don't respect them. Respect only comes from proving ability is there: and I'd be lying if I said we think there's a lot of ability among the journos.

One or two well-known journos are real "establishment" types. They write what they think we want to hear. Their motives are very transparent. We have even less respect for them.

RICHARD BECHT

> 'I don't think a journalist is any less of a judge of a game of rugby, or who a good player is, just because he hasn't made it to All Black level.
>
> By dint of the job, a journalist gets to watch a lot of rugby. If someone has a passion for sport, as most sports journalists do, and he follows a game for a long period of time, he will be as analytical as he can.
>
> Having worked in both mediums, I know that television is the one with the most impact. You'd think it's much easier to offend with the written word than it is on TV, but television is where the public really responds.
>
> Sean is good on television. Unlike a lot of All Blacks, he makes himself available for interviews. If I have a criticism, it's that from a journalistic point of view he's too much a diplomat. He's almost statesman-like.'

While nothing's been as savage as the kicks I took after the second test, I've certainly had my share of knockers over the years. The "third winger" tag is the most common criticism of my game. It started because I've scored a lot of tries for Auckland and the All Blacks. The implication is I'm not pulling my weight in the tight stuff if I'm out on the wing. Hookers aren't *supposed* to score tries at the end of a backline movement. Some people ask me sarcastically, "Why don't you have cauliflower ears?" I tell them, "Wingers don't get cauliflower ears."

Loey's sussed it out. He's scored an incredible number of tries for a front row forward (50). But Loey mostly scores his in the tight, where it's "more acceptable" for a front-row forward to dot down.

Under Laurie's era of coaching I am a different style of player from my younger days. He uses me as a designated runner, a bit like a league forward whose principal job is to get over the advantage line.

ANDY HADEN

'People who criticise him for being loose wouldn't know anything about rugby. Fitzpatrick has that priceless quality of judgement; he can turn a game with it.

He knows damn well if his pack is getting beaten and he's needed there. But he's always thinking, 'How can I best contribute? Is it running and diving into this pile of players, or is it adding to the end of the backline?'

If you can see the ball is being won quickly and that your becoming the extra man gives your team the overlap, then it is smarter to stay on the wing.

A lot of critics don't understand that type of thinking.'

BRONWYN FITZPATRICK

'It first hit home to us how flimsy the All Black life was when Gary and AJ were dropped. The way Richard Loe's been treated was another reminder how quickly fortunes change. These people were close to us personally. Like all friends, you share their bad times with them.

I remember when Buck Shelford was dropped, we didn't know what to do. Should we phone or not? Did Buck want to be left in peace or hear from us? It felt like a friend's mother or father had died: should you leave them in peace or call? With Buck we waited, and rang a bit later. Now, I wished we'd rung straight away. When the Whettons were dropped it was straight in.

And now here Sean was, possibly in the same boat. Before they announced the third test side, part of me wondered if *we'd* soon be getting commiseration phone calls.'

If events had gone against me, I would've accepted my dropping without any bitterness.

And if they'd picked Norm Hewitt I wouldn't have had any complaints, either. He's a fine player.

In the end, the selectors *did* make changes for the test. Thankfully, I wasn't one of them.

LAURIE MAINS

'After the loss, Sean copped an unnecessary amount of unfair criticism. But he was never in danger of being dropped. After all the service he's provided for New Zealand, you never drop a loyal player like him after one bad performance.'

LOUISE FITZPATRICK

> ‘Before they announced the [third test] team, it was the most worried I've ever seen Sean about keeping his place.’

At Eden Park the number 50 featured in my career again: this was my 50th consecutive test match. Unlike at Christchurch, this milestone went unrecognised. More serious matters were under debate.

When the team assembled, everyone was pretty down. Laurie outlined where we'd gone wrong – he'd watched a video of the second test and discovered 60 unforced errors – but this wasn't a session where the finger gets pointed. Sometimes they're necessary, especially if the team's getting a bit swollen-headed over its ability. One look at us and you could tell this didn't apply here. We were grey-faced, tight-lipped . . . An extensive post-mortem could definitely wait for another time.

LAURIE MAINS

> ‘Without a doubt it was the worst week of my life.
> On the Sunday and Monday I felt so ashamed at that All Black performance.
>
> First off, I didn't blame the players. I wondered if I'd provided the right environment for them. I really asked myself some hard questions.’

Laurie's number one priority was building up our confidence to make sure we won the decider.

In light of the progress we've made since, it's interesting to note that most of the boys weren't as switched on as they needed to be.

Thorbs was astonished to discover only four or five guys had watched the test. As he said, and I agreed, it was virtually their careers at stake – yet most players hadn't taken the time to assess their own performances.

In the first two tests we played the wrong game plan. We tried to take the Lions on in the forwards, to wrestle possession from them. They were too strong for us. So we had to change.

Laurie's new tactics were precise: we had to draw in their big forwards who stayed out in the backline. This would give our guys room to move. To do this we needed to move the ball faster than we'd been doing and really stretch and tire out the Lions' big men. *That* required our fast guys, players like Michael Jones, to produce big games, certainly a lot better than anything they'd shown in the series.

We'd seen in two tests that the Lions had just the one string to their bow: they could only play possession rugby. They'd win the ball, make a couple of passes, set the ball up, win it again. If you can't dominate it, this style is very effective. In Christchurch the Lions made too many mistakes to ram home their advantage, but in Wellington they were more disciplined, we couldn't counter it, and we lost.

Of the criticism we took, maybe there's justification in criticising the speed of our tactical response. McGeechan had obviously studied tapes of our games in 1992, and their drift defence was difficult to break through. We took too long to counter it.

PETER THORBURN

'There is no mystery about a game plan, although some people talk about it as though it's holy. A game plan is nothing more than the options a team takes into a match, options that you've concentrated on in training.

What a team needs more than a game plan is having the 'shot-callers'.

A coach will put his mark on a team by outlining how the game will be played under certain circumstances . . . but once the game's started a team cannot rigidly stick to one formula. It must adapt. That's where you need your shot-callers – to say what to do and when is the right time.

In Auckland we had to relieve some of this pressure from Sean.'

I accepted responsibility for the on-field tactics in the second test – as in any test. But the reality is the hooker can never be the main strategist in any team. The position has limits: for a start, you can't see the bigger picture. That's why the key tacticians are the number eight/halfback/first-five combination. They have the best view.

There were no private one-on-ones with the guys. I spoke a lot with Laurie, JK, Foxy, but that's something I've always done as captain. I'm a big believer that you don't say much unless it's necessary. That week it definitely wasn't necessary. New Zealand expected nothing less from us than victory. Everyone knew it.

DOC MAYHEW

'In terms of preparation, the week wasn't incredibly different from any other test. Laurie handled it well. He actually backed off a bit and gave other people, like Peter Thorburn, their say.

It was a tough week for all the players, especially Sean. I think in his time as captain he's lacked a solid support structure of experienced players to rely on.

I was privy to a lot more information from Sean than before. He knew he could trust me, bounce ideas off me, knowing I wouldn't divulge anything.'

GRANT FOX

'It was a hell of a week, a shit of a week, one of the most intense build-ups I've ever been involved in. If I compare it to another vital game – the 1987 World Cup Final, for instance – the difference was then we'd played well throughout the tournament. Everybody loved us.

This time we'd hadn't gone well in either test and the outside pressure, the public scrutiny and external criticism, was unbelievable. Seany and I talked about this, and especially how he was under the microscope.

I can't remember if I offered him any specific advice. It was more talk like, 'Just lead from the front, mate. You're so good on the rampage, it lifts all the guys . . .''

The pressure on us was what Thorbs calls "uncontrollable pressure" – pressure based on other people's unrealistic expectations. No matter how well you play, the expectation is you could still have played better. Nothing in life is ever perfect – but somehow the All Blacks are supposed to be the exception.

World rugby standards have levelled out. Except the New Zealand rugby public won't fully accept this. To them, every test has to be won as handsomely as it was in the late 1980s. As each passing year demonstrates, that was a freak era.

People say there's one way to relieve the pressure – keep winning. But that is so simplistic, it's hardly worth responding to. What this really means is that they're sitting back and waiting for you to fail. As you will. Because no one can win all the time. Not any more.

PETER THORBURN

'The public expectations of what a coach can, and cannot, do are badly misunderstood.

Any coach who tells you *he's* motivated a team to victory is, frankly, talking rubbish.

A coach cannot do it on his own.

He can train the team well . . . he can pick the right players . . . he can motivate them in a number of different ways, whether it's in the team talk or on an individual basis.

But the last 10 per cent a player needs to produce his best – and I'd argue this is the crucial 10 per cent – must come from the player himself. No external motivation can do it.

Whether he's playing for his wife or girlfriend in the stand, his ego, his ambition – whatever – the player must produce it from within.'

JAMIE JOSEPH

> 'That week was probably the most intense of my life. Nobody rated us. All week long we were rubbished by the media. I remember talking to Earle Kirton who said, 'If we don't win, there go our jobs – and probably some of the players we've developed.'
>
> That comment really sunk in deeply. It was the first time I'd really thought that my career was at stake . . .
>
> The day before I was so nervous I walked into the team room and got six cups of coffee one after another. I'd take one, have a sip, then go back and refill it.
>
> I didn't even know I was drinking coffee.'

As Saturday loomed closer, I was troubled by a recurring nightmare.

It centred on an incident in the final stages of the second test. An All Black dropped the ball, and I heard Foxy groan, "That's the series." He hadn't realised *I* was that All Black.

Several times during the week I kept dreaming of Foxy's words: "That's the series." It played in my mind like a scratched record, over and over again.

I know the possibility of failure is a very powerful force for sportsmen. It's *huge* for All Blacks. I've played in lots of big games, seen lots of different motivation techniques, but nothing – *nothing* – has had more effect on me than what was at stake in the third test. I wasn't alone. Big game veterans, like JK and Foxy, didn't crack a smile all week.

The fear of losing is an All Black's biggest fear. All Blacks always remember the games they lose while other teams, like the Welsh, always remember the games they win. A Welshman says, "I remember 1953, that's when we beat you." Whereas an All Black thinks, "Oh, 1953. Yeah, we lost."

It's an attitude that's bred into our players. When you consider how sophisticated sports psychology has become, it's probably not the best form of motivation. But I think it's as integral a part of our rugby as the black jersey and silver fern.

My biggest worry was my self-confidence. It had taken a direct hit. For the first time ever, I wondered if I still had "it". Did I still possess the ability to perform at the highest level? Or was I on the decline?

Thoughts like these are like cancer. If you let them linger they spread and destroy your self-belief. I'd never been an unconfident All Black before and I'd seen enough players come and go to know those who couldn't shake off their doubts never lasted.

I had to get rid of mine before the test.

I'm not the sort of person who wears his heart on his sleeve. I prefer to ride out the bumps alone, in private. Laurie guessed what was on my mind because one day he spoke to me about my form and ability.

His message was: forget the knockers, just play my own game, I was still a good player. I needed to hear it, to know he still had confidence in me. It was a small thing, but it worked. An excellent example of man-management.

LAURIE MAINS

> ‘Sean's as tough as old boots. All he needed was a bit of reassuring to believe in himself. I isolated two or three areas of his game and moved to take the pressure off him. Calling the line-outs was one. We gave it to Arran Pene.’

That week Thorbs' influence was incredibly valuable. He's another very good person at man-management. He spoke soon after we assembled and it had a very big impact with the guys.

PETER THORBURN

> ‘I asked them to consider if maybe we were digging our own graves by adding to the tension *ourselves*. And I gave them this example from what I saw before the second test.
>
> In the bus on the way to the ground we stopped at a set of lights. Staring out the window I noticed a father and his two kids were waving at us, obviously cheering on the All Blacks.
>
> I turned and looked around the bus. Everyone was sitting with their arms crossed, straight ahead, ignoring the family.
>
> I thought, 'Why can't we give them a wave or a smile? Why are we so uptight? What person needs to be that tense and affected two hours before a game? *Especially* a big game?'
>
> Frano Botica has told me how at Wigan, their dressing room is full of noise and chatter until about 15 minutes before the game. Then the coach comes in, says, 'Right everyone . . .' and they immediately switch into game mode.
>
> I compare it to driving to work in the morning. You have the radio on, you're whistling away, enjoying the songs – and then you arrive at work and you switch on to what you have to do.
>
> What's the point in driving to work and worrying all the way? You can't do anything, except get more and more wound up.
>
> Why do we have to focus like madmen before big games? It's counter-productive, but ritualistic.’

We trained at Sacred Heart, my old school. It was a great call. The brothers and the boys were tremendously supportive of the team – and me. I felt an extra shot of confidence being among such familiar surroundings.

One afternoon we went cruising on the harbour, down to Motuihi. Thorbs took us on his boat, a 20-metre launch. There was food and drink, though not too much drink. The only people on board were the team and management. No outsiders, no one who shouldn't have been there.

The concept was very simple: we needed private time, without any interruptions. The guys fished, unwound, had a laugh. For a couple of hours we even forgot about Saturday's test. The only one who didn't go was Lee Stensness, the debutant. He gets sea-sick.

DOC MAYHEW

> 'The build-up was one of the few times we felt the public really got behind the team. We got faxes from all over the country, and, during the national anthem, the crowd sang with one voice.'

If the players were uptight, Laurie and Earle were dying a thousand deaths in private. They judged themselves as hard as any of the guys. I think they were angry they hadn't reacted more quickly to some of the Lions' goings-on. They both worry about letting down previous generations of All Blacks, and the idea of a series loss to the Lions would have been awful, especially for Laurie, who'd been down that road as a player in 1971.

Laurie will go to amazing lengths not to let his worries or anxieties be passed on to the team. Sometimes you'd swear he hasn't a care in the world judging by his external appearance.

The day before the test he and I had a brief chat before the team went to Eden Park for our usual "suss out the ground" walk-through. Laurie was all frowns, his face a picture of worry.

But 10 minutes later, in the team talk, he radiated only positiveness. He was smiling, joking – I remember he walked into the team room and cracked a joke at JR. He exuded confidence. I couldn't believe the change in him. And I knew he was forcing himself through every minute. Gutsy stuff.

The atmosphere on the bus heading to the ground was like prisoners lined up on Death Row. No one said anything. Laurie stood up and walked down the aisle: "C'mon you guys, loosen up." And he went down the whole bus, making the players talk, forcing them to lighten up. Slowly a voice was heard. Then another. The tension eased.

The rest of Friday dragged. I didn't say much at the press conference. At the captain's talk that night we gathered in the team room. It was a short message: I stressed everybody had to play for themselves and the people who'd shown faith in them, especially the selectors. Laurie in particular. "They've chosen us to do the job. Let's pay them back with a win."

I said I was the worst offender with a poor performance in Wellington, and made a commitment to the guys to give 200 per cent tomorrow. Foxy said something but I forget the specifics.

The actual words didn't matter. The time for talking was over.

> *"I wanted to come back and prove that what I had gone through had made a difference, to justify this kind of suffering."*
> – Keith Richards

The test followed a similar pattern to Wellington. One team quickly shot out to a lead – then the other side clawed its way to victory. This time it was the Lions who were up 10-0, a lead that was always flimsy.

In the All Black side no one panicked.

Then Lee Stensness, in a very classy performance, put in a perfect little chip kick from which Buncey scored. The resolve in the guys hardened and after I scored my try we were in front, 14-10. As the ref confirmed the try, a single thought flashed through my mind: *"Yes."* There was no way we were going to let them back now.

At Eden Park we won our share of quality, set-piece possession. We upset the Lions' defensive pattern by forcing them backwards. Our loose forwards were far more aggressive and committed, and we concentrated a lot more on rucking than mauling. Rimu played a huge game, driving up the middle and constantly breaking the gain line. Robin won a ton of good line-out ball and Ice was everywhere.

Our scrum was unrecognisable from the unit that was so easily dominated in Wellington. This time the Lions could not match fire with fire. Brain Moore really struggled. Olo and I targeted him as the weak link in their front row – Popplewell and Leonard are excellent props – and really worked on him. We popped him a couple of times. With about 20 minutes to go, we knew he was gone: he stopped talking. All game long he'd been mouthing off. Now he had nothing left.

Because the tight five were performing, the backs had the room they needed – the first time in the series. Foxy had a brilliant game, kicking for position, not touch, which cut down the number of line-outs with a Lions throw. Jon Preston scored a wrap-up try . . . that was the ball-game.

What made the result so satisfying was that we defeated the cream of British rugby. Forget their appalling provincial record: the Lions' test team was in another class. It contained the best players in the United Kingdom. The possible exception was Jeff Probyn, but Jason Leonard proved an excellent tighthead.

Consider their talent. Gavin Hastings – a great captain and an inspiring player; Ian McGeechan – the best coach they had, by miles. In Ben Clarke and Martin Bayfield they had world-class footballers. Clarke was consistently able to get over the gain line and Bayfield, the tallest lock in world rugby, won a mountain of good ball. Their outside backs, the few times we saw them, were fast and skilled. The improvement in Ieuan Evans from when we first played him in 1987 was incredible. He looked a completely different player. Even JK was impressed.

They were good – and they lost. Yet the All Blacks never got due credit for our victories, which really disappointed me. Our recovery from second test disaster to third test success showed our class, how capable we were at bouncing back. Psychologically, it was a huge boost to the team's coaches and players. We had proven to ourselves that when it really mattered we had the ability to raise our game and win.

The momentum was with the Lions. We met them head on, and snuffed them out.

In Auckland they didn't really have anything new to offer. They obviously underestimated our ability to rethink our game. Tactically they just relied on us to make mistakes.

Some people said if there had been a fourth test, the Lions would have won; that if they hadn't made so many unforced errors just before half-time, they'd have succeeded at Eden Park.

Rugby is full of "ifs". It's a pointless debate. History shows this was a three-test series and we won. End of story.

Almost.

I'm not a hypocrite. I hadn't enjoyed the series, and putting diplomacy aside for a moment I said so at the final press conference. The Lions were very negative, I told the journalists; they weren't a good advertisement for the game. Our crowds found their rugby boring; so did the New Zealand players.

My comments weren't intended to win friends or influence people. I wasn't concerned. Even though our attacking game was not as coordinated as it might have been, the All Blacks were the only team attempting to play rugby. The Lions, like the British sides we would meet in a few months' time, only cared about winning – and they didn't give a damn how.

> *"We're a nation of low self-esteem, with not enough sense of history. That's why when we don't do well at something like rugby, which we care so much about, we have to blame someone for taking away our good feeling."*
>
> – Peter Thorburn

ONCE THE SERIES was wrapped up we were back in the public's good books. The country basked in the win.

Publicly I thanked New Zealanders for their goodwill and I meant every word. The support for the team in the lead-up to Eden Park was marvellous.

I hadn't completely forgotten the savaging of the previous few days.

It was great to be flavour of the month again. But I was under no illusions. The lines were clearly drawn: we would be heroes as long as we kept winning. In a fortnight's time we would play Australia at Carisbrook. A loss there . . . well, the reaction didn't need spelling out.

The media didn't know what to do: certain journos who had really got stuck into me were quite red-faced. Several rang up looking for my reaction to the selection of Nick Farr-Jones in the Australian team. I was polite; there's no point in making things personal when you have to deal with them again. But I could hear the discomfort in their voices. "Ah . . . er . . . excuse me, Sean, would you mind if . . . um . . ."

There were lots of people who had to do U-turns over their attitudes from the Lions series – including most talkback radio callers. Of course, no one ever admitted to me *they'd* gone over the top. I had friends 10-deep on every street.

I've sung *God Defend New Zealand* all over the world. It still sends an incredible shiver down my spine. When I'm standing on the ground before a test and hearing our anthem I feel a real surge of emotion: I'm playing for many people – my family, my friends, those thousands of strangers watching and cheering us.

I do find, however, a streak in New Zealanders which disturbs me. As much as they'll give us fantastic support when we need it, they'll switch sides without so much as a blink. Overseas the All Blacks are lucky to hear even token applause during a test. In New Zealand, I've been astonished to hear our crowds cheer for Scotland and Ireland *against* the All Blacks. Sometimes, Kiwis are so enthusiastic their players must wonder if they're not back home.

This fickleness gets to me. The All Blacks are New Zealand's only consistently successful sports team. Nothing else comes close in our history, except for the brilliant efforts of individuals like Susan Devoy or Peter Snell.

I love cricket. It's a great game. But the double standards by which the New Zealand cricket team and the All Blacks are judged is a joke. It's regarded as "acceptable" when New Zealand's cricketers draw a test or narrowly lose a one-dayer. The occasional victory is treated as a cause for national celebration.

But with the All Blacks, nothing else will do except an outstanding victory. *Every* game. And it's not possible.

I respect people's right to criticise us. I just wish they'd remember the good times more often, get some balance in their criticism. Unfortunately, New Zealanders' memories are embarrassingly short.

Every time it's the same old story: the All Blacks play badly, or lose – and New Zealanders take it personally. The levels of abuse which follow are pathetic. It portrays a real ugly side of the New Zealand nature.

I understand that pressure is part of rugby. Every player has to deal with it. At club level you've got to satisfy the coach, the club hierarchy and the local population. The suburban paper and friendly local sponsor have a bearing, too.

At rep level, you've got these pressures – and a few more. You're appearing on a national stage, and TV now plays a much larger part. Auckland players cop a bit more of the spotlight because we're successful and our union's larger than the rest; we've also got New Zealand's biggest newspaper and a number of high-profile sponsors to satisfy.

As big as rep rugby gets, nothing prepares you for life as an All Black. It seems *everyone* has an opinion about the All Blacks, and they feel entitled to express it, no matter how bluntly.

The extent to which the national mood is dependent upon whether the All Blacks win or lose worries me. What sort of narrow-minded, empty lives do our critics have?

I've had several discussions about pressure with the All Blacks' chief sponsor, Kevin Roberts, the boss of Steinlager. Kevin argues his pressures are greater because he runs a large, international company and his decisions involve millions of dollars and people's livelihoods.

I tell him that while you can't relate my pressures to sums of money, they are more closely scrutinised than his. He doesn't know what it's like to feel the whole of New Zealand on your back . . . to deal with all his peers or the man in the street saying what they think about his every decision – I've got a whole country looking at me telling me in no uncertain terms how I'm doing.

I don't know if this situation will ever change. What's undeniable is after every All Black victory, 99 per cent of people I meet seem happier. The girl at the hotel check-out; the cabin crew and passengers on the plane; the taxi driver taking me home from the airport . . .

When Jim Bolger visited our dressing room after the third Lions test, he told me that if he'd called a snap election on Monday, National would have bolted home. I think that says it all.

CHAPTER THIRTEEN

Over-Paid, Over-Hyped and Over Here

"Many of the young men attracted to the sport are possessed of a bit of devil . . . the same youthful enthusiasm that motivates these players on the football field will occasionally overflow away from it."

– Andy Haden, *Boots 'n All!*

ONCE, touring was the ultimate rugby pastime for me.

Like most players, I anticipated a tour months ahead. Regardless of your age, ability, or the intensity of rugby involved, you know touring meant fun. Like JK says, touring's not a holiday – but it's not like going to work, either.

It won't come as any great surprise to learn I found All Black tours the most prized.

I've been on nine overseas trips in national colours, visiting places as diverse as Japan and Canada. They've provided stand-out moments of my career – many of which have absolutely nothing to do with rugby.

In terms of "unforgettability", however, the All Blacks' 13-match tour of Scotland and England sits at the top of the list. Unfortunately, it's there for all the wrong reasons.

The tour from hell.

It promised so much – it should have been one of the best ever because we'd prepared so well. Sadly, it will mostly be remembered for its bitterness, recriminations, and maligned reputations.

The short version of the tour is easy enough to describe: the All Blacks overcame a murderous itinerary, were "heroes" until we lost one game, and then the media and public went bananas. Along the way we were unfairly and unjustly accused of many wrong-doings by the English press.

There is a longer version.

> *"There are always bound to be a few disappointments on tour, and one gained the impression that Sean Fitzpatrick went through the motions as captain at the expense of a more inspirational role."*
>
> – A post-tour review in *The New Zealand Herald*

IN TRUTH, I WASN'T looking forward to the tour with my usual enthusiasm. International and domestic rugby during 1993 drained me: I was dog-tired. My body was sore. During the season I needed a discreet operation to remove bone fragments from my elbow; wandering fingers poked and scraped an eyeball twice; and I was carrying persistent aches and pains which needed a full summer to heal. I'd already been overseas six or seven times during the year, for rugby trips or work reasons, and the thought of flying around the world and stepping into a British winter didn't exactly turn me on.

Nonetheless, I was fit enough to last out another few weeks. This tour was vital to our World Cup plans: it offered the selectors their last opportunity to take away a full All Black squad before the 1995 World Cup. It would make, or break, several players' careers.

By any yardstick, the All Blacks had enjoyed a successful season. After knocking over the Lions we creamed Australia to regain the Bledisloe Cup and then, against a physical and combative Samoan side, our control never wavered.

Three different international opponents, three contrasting sets of tactics – three successes.

Even this record didn't satisfy the critics. They moaned our backs weren't seen enough any more, that our wings never got the ball. They complained that JK hadn't scored for the All Blacks all season, that Inga was a loose forward in all but name . . .

We knew it wasn't blemish-free rugby. Too often we'd drift in and out of a game. I put that down to inexperience. The more top-level, high-pressure rugby a team plays, the more mentally hardened it becomes. It's something which develops during a tour.

A number of the guys felt stale. I was disturbed at how many times we'd had to peak already: for the Super 10, the trials, the Lions, the Bledisloe Cup, Samoa, for the National Championship finals.

No All Black team had ever followed such a demanding domestic programme.

The core of the tour party picked itself: it would comprise those players who helped win the last three tests. Except we needed a new first-five. I'd known Foxy was pulling out of rugby but said nothing. It was Grant's wish that he make his intentions public in his own good time, a stance I respected totally.

GRANT FOX

'I made up my mind after the North Harbour game (22 August) and told Laurie immediately.

I was going to Britain for work reasons for three weeks anyway, but there was no way I could've mixed business and rugby. Business-wise my time was so limited; I was now managing a company which is quite different from being on staff, and rugby-wise, I wanted to do the right thing for the All Blacks. They needed to blood a new first-five and a touring environment is the best of all. If you can't play on tour, where you eat, drink, sleep and breathe rugby, you can't play anywhere.

I hadn't shut the door entirely on playing again. But when I was sitting in the grandstand at Murrayfield I felt no pangs of the 'I want to be out there' sort. It was probably at that moment in Edinburgh I came closest to knowing it was time to retire . . .'

As far as I was concerned, the only question marks were over a couple of the fringe selections. Or so I thought.

JK was a real shock.

I couldn't believe it when Laurie told me his place was in jeopardy.

The selectors admired JK as a person and for his off-field mana, but I knew they had persistent doubts about the effects of back-to-back seasons of "spaghetti rugby" on his form. Admittedly, JK hadn't played too well for Auckland in a few matches but he is a big game player who I knew still had the goods.

I argued that his experience was essential for a UK tour. Without JK and Foxy I was the longest surviving All Black in the squad. Zinny had been in the side since 1987, and we get on well, but I made it clear to Laurie I wanted JK there too. We were light on wise old heads. He was a mate, and, most importantly, he was someone I could trust. Captains need support from people they know. Laurie heard what I was saying, but I think his mind was made up.

On the day the team was announced I phoned Laurie one final time to plead JK's case. "Sean," he said, "we're right in the middle of selecting the team . . . I'll call you back." The news was bad for JK.

Once their decision had been made, as captain I had to bite the bullet and accept it. I threw my weight behind the team. JK handled his omission with great public dignity, which went down well with everyone. I know Laurie really respected him for the way he reacted.

GRANT FOX

‘I could see Sean’s point of view. A tour is full of intensity and pressure and experience is a vital ingredient. Youthful enthusiasm, while an admirable quality, doesn’t win tests.

Enthusiastic younger guys take time to develop. They’re not automatically able to step into the breach. They’ve got to evolve.’

LAURIE MAINS

‘JK’s omission was a very difficult decision but I looked at the make-up of the team and felt Sean still had plenty of friends – guys like Olo, Michael Jones, Robin Brooke, Zinny – to help him with the on and off-field pressures. The tragedy for Sean was that Michael and Robin got injured. That put a huge amount of pressure on Sean, pressure he handled remarkably well.’

For the superstitious there were some ominous signs before we even left the country.

From the original team two guys had to pull out. First, Jonesy broke his jaw in a freak training accident with Auckland, and then Walter had to withdraw with a leg injury.

Some of the other guys weren’t fully right from knocks they were carrying either; Bull Allen, for instance, was coming right after a broken jaw and Lee’s knee wasn’t 100 per cent right either. Disappointingly, one or two weren’t as fit as they might have been – or, at least as Laurie wanted them to be. The rest of us suffered the usual, gruelling, “welcome-to-the-tour” sessions that are Laurie’s specialties. For those fitness offenders, however, long, extra runs after practice were the order of the day.

Then the NZRFU threatened to torpedo JR and Rimu’s tours with an 11th hour, 59th minute judicial hearing. They were cited on a charge of foul play. Luckily, they were cleared, but the timing was awful: it was the last thing the team needed.

As they’ve done so many times before, my family came to farewell us.

Dad reminded me how, 40 years earlier, he was in a similar situation preparing to head away with Bob Stuart’s All Blacks. As he’s reminded me quite a few times since, rugby tours were very different affairs back then.

“Horseplay and wrecking have come to be accepted as part of the average rugby player’s behaviour over the years but we should always be careful that wrecking remains a private affair, rather than spilling over and affecting any third parties. What is described as high spirits in a rugby player is called hooliganism by the world at large . . .” – Peter Wheeler, *Rugby From The Front*

MY FATHER WAS A member of only the fourth New Zealand team to visit Britain, or the "Home Unions" as they like to be known. Dad's team was away from home for six months. We were the twelfth All Black team to visit the UK. We were gone for nine weeks.

BRIAN FITZPATRICK

'There was huge excitement in the country over the tour. Talk of it went on for months. International rugby was less frantic then – it was also less frequent. The All Blacks hadn't played a test for over a year [13 September,1952, to 19 December, 1953].

I remember that trial form counted a lot. You had two sets of trials, one in the North Island, one in the South – and then a final trial of the best players at Wellington. The pressure was huge. You knew bolters might make the team, players who came from nowhere. Many a chap played his way in, or out, on the basis of just one good or indifferent game.

The team to Britain was announced under the stand at Athletic Park after the main trial. I wasn't too surprised to see my name there: you had a gut feeling if you were there or not. I was more surprised when I was picked for the North Island for the first time a couple of years before.

It was more or less whispered to me to keep myself fit. Before the final trial Tom Morrison [a NZRFU councillor] asked me to try on some sample gear. This was a big hint, but I never asked Tom to his face if this meant I was in – you didn't do that sort of thing in those days.

In fact you never believed it until you heard your name called out. Afterwards, there was a celebration party. I can't remember the specifics, but I'm sure it lasted a matter of days.'

My first All Black tour was to France in '86. I was 23 years old. Dad's All Black career was over by the same age – he got out of the first-class scene after the tour to concentrate on work and family.

I'd already sampled the magic of touring when Graham Henry invited me with the University seniors on their pre-season team-building tour of Australia. I was still in third grade, just 19 years old. Damian Fox, an old family friend, was also in the team. Mum gave him strict instructions to look after me. Unfortunately, Damian forgot them as the plane took off for Sydney.

That tour was such an eye-opener for me. Grant Dickson flew all the way back from France just for it. I thought he was keen. He was – and it wasn't for the rugby. Like so much in my career, I trace a lot of bad habits back to those days with University. And most of them started on that first tour.

In 1985 I was chosen for the New Zealand Universities tour of England, Ireland, Italy and France. This was definitely one trip not to be missed. Kirky was the captain and a young guy called Mike Brewer one of the loosies. Auckland's University club provided nine of the 25 players, so it was almost like an all-expenses paid holiday with your mates.

In rugby terms it was a successful trip: 11 of the 12 games were won, including all three "tests". I played in two of the "tests" but got dropped for the last one, against French Universities.

I wasn't too disappointed. In terms of fun, it was the best tour I've ever been on.

There were some hilarious incidents, most of which can never be told in public. I do remember one spectacular formal dinner after playing the French Universities.

Both teams were seated down either side of a huge hall. As we ate, someone threw a roll or something and then everyone flipped their tables up as a barricade. Next thing a full-scale "food war" broke out. Red wine was poured down people's backs. The president of the French Universities got hit in the face by a custard pie while giving his speech . . . it was absolute mayhem. Our hosts were into it as much as us. A great night. Thank God we didn't have to clean up the next day.

Ireland was another non-stop party. Because of bad weather our game in Belfast was cancelled. I don't think we even noticed.

In Galway we were billeted into the bosom of the community – in one player's case, literally.

The team bus was due to leave town at 9.30am the next day. But one of the players had met a girl at his billet – and he never made it by the scheduled departure time. We waited, and waited, but there was no sign. So he was left behind. Eventually, while we were training in Dublin – on the other side of the country – the missing player turned up.

Our coach did his nut. "This is not good enough. The team depends on unity to work. We have to stick together or else we won't succeed. So, make your choice: are you for us or against us?" The player didn't miss a beat.

"I'm really against you coach," he says, "because I had such a great time last night. I really wanted to stay down there."

When he said this everyone just burst out laughing. We were in fits. It summed up the joy of touring without real pressure. In an All Black team you couldn't do that and get away with it.

We were high-spirited but we didn't break much. Certainly not compared with what some teams have done in the past. Andy Haden has often told me how, at the beginning of his career, "wrecking" was considered part of general rugby behaviour.

Wreckers disappear from rugby teams the further up the scale you go.

When I first started out the species was not yet entirely extinct at first-class level.

On my first Auckland tour one of the forwards was a real wild man. One evening, I was talking to JK in his room when this player walked in, picked up a bottle of red wine and threw it at JK. A *full* bottle. JK ducked but it smashed all over the wall. Then he left.

You hear some amazing stories of legendary wreckers. The sixties and seventies must have been wild times.

Grizz told us yarns about how teams would go ape after Saturday games. They had huge nights – and hotels bore the brunt. He said the next morning every door in the hotel was swinging off its hinges . . . the hotel floor was full of water after the team had turned on the hoses and had a big water fight. They'd smash lights, tip pianos into swimming pools – and nothing was ever said. The manager just paid the bill on his way out and 90 per cent of the time it was treated as par for the course by the players, the managers, and, incredibly, the hotel.

That sort of behaviour is unheard of at top level today. Any All Black who did that now wouldn't last a day on tour. He'd be sent home in disgrace.

Times change.

"Over-Paid, Over-Hyped and Over Here."

– A headline greeting the All Blacks on arrival in the UK

AFTER YEARS OF DEBATE with the NZRFU, the All Blacks were finally given the green light to fly business class to the 1991 World Cup. It was a decision a long time in the coming, but the benefits were immediately obvious. Now on long flights we always travel business class in the upstairs cabin of a jumbo. It's private and roomy – not an inconsequential matter for athletes who really need their leg space.

I grabbed as much sleep as you'll ever get while travelling 30-hours non-stop but, even so, tiredness wasn't the reason I was feeling apprehensive when we touched down at Heathrow. The Lions series had been a dog to play in; there was little chance the rugby in Britain would be any more enjoyable.

Worse, I knew the off-the-field pressures would be intense.

Britain has so many advantages: we speak a common language, you visit some great places, play in marvellous stadiums . . . there's a lot to see and do.

The downside is that you never feel entirely at ease. Perhaps it's the bad weather, the lack of sun, the numbers of people everywhere . . . but most places seem boxed in and claustrophobic to New Zealanders used to blue skies and open spaces. It's hard to relax 100 per cent because there are too many prying eyes, notebooks, tape recorders, long lenses. At the back of your mind you know a single indiscretion or a mistake will be put under the spotlight and scrutinised like nowhere else.

A tour of England is like waging battle on two fronts: on the field, where the standard of rugby has improved out of sight, you face tough, competitive opposition. Off-field, you have their media to deal with. It's a toss-up which is meaner.

It's noticeable that since England made the 1991 World Cup Final, rugby receives a lot more coverage than before. This made the All Blacks, who have always enjoyed a huge profile there, real drawcards.

There were about 20 journos following the tour: triple that number for the tests. We knew we couldn't expect any favours – you only have to look at the way their royalty gets treated to know anything's fair game. Obviously, they don't let the facts get in the way of a good story.

Our management was very aware of the potential media booby traps and warned the players to be extra careful about what we did on and off the field.

The best response – in fact the only one, we told the guys – was to be successful.

GRAHAM PURVIS

> 'I'd been over there in '89 and at the World Cup and you knew anything you said to anyone could be printed in the press. Matthew Ridge was in a bar once and said to this guy he was looking forward to leaving Wales. The next day, his remark was a quote in the paper.'

LAURIE MAINS

> 'I was obviously extremely wary of them but, nevertheless, our strategy was to be non-provocative, friendly, not antagonise anyone off the field – in short, to do anything we could to promote rugby.'

In an effort to smooth the way, I'd met as many of the British journos as I could earlier in the year. Most of those covering our UK tour had also been down with the Lions.

We first met informally a couple of days after Auckland lost the Super 10 final to Transvaal in Johannesburg.

I was knackered. The meeting was at night and I'd only got back that morning. The last thing I wanted to do was to attend a rugby function but the gesture seemed to go down well with the Brits. We were deliberately looking ahead to the UK tour even then: we wanted the British media to feel comfortable with us, to see what we were like as people, so that when we got to their shores they'd be far less likely to hunt out sensational stories.

Give us 10 out of 10 for the theory.

STEPHEN JONES

'We met at Stu Wilson's pub. Sean was phenomenally impressive. It was a remarkable 'do', in many ways. We knew he'd been invited, but as he'd just flown non-stop from South Africa, none of us expected him to turn up.

He arrived a little bit late, but he was bright and cheerful. He spoke to us all individually, was courteous and frank. He worked the room brilliantly.'

The British sports press come in two categories: the quality dailies, which supposedly concentrate on the game, and the tabloids, which seek out the sensational. If you ask me, it's getting harder and harder to tell the two apart. The frequency of malice seems about the same, it's just buried in longer articles in the quality press.

We believed the All Blacks were being set up. Their media's position was abundantly clear. They'd aimed their guns, we were the target – they were just waiting to fire the first shot. You didn't have to be a *Mastermind* winner to see it.

An impartial viewpoint wouldn't have helped their newspaper sales. Actually, I think they resented our success. The majority had rarely seen an unsuccessful New Zealand team. For years they'd only had crumbs to feed off, like the Lions' second test victory. The last time British teams *really* cleaned us out was in 1983 when the All Blacks didn't win a test on tour.

I'm certain their bias was premeditated. For example, before even the first game, the London *Sunday Times* ran a big feature with diagrams of how All Blacks allegedly infringe: a reader's guide to "spot how the All Blacks cheat". It even claimed I purposely threw the ball in crooked. The story didn't deserve to be tomorrow's fish and chips wrapper, but it reflected the consensus of opinion already stacked up against the All Blacks.

The first hurdle we faced was the arrival press conference. We'd rehearsed the likely questions but I was wary in case they threw us a real ropey one from left-field. The last thing any of us wanted was a faux pas on day one.

Thankfully, the press conference went smoothly. They asked us about the itinerary; the lack of experience in our ranks without JK, Foxy, Ice; our goals for the tour . . . it was pretty run of the mill.

The only hiccup was minor. Their officials had a fit when Paul Sissons, our Steinlager rep, whacked up a big Steinlager banner behind the conference table. The old boys told him, very clearly, "This is not your press conference . . ." and ripped the sign down in front of all the journalists.

It was a storm in a tea-cup. Even the English media couldn't understand what the fuss was about. Steinlager, of course, were thrilled by the free publicity.

"If yous lie on the wrong side of a ruck, yous shouldn't expect a handwritten invitation to move to somewhere out of the vicinity before a Te Kuiti Tap Dance is run over your body." – Loosehead Len

THERE WAS A LOT of tension and expectation within the team before the opening game against London. Training was a bit scratchy. The "experts" considered a loss a strong possibility.

Instead, we blitzed London.

Suddenly, the All Blacks got a compliment or two. Perhaps we weren't such bad players after all. Perhaps we *could* play a bit. Perhaps we'd been written off too early . . .

We understood the need to develop good public relations. PR is an essential fact of rugby tours these days and a team overlooks it at their peril.

It was a deliberate ploy to perform the haka. Each tour this issue is taken on its merits. In 1992, for instance, it hadn't been used in Australia, except before tests, because the Aussies showed scant respect for it. The British crowds, on the other hand, seem enraptured by the haka. Our decision drew widespread approval. We got a huge cheer at Twickers when we performed it in the opening match – though it was a different story a few weeks later. The BBC used it constantly in their TV rugby promos. Inga was the one they always focused on, the out-and-out "haka star".

We even courted the media, hosting an early-tour function and agreeing to a female reporter from the *Daily Express* newspaper going behind the scenes with us for a few days. We suspected she was looking for dirt. We knew there was none; she was welcome to join us. And she was honest enough to see the truth and tell her readers in a high-profile feature story.

Our second match, against the Midlands, was less spectacular. It went down to the wire before we won. Disappointingly, instead of commentating on the exciting finish, their coach, Dusty Hare, labelled us "cheats". But the story died a quick death. The press gave it a bit of a sniff and passed. We breathed a bit easier. We wondered if we'd overestimated their hostility.

The answer came, once and for all, in the match against South-West Division, at a town called Redruth. I suppose we should have been more suspicious playing on a ground with an area named "Hellfire Corner".

During the game their centre, Philip de Glanville, was caught in a ruck. His cheek was ripped open, and he received 15 stitches near the eye. At the time it was seen as an unfortunate injury, one of those things.

The next day the media went berserk. De Glanville claimed the All Blacks had deliberately stomped on him and trial-by-video began. The ruck where he got hurt was replayed. And replayed. On the "evidence" of TV, the "guilty parties" were either Kamo Jones or *me*. Together and alone we stood accused of deliberately kicking.

I was shocked to be fingered when I hadn't done anything wrong. For a few uncomfortable days I felt like Public Enemy Number One.

The truth is no one knows whose foot cut de Glanville. It might have been me, it might have been Kamo, it could have been someone else. No matter how many times you watch it – and I've watched it more than I want to – there is no clear evidence.

Not that I'm using inconclusive TV highlights to hide behind. I've said before I am a competitive, physical player; I have no qualms admitting that. But I am *not* a dirty player, I will not do *anything* to win. I know where to draw the line. I could still look myself in the face after the game.

We didn't duck the issue. As I said publicly, "The head is always sacrosanct. No player – let alone an All Black – would want to go out and stamp on someone's head."

GRAHAM PURVIS

> 'I thought Sean handled it really well. He was on live TV, being asked these curly, twisty ones, and he took them in his stride.'

The All Blacks were just as sick as anyone else at the possibility a player might lose an eye. De Glanville's injury looked grisly. But rugby's a contact sport; accidents do happen. In my captain's speech that night I apologised to Phil. That was 24 hours before the mother of all rows broke out.

De Glanville himself said on TV that some All Black – unnamed – should be "sent home" for causing the injury. Then his father got in on the act, going right over the top: "Is it going to take someone's death before something is done?"

Obviously the de Glanville family were upset about the injury. Possible eye loss is an emotional topic. The last thing we wanted was to get into a public row with them. We bit our lips.

But the British media wouldn't let the matter die. You could almost see them rubbing their hands in glee. For a lot of our guys this was the first time they'd seen at close quarters how savage the journos could get. The controversy didn't worry the guys too much. All Black teams can shut off from outside pressures very well. For a start, we don't read the papers.

JAMIE JOSEPH

> 'Fitzy's a leader. He couldn't be seen to crumble by the guys – and he didn't crumble.'

LAURIE MAINS

> 'The irony was that at the same time we were taking real stick for the de Glanville incident, a game between Midlands and

London Counties had a five-minute brawl that involved about 15 or 16 players . . . that got no exposure, by comparison. The way the two incidents were covered made us realise how heavily the odds were stacked against us.'

The de Glanville row illustrated the difference in British and New Zealand attitudes to rucking. Their guys are specialists in killing the game by lying on the ball. They wouldn't get away with that in New Zealand.

The ruck is as legal in rugby as the line-out. Its purpose is to recover possession of the ball quickly, thus maintaining the momentum of attack – a principle of rugby, especially New Zealand rugby. It's our national style – and extremely logical. Forwards remain on their feet and don't need to pick themselves up off the ground all the time, like the Poms. If you have to wait for slow ball, the opposition has more time to stack their defence.

My try against Australia in the Bledisloe Cup game three months earlier was the perfect illustration of the beauty of the ruck. It was on the sixth phase that we scored: their defence could not cope any longer and finally gave in. I was on hand to score.

Because we wouldn't admit to any wrong-doing the media got stuck into us. Former Welsh internationals in particular led the charge. Phil Bennett called us "cowards". Gerald Davies criticised us for "inexcusable behaviour". JPR Williams, of Bridgend fame, also had a dig.

The few lone British voices of support, from Bill Beaumont and Ian McLauchlan, were much appreciated. Bill knows the difference between stamping and rucking. One of the rare times I can remember a British ref agreeing with us was Clive Norling in the All Blacks-Barbarians match in 1989. Rees, their flanker, was lying on the ball. We rucked him off it. He squealed to the ref. "Well, roll away you silly boy," said Norling. He understood there was nothing malicious in our actions.

The de Glanville incident highlighted the double standards of the British press. When the Lions played North Harbour, Dean Richards jumped up and down on Frank Bunce's ear. It almost took his ear off and needed 11 stitches.

Frank accepted this "occupational rugby hazard" uncomplainingly. From where I was sitting at Mt Smart it seemed intentional. Yet no one in the Lions management said boo. They showed what they really thought by making Richards captain for the next game.

The All Blacks weren't allowed such latitude. We were now, officially, "heavies". We were called to a "ruck summit" with their officials which was as inconvenient as it was pointless. It was nothing more than a PR stunt done for the English media. It achieved nothing.

CHAPTER FOURTEEN

The Touring Life

"These All Blacks have developed [cheating] into an art form which seems to have entirely fooled our Northern Hemisphere referees . . ." – Clem Thomas, *Rugby World*

AFTER THE DE GLANVILLE fuss, the controversies kept on coming. The next complaint: the All Blacks perpetrated late tackles.

On every tour a couple of ill-timed tackles will inevitably occur, and if we're in the wrong we'll say so. For instance, John Mitchell admitted he'd acted rashly in one tackle against the Scotland Development XV.

But deliberate late tackles? That was rich. British sides seemed totally bamboozled by our defensive capabilities. Their backs showed that under pressure they could not pass accurately. The few attacks they mounted were easily countered by a well-organised defence, which ours was.

The stats confirmed this. On tour we scored 42 tries in 13 games and conceded just five – and we kept the Barbarians scoreless for the first time in their history. No prizes for guessing which team made all the play. As entertainment, our matches were far better to watch than your typical British club game – and certainly in another class to the typical Five Nations international.

Incredibly, the quality of our defence was used against us. The British refused to accept it could be explained by something as obvious as superior ability. Somehow, the idea was floated that to stop tries we happily conceded penalties.

British opposition was invariably negative. They feasted off our mistakes instead of trying to create opportunities for themselves. A narrow loss seemed to be their first priority rather than attempting a win.

A constant annoyance wherever we went was the spying at our training sessions by English coaches and scouts. They were incredibly organised: they brought along clipboards, stopwatches, even video cameras – they had the works. They learned our calls for bringing the fullback into the line, when we'd pick up and drive . . .

In the end we resorted to non-public training sessions. It was the only way we could get any privacy, or develop our moves.

You wondered at times if an orchestrated campaign to unsettle the team was taking place, masterminded by English rugby's hierarchy. Dusty Hare had already had a go at us. After our next two victories, Paul Ackford, the former England lock, accused us of cheating. Mike Slemen, the assistant England coach, complained of "gamesmanship tactics". The North coach, Dick Greenwood, called us boring. Ernie Kirton summed up our point of view when he said, "Such talk doesn't annoy us – we just look at the credibility of the people saying these things."

But I think we were more affected by this blatant negativity than we admitted.

It was unfair: we were doing all the right things off the field. We were approachable. We had exemplary standards of behaviour. We visited schools. We signed autographs by the hundreds – one count estimated the team signed 1400 autographs by the end of the tour.

None of this seemed to count for much. Even though the All Blacks drew capacity crowds, the animosity stirred through the media had its effect. They seemed to despise us for being so successful. Every time I led the team out I felt a blast of hostility greet me.

Thankfully, we were a close-knit team.

> *". . . if you're a young guy coming into the All Blacks with no commitments, you'll go anywhere and have the time of your life . . . as long as you're playing good rugby. That's the first priority – playing good rugby."*
>
> – Garry Whetton, *Brothers In Arms*

ALTHOUGH THERE'S A CERTAIN mystique that comes with the territory, touring with the All Blacks is like working in any job, except you're on the move all the time. You're not always consistent; some days are definitely better than others. That's why the composition of a touring team must go beyond playing ability. Getting on with people you don't care for is part of successful touring. The best All Black teams are those which pull together on their own initiative. In 1993, despite the barracking from the crowds and the media, we had one of the more harmonious sides I've been part of.

One day we went to the Sportsmans' Club Association for a luncheon. It's traditional; they host every touring team. They were a pretty toffee-nosed lot.

Basically, they treated us like second-class cousins. "Colonials." You'd have thought we were straight from the bush. We felt insulted, but no one over-reacted. We just smiled and put up with it.

During a speech, full of "let rugby be the winner" remarks, Ric Salizzo had heard enough. "That was a great cliche," he said. This "hear hear, old chap" sort of guy looked at him. "So you actually use that word down there, do you?" Another old guy went on, "So you're one of those *Maori* people, are you?"

The team was not impressed, but we got a laugh from it. "Hear, hear . . . hear, hear" was the big call among the guys for the rest of the tour.

At that same "do", Norm Hewitt copped a few laughs when he was called across to meet Sir Edward Heath, the former British Prime Minister. Norm misunderstood. He thought he'd been offered "something to eat". He shook Sir Edward's hand and said, "Nice to meet you, but where's the food?"

JAMIE JOSEPH

> ‘I think most of the guys were humorous in their own way but only Dicko [Richard Fromont] was not intimidated by Laurie's position. He was always looking for a laugh, even before a game.
>
> I think more of us needed to be like him. If I ever go on another tour I think I'll do very well because I've realised touring is about being yourself. But there are a lot of subtle pressures in touring. You don't always get feedback when you need it.’

For a team to achieve harmony, you've got to work at it every day. There are 30 healthy – sometimes one or two over-healthy – egos to deal with and some will inevitably get bruised: everyone knows that only 15 can make the test side, and not all disappointments are handled with a smile.

I've always found the key to success is finding your touring rhythm as soon as possible. This means giving your all as a player and trainer. The happy tourists are those who understand this and don't try to cut corners. If the breaks don't go as planned, they at least know they've tried their best.

This team was young, and eager to do the right thing. They tried hard at everything: training, playing, fitting in.

GRAHAM PURVIS

> ‘You are like family. You will bicker among yourselves but if an outsider criticises anyone, you always back each other up.
>
> If you saw one of the guys bailed up in a corner by a ‘Saturday night All Black’ and giving the old tug on the ear – the international sign for ‘I need a bit of help’ – you’d go across and help. If you don’t . . . well, before you know it things might lead to an argument . . .’

Tours are built around daily training. It’s time-consuming, so you have to use spare moments wisely. It’s a fallacy that you’ve got a lot of extra hours to kill. As a rule you’re only in a town or city for three days, and that includes travelling and playing.

After the first couple of games, the basic Saturday/Wednesday line-ups settle down. This affects the social balance of the party: the 30 guys can rarely go out for a big night together. While one group is ready to let off steam, the other is preparing for the forthcoming match. You can go through a whole week and never see the other guys, except on the team bus. When group opportunities do come along, you grab them.

Tests are great days, but usually the best time to relax with your teammates is if you’re a “dirty dirty” – not required in the next game. In the UK we insisted the dirties leave the hotel in the evenings. Times spent together going out to dinner, or having a drink or two at a pub, are vital for building team spirit.

ANT STRACHAN

> ‘I’ve only been on one but I don’t know if Joe Public would get that big a surprise if he could see what happens on an All Black tour. The guys train every day, go out in small groups together, which they enjoy, attend a lot of functions which they usually hate . . . they have a few court sessions and nights on the turps. I don’t think there’s much that’s a real eye-opener – it’s a rugby tour, after all.’

As captain, I tried extra hard to make sure no player felt left out. But it’s more than one man’s job. That’s where John Mitchell was excellent with the Wednesday team. He basically took them under his wing and helped them build their own identity. The Wednesday guys set a goal to go through unbeaten, and they did. The support they gave the test side before the internationals was superb.

An All Black gains peer respect from his off-field performance as much as his playing ability. I agreed with John Sturgeon’s approach when he was manager. He always congratulated, individually, every new All Black. He’d say, “Welcome to the All Blacks. You’ve joined a wonderful team. But how well you do now is largely your concern. It’s up to you to mix and mingle and get to know your fellow players." He made it quite clear that a player was to get off his backside and make friends.

If somebody sits in their room all day it's just hopeless. It's only happened once or twice in my time and those who do get told pretty quickly such behaviour is not acceptable. The key to making it as an All Black teammate is simple: you've got to get on with people, even the ones with whom you don't have much in common.

I connect with my teammates most of the time, but if you clash with someone then you just keep out of their way. It is so important not to let rifts develop or problems fester.

One of the unsung heroes of All Black morale since 1988 was Doc Mayhew. He had an intuition for when the guys needed a laugh, or maybe a bit of a private chat. It helped that he played club rugby too: he could relate to the guys' needs. This was his last tour, and countless times he showed how much we'd miss him.

GRAHAM PURVIS

> 'Doc was the sort of guy who, if you had crook guts and he was in the middle of his dinner, would get up straight away to get you some pills or something to cure the problem.'

Doc loved the All Blacks and was an integral part of the team. His enthusiasm was contagious; we knew he'd go to any lengths for the team. I'll never forget his first tour, to Aussie in '88, when we drew the test. Doc was on the touchline and for most of the game had to endure this loudmouth in the crowd who kept abusing us.

"You're useless, All Blacks, bloody useless," this guy kept on mouthing. He never let up.

By the final whistle Doc had reached boiling point. As he walked off the field, he spotted the guy and slammed him.

That's passion.

> *"It's taken me 18 years to learn to play rugby and I'm still learning. Why would I want to go and learn to play another game after all that effort?"* – *Inga – The Winger*

IF THEY'D REALLY WANTED to create headlines, the journos missed the scoop of the tour. For weeks I'd known that Inga had signed to turn pro.

For months it was an open secret Inga was the target of rugby league.

In the build-up to the Bledisloe Cup test earlier in the year the news broke that Inga was being chased by Wigan. When I first learned of their interest my reaction was: "Good for him, if he wants to he should go." I just wished they'd saved it until after the test.

Rugby league's interest in All Blacks has never worried me. If a player wants to switch codes then good luck to him.

I'm not anti rugby league. I enjoy watching big league games – like I enjoy watching lots of top-class sport. I'm not "league-o-phobic" at all – in fact part of me would like to have played league, to see what it was like. I'll probably attend the Auckland Warriors games in the Winfield Cup.

I'm glad the days when the two rugby codes were arch-enemies have disappeared. I've played golf from time to time with the Warriors boss, Ian Robson, and he's excellent company. It wasn't that long ago the All Black captain and a rugby league administrator being seen in public would have created a scandal.

GRAHAM PURVIS

> 'Officially, no one knew. But Inga and I became All Blacks in the same year and we shared the same seat level in the bus. We talked a bit about a few things . . .
>
> It was a bit of a no-no subject. It was never discussed openly during the tour. Laurie was very strict about that.'

I learned of Inga's switch in a roundabout way. We arrived in Gateshead, and that night I phoned Bronnie back in New Zealand for a chat. During our phone call she mentioned a rumour that was doing the rounds at home. According to the Auckland grapevine, she said, Inga had signed a deal with Wigan.

After the call I went to Inga's room. I couldn't believe he had signed because there hadn't been any obvious signs of him talking with guys in suits. But I bluffed him: "So, when are you going?"

Inga looked up, shocked. "How did *you* find out?"

He told me the whole story. In Liverpool, when we played the North, he and Eroni visited Wigan to have a look around. Later, Inga and his agent went through the deal at a pub. They wanted somewhere discreet to duck away. When they walked in, the first person they saw was Earle.

I told Inga that, whatever he did, he should not let the news slip out. And I advised him not to tell Laurie just yet – he had enough on his plate.

Inga followed my advice perhaps too well. The next day Laurie told me he'd heard a whisper that Inga had signed, so he had him on about it. Bearing in mind what I'd suggested, Inga denied it. Laurie shook his head. "Those media guys . . . they never let up, do they?"

Inga's decision was never formally discussed within the team. I supported it – I thought he'd have been a fool to turn that sort of money down. If I had a disappointment it was that he hadn't let us know earlier. He was preventing JK from being in the team.

But Inga swore to me that nothing was finalised until he arrived in England. I had to take his word for it, but before the Barbarians game, his last as an All Black, I told him in no uncertain terms: "You owe us a big one today."

"Why is it we go to pieces when we meet these people?"

– England coach Dick Best, before the New Zealand-England international

BY THE FIFTH GAME, against England A (England's 2nd XV in all but name), Laurie had settled on the probable test line-up for the Scottish international, now just a fortnight away. With one exception – JR in on the blindside – it was the test team.

The big talking point among the public was the choice of first-five, Marc Ellis getting the nod over Stephen Bachop.

Bach had started with a blinder against London but then turned in a pretty ordinary display against South-West.

That's the fine line in international rugby these days. You could argue that one "off-day" sealed Bach's tour – he played some great rugby in later games – but he conceded the initiative to Marc. His next chance would only come if Marc's form fell off. Marc knew this and kept producing the goods.

As a captain, I thought this rivalry for places was excellent. It's just what Laurie and Earle wanted too. They hadn't forgotten how the complacency of the first choice players in 1991 had hurt the team.

JAMIE JOSEPH

'Fitzy was really good to me before they picked the test team. I'd only just come back from injury and it didn't look good for my chances. I thought I needed to produce a big game in the midweeker before the test.

It didn't look good for me: the coach's body language wasn't the best.

I was really intense, but Fitzy came up to me and said to get stuck in, to play my own game, ignore the pressure. He said a few extra things too and I ran onto that field much more confident.'

Edinburgh was cold and grey, but we had a lot of support from home. Many of the guys' wives and girlfriends were over following the tour too, and Bronnie flew into Britain just in time. Mum was with a tour party but I hardly saw them, so intense was the build-up.

We were now down to the business end of the tour. There were only three big games and then 1993 was history. As tempting as it was to think of summer, we forced such thinking away.

First we had to deal with Scotland at Murrayfield.

LAURIE MAINS

'The week before the test we played Scotland A which, as things turned out, had a huge influence on the tour. That day the guys thought they'd done well, given it their best shot, but on viewing the video I saw our team was still some way off the pace.

As a result, we had a much more intensive build-up to the test than we'd planned. After the way Scotland A played, we knew Scotland were confident they could beat us. We were very worried – but we thought Scotland were better than they actually were.

Our intensity was so good that it culminated in the performance we delivered at Murrayfield.

The problem after such a big build-up, and then such a fantastic result, was that we eased off. Earle and I were worried in case a little bit of complacency crept into the side. We warned the players not to let the result go to their heads.'

On paper, the Scots were no pushovers. Six of their side were 1993 Lions. Kilo for kilo, Scotland's pack matched our forwards in size and there was a lot of timber in their lineout. They even turned a lock into a loosehead prop in a futile attempt to unsettle our scrum. But they didn't use what ball they won well – and they couldn't match our hunger for possession.

A 51-15 test scoreline . . . it felt like the old days. And we'd done it without JK, without Foxy, without Michael Jones or Bruiser or Loey, any of the great names.

The new men played like veterans. Goldie's magic run of form continued, a Marc Ellis try went through six pairs of hand, and Steve Gordon produced a grafting, gutsy display.

I couldn't remember a recent test I've played in with more pleasure. Seven tries were notched up. The All Blacks were the first team to post a 50-point total against Scotland. It was a fantastic team performance.

The Scots were disappointing. They weren't fit enough, and some of their senior players did themselves no favours with lack of effort. Not that I particularly cared about Scotland's problems. I was happy that, after two hard years, we'd finally turned our obvious potential into a quality performance.

This was our seventh test win from the last eight.

If I had any unease after such a victory it was at the sudden and fulsome praise we now received from the British media. Their praise was too magnanimous, too laced with glowing adjectives . . . there was talk of the All Blacks adding "a new dimension" to rugby. It was so exaggerated. We'd done the fundamentals – staying on our feet, running hard and straight, supporting the ball carrier – extremely well, but we hadn't discovered anything new.

Perhaps I was being over-cautious. But I didn't trust their media just because they said a few nice things about us. I knew they would switch again without a blink.

We had a great night in Edinburgh.

On the Sunday, a somewhat bleary-eyed All Black team headed south. The tour "biggie", the English test, was now seven days away. The call went out to forget the Scotland result. England, as everyone knew, was the game we had to win.

Olympix

're drinking their beer here. Steinlager – a tremendous sponsor for the All Blacks and New aland rugby.*

Rob Tucker

other great All Black sponsor is soft-drinks giant Coca Cola – my new employers. With Coke) Tim Woodward.

The 1993 Lions were written off by too many people, too soon. Battling away in the first test.

Taking the field for my soon-to-be-worst All Black performance, bar none. Second test, vs the Lions.

Olympix

eet success. The Lions are tamed, and the series is ours.

Grilled by the press – again (this time after losing to France). The public bagging of the All Blacks has reached ridiculous levels.

BELOW: As time will prove, this is a very talented All Black team. It just needs more confidence (third test against South Africa, Eden Park).

Peter Bush

t the party begin . . . I start celebrations after our historic second test and series win over Boks . . .

Peter Bush

Andrew Harvey

The biter. Johan Le Roux

LEFT: The bite

BELOW: If only more New Zealanders would support us like the crowd at Athletic Park – second test, versus South Africa.

Peter Bush

ing up for Bledisloe '94, our sixth test in nine weeks. A killer schedule.

Peter Bush

tense moment in Sydney against Australia. The Wallabies have been our toughest ernational opponents these past few years.

Bronnie and Grace mean everything to me.

CHAPTER FIFTEEN

National Disaster

"We got it right. It is incredibly satisfying." – Geoff Cooke

"In New Zealand this will be a national disaster."
– Laurie Mains

THE GOOD NEWS ABOUT losing to England 9-15 was that we didn't concede a try.

There wasn't any other good news.

What's worse, we deserved to lose. There are no sour grapes: we never fired a shot all day. Looking back, I know it's a game we should have won, even comfortably. It was like a replay of the second test in Wellington: even though we knew the prize was at hand, we failed to deliver. When you're the better team, with the better players, such failure is devastating. The scoreboard shows they scored more points than us, but we knew we handed the test to England on a plate.

DOC MAYHEW

'The week before the test was non-stop. On Sunday we flew down to London where we changed hotels. Laurie didn't want the team distracted by staying in central London, where we were booked, so we moved out to the Surrey countryside.

On the Monday it was snowing, so all we could do was a bit of touch rugby for training. Then we met the Queen and Lady Di.

On Tuesday we drove down to Gloucester, for the game against the Emerging Players. There was a severe spell of cold weather in Britain around this time and there was a lot of doubt the game would even go ahead. That sort of uncertainty isn't ideal in test week, even if the test team wasn't directly affected.

By mid-week we were back in Surrey. We trained at Sandhurst Military Academy. Our hotel was great – however it was a million miles out of London. I think this was a disappointment to a lot of the guys who hadn't spent much time in central London before.

I understand Laurie's thinking about getting the team away from distractions, but I wonder if it has a counter-productive effect.

In the Gary Whetton era, for instance, the senior players would come and go pretty much as they pleased. And on Friday nights before a test it became a bit of an unspoken tradition with a few of the guys to have a port or two. It relaxed them.'

LAURIE MAINS

'On test day, the build-up was less than ideal. Just before I was about to give the team talk, Neil Gray told me there had been a road accident and we had to leave early.

This meant I had to cut down to only four or five minutes what I intended to say. The journey was a lot longer than usual and instead of getting to the ground an hour before kick-off, we arrived 20 minutes late.

Once inside the ground we had to rush our routine. Effectively, because of the delays, we took the field half-cock.'

The atmosphere at Twickenham was absolutely incredible. Although England were the out-and-out underdogs, the "Twickers" crowd inspired them by singing their absolute lungs out.

They didn't like us and made that very clear. When we performed the haka they totally ignored it, singing over the top of us with their "Swing Low, Sweet Chariot" number.

There's no mystery about our loss: the explanation begins with the forwards. The tight five had no fire, the loosies were off the pace and the line-out – yet again – was a mess. The quality of ball delivered to our inside backs at the line-out was the worst we'd served all year.

We won only 50 per cent of clean ball on our throw. We didn't protect Kamo well enough. Wherever he went in the lineout they had a guy who stood just behind him, pressuring him.

England were smart. They selected taller guys and had an extra jumper than us – four big men to our three. The man we thought might be a weak link was Nigel Redman. He is quite a bit smaller than his teammates but he played superbly. The sequence of line-outs he won after the break were a turning point.

To state the obvious: without set-piece ball a team is incredibly vulnerable. There are 40-odd lineouts in every game so you have to compete or you struggle. If the opposition tackle like men possessed, as England did, your task is even more difficult.

We were never allowed into the match. There were no rucks for us to get into, we barely got over the gain-line – their defence kept knocking us back. They weren't good enough to finish us off though; we were always in with a chance.

When JT almost scored with 15 minutes left I thought we had cracked them. But we let the advantage slip almost straight away and England hung on as the clocked ticked down . . .

With five minutes to go I wasn't panicking. I still thought we would win. And if anyone was to score the winning points it would surely be Goldie. His tour had been so *Boys Ownish* that a last minute try to save the day would surely be in the script. However, it wasn't to be . . .

Our defeat at Twickenham was, ironically, Grant Fox's answer to those critics who'd bagged him over the years as just a superboot. In every test he played, Foxy was the cool head on the park. He called the shots. Now he was gone, New Zealand suddenly woke up to what they'd taken for granted since 1987. At Twickenham our tactical kicking had shortcomings.

Another lesson for us was that too many players stood back and waited to be told what to do. Laurie and I had worried about this all year: the All Blacks need players, all players, to take a leadership role upon their shoulders. They can't rely just on me. In '88 and '89 that instinct came naturally to the side. The All Blacks of 1993, especially in the second Lions test and against England, lacked personal initiative under stress.

After the game, someone pointed out I had now set a world record of 54 consecutive tests. I was proud to have taken it off Gareth Edwards, a player I admired tremendously as a kid. But the defeat overshadowed it. On match night the achievement meant nothing to me.

I was annoyed because the Poms saw victory as a triumph for their dour, safety-first, full of commitment, totally dependent on Rob Andrew's boot style of rugby.

That's their choice: it's not compulsory a rugby team has to score tries – or even move the ball wide. But it's the sort of rugby which makes lawn-mowing look exciting.

Ironically, it's England who will lose out in the long run. They have some tremendous players – Clarke and Rodber to name but two – and they're much fitter and more organised than previously. They've taken a leaf out of our book there. Tactically, they're very limited and I'm sure history will confirm their limitations. A team that's only based on defence is a team with tunnel vision.

And, after all the talk we'd endured of how the All Blacks deliberately conceded penalties to prevent tries, it was noticeable that England infringed at will in the last few minutes to keep us out. Strangely, this wasn't a big point of discussion in the local press.

JAMIE JOSEPH

> 'We went to two or three luncheons before the test which is unheard of in test week. At every one we heard how great the All Blacks were, how good our captain was, our coach, our forwards . . .
>
> Right from the test dinner after beating Scotland people came up to us and said, 'You're going to beat the Poms, they haven't a chance . . .'
>
> I think you carry a bit of that praise in your head, even if you don't want to. We tried to play the win down but when every second person you meet is saying, 'Great game, great win, I pity the Poms' – it's hard not to be affected.'

Back in the dressing room I said to the guys, "This loss means you'll each have a rock on your back all summer at the beach. It's an awful feeling – don't get over it in a hurry."

The loss hurt us; I warned the team not to show the Poms how much. "Wear it on the chin, show them we can take it," I said. "For God's sake, don't spit the dummy."

Privately I kept thinking over and over, "How could we let them win?" Doc Mayhew said it was a worse feeling than Dublin in '91, because at least the Aussies were a good side. Ginge Henderson tried to lift the guys' spirits, saying, "I'd rather be a losing All Black than a winning Pom."

There were some positives. The guys reacted with style. Everyone dressed immaculately. We signed more autographs, posed for pictures with people. There was no whingeing about England's victory – we accepted the better team won on the day, and said so.

The bus journey from Twickenham back into central London for the after-match took a couple of hours. The traffic just crawled. I sat next to Olo who was even quieter than usual – like everyone, he was at a loss to explain our performance.

Neil Finn helped lighten the atmosphere. After the game he made a gesture which the boys really appreciated. It was his only night off on a Crowded House tour, his voice was really sore, but he stuck his head in the dressing room and offered to sing us a song. He stayed with us as we headed back to town. While Neil played guitar, performing a spontaneous acoustic solo "concert", we sang Split Enz and Crowded House favourites like "Don't Dream It's Over", "I See Red . . ."

Neil's gesture was brilliant. It didn't cure all our blues, but it sure helped restore spirits before joining the England team for the official dinner.

It takes a good loser to be a good winner. When we arrived at the function you'd never have thought we were the defeated team. We were smiling and talking to everyone. Inside, every minute hurt, but publicly we carried ourselves with pride.

'Fitzpatrick's racist abuse of Victor was not on'.

– Brian Moore column, *[London] Sunday Times*

IT'S NOT EVERY DAY you wake up to find your name splashed across a famous newspaper announcing something you didn't do. It's even worse when your body's aching and sore, and your side has lost to England, the most arrogant rugby team in the world.

On the lower front page of the sports section of the *Sunday Times* was an ominous headline: "Brian Moore slates Fitzpatrick, page 9".

Page nine was unbelievable.

In an "exclusive", Moore, the English hooker, accused me of calling Victor Ubogu a "black bastard".

For the record, I never said what Moore claimed.

After I got over the surprise, I felt disappointment at his action rather than anger. To break into print and create an issue out of nothing revealed more about the character of Brian Moore than my alleged racism.

In his column, he stooped low for no good reason. He wasn't advancing the cause of rugby in any way. It wasn't as if players would suddenly keep quiet on the field. It's never been that way, never will. Test rugby is a real battle and there's an inevitable amount of "effing and blinding" which goes on. The unwritten rule is that what's said on the field stays on the field. It's laughable for him to say I cracked racist remarks when there are nine Maori or Pacific Islanders in the All Black team.

DOC MAYHEW

> 'It wasn't an issue within the team at all. No one took it seriously for a moment. Rugby players abuse each other all the time. All Blacks are classic sledgers – especially at each other. At training, for instance, teammates slag off each other at any opportunity.'

We got Ric Salizzo to make a press statement. I denied Moore's claim and added I didn't want to take away from England's performance by getting into a public slanging match with one of their players.

Later, Ubogu publicly said he didn't hear me make any such statement. "If that is Fitzpatrick's true stance I don't think half of his team would be playing with him," he told the press.

I suspect the only reason Moore dared say anything was because England won. If they'd lost he wouldn't have said didley squat. At the test dinner, he never mentioned anything. Neither did his captain, Will Carling – and I sat at the same table as him. We got on well.

That's what sticks in my craw about Moore and Carling. They attended the after-match dinner and sat there, all angel-faced. They never mentioned anything either in public, or to me or the team management privately. If they felt so strongly about things, that was the appropriate course of action to take. They could even have made an official complaint. Instead, I had to read the paper.

I have no respect for people who behave in such an unprincipled way.

Moore's motivation is impossible to know. It's no secret there's no love lost between us. He knows I don't particularly rate him. I guess he shot his mouth off because, like a number of English players, he has a column to produce and he obviously needs sensational material to fill it.

To me, this was a very ugly pay-day.

LAURIE MAINS

> 'This was a public indication of the measure of the England player who claimed it had been made.'

We were still dealing with Moore's charge when the crap really hit the fan. JR was picked up by TV walking on the English halfback's leg.

DOC MAYHEW

> 'We weren't aware of the [row] until the Monday. We went down to Plymouth on Sunday afternoon, and none of the guys were exactly queuing up to catch a replay of the test on the BBC rugby show. So we weren't aware of what was being highlighted on TV.
>
> With hindsight, which is a wonderful thing, I think we handled the situation poorly. I have a lot of respect for Jamie Joseph as a player, but I think it's fair to question whether we did the right thing for him, or the team, by our response.'

We watched a video of the incident and it was clear that JR had done a silly thing. We told him so and Laurie then took him aside for a private word.

Though we didn't announce it to the media, Jamie was told that as a disciplinary measure he wasn't in contention for the Barbarians game, the tour finale. You could see he was upset but I admired his handling of the situation. He accepted his discipline with dignity.

If we'd publicly dropped JR he would have been hounded and criticised by the English media for what remained of the tour. So we deliberately kept our response in-house.

In PR terms we'd have come out better for reprimanding him publicly but team spirit isn't built that way. After what happened to Loey in Australia after the Carozza incident, management was adamant Jamie wouldn't be set up the same way.

Is it siege mentality? Maybe. A touring team becomes like a family. Criticising the team is like criticising the family. You close ranks when it happens. If someone is injured, or goes home early for any reason, it's like a death.

And maybe there was a bit of bloody-mindedness in our decision too. Deep down, we didn't want to give the English press the satisfaction of putting the boot in again.

LAURIE MAINS

> 'I'm not going to defend our decision in terms of whether it was the right one, but my feeling is I'd do it again for the player's sake. The media would have torn him apart if we'd made our decision public, and we weren't going to let that happen.
>
> What made the pressure worse was that we didn't act as we planned to. In-house, we agreed we'd make a one-line response to the issue when we named the team to play the Barbarians. That was all, we didn't want to flame the fires. Ric Salizzo was supposed to do it but our manager decided to handle it instead. He got questioned, and he said some things we'd agreed wouldn't be discussed.'

"If something can go wrong, it will." – Murphy's Law

WITH NOTHING LEFT but pride to play for we finished the tour with two wins and a good three-try-to-none thumping of the Barbarians in Cardiff.

The consequences of the English loss still lingered. Incredibly, a *third* row broke out. Unlike the others, the heat from this was generated back in New Zealand. In terms of fallout, it was probably the most damaging of the lot.

I'm referring to the decision to call Mike Brewer into the tour squad as a replacement for Matthew Cooper.

Bruiser joined us the day before the English test and was put straight in the test reserves as cover for all the loose forwards. This meant we overlooked Liam Barry, the remaining openside flanker. Because of Bruiser's experience, and versatility, the decision made sense. He was fit, available, and answered a need. If we'd won that test there wouldn't have been a peep out of the public. But it's the same old story: the All Blacks lose, so there has to be a scapegoat. Anything will do. The same weekend New Zealand's cricketers suffered a record loss to Australia at cricket. The public outcry about that was minimal.

It's not as if we kept the NZRFU in the dark about Brewer's inclusion. They knew what was happening. Eddie Tonks, who was in Britain, told us he wasn't happy but we were the tour management so he'd respect our decision and back us.

Mike was uncertain if he was doing the right thing. He didn't want to take anyone's place and told us so. Laurie said we'd carry the can.

Liam was not an option. He was specifically picked for the tour to learn. He knew that – Laurie told him before we left. Liam was never in the running because he wasn't experienced or strong enough to handle a test yet. When Ginge pulled out we needed players capable of matching the Englishmen's strength.

People might raise an eyebrow at such a hard-nosed attitude. It wouldn't have done to act like that in the "old days". But these aren't the old days any more. I make no apology for what we did. Everyone knew the tour's success or failure would be judged on one game – the English test. So it proved. Test rugby is about putting the best players on the park. As he's shown by forcing his way back into the All Blacks this year, Bruiser is a frontline test player.

Naturally, Liam wasn't too thrilled at what happened but he's since shown the world his depth of character. He bulked up over the summer, approached 1994 with real aggression in his game, and is already a far superior player to the promising rookie who went away to Britain.

In years to come I think Liam will prove he has "it", the mystery component all great All Black players need. And I'm sure this experience, painful though it was, will have helped.

GRAHAM PURVIS

> ‘The DDs were getting ready to go to a function when we were told the deal: Mike's coming in.
>
> Liam was obviously very disappointed. So were all the DDs – there were about nine of us, and we were very close. As one of the older members I took Liam aside and said, 'Look mate, obviously you feel deflated, you've had a little bit of confidence in your ability knocked out of you. But accept it. The coach is the one picking the team, it's his decision. Don't get down – and remember, you're going to be an All Black a lot longer than he is coach.'
>
> The DDs had quite a few beers with Liam that night.
>
> The day after the England test, we got held behind for a talk with Laurie. He said, 'Well, let me have it.'
>
> There was a bit of silence then I said, 'OK, we've all had a bit of a spit at you, a bit of a spit at the world. It took about quarter of an hour – then we went out and had a good time. And here we are back at training this morning.'
>
> Then Liam got the shit off his chest, called Laurie what he wanted to – and that was that. In Laurie's defence, he listened to

us, let us have our say. It was smart, it prevented the guys bottling and brooding.’

I'd still support the same decision today about bringing Bruiser into the English test. The mistake we made, and one which I realise now, was in picking Brewer in the reserves against the Barbarians a week later.

It amazed me the depth of anger that people expressed after I shook Mike's hand when he replaced Blair late in the match. This was my way of supporting him, publicly, for all the stick he'd copped that week. If it caused a few tut tuts, I can live with it.

When I got back home I found it difficult to stay quiet over one or two particularly stupid remarks. I'm glad I didn't bother to respond. Once again, the intensity and length of time that was spent on this "issue" made me wonder why New Zealanders don't have more important issues to worry about.

Laurie's off-the-cuff remark about not caring what people thought about the decision has been taken and used against him out of context. I think it should've been viewed with more understanding. It was a reflection of how much strain we were under in those final days.

Like the Jamie controversy, we'd been pushed around by the media so much that we'd reached our limit of tolerance. There was a "stuff you" attitude about Laurie's comment which the whole team shared. We were wrong – we were also human. In other words, we'd had enough.

Adding to the strain were the internal tensions within our management. Neil Gray tried hard but he and Laurie weren't a natural partnership.

It's not just players who need a strong manager. Coaches need their support because they've got enough on their plate. Politics between a coach and a manager are not uncommon which is surprising because they need each other's support. The coach knows the manager is one of the councillors who vote for his appointment – naturally, he doesn't want to get off-side with him. The manager, on the other hand, knows his chances of going on another tour depend upon the team being successful.

A bit of this friction went on between Neil and Laurie in the UK. Because of the undercurrents between them, it was another reason why Laurie couldn't fully relax. That was felt by the whole team.

Originally I thought Neil was quite a good manager but in Britain I was disappointed in him on a couple of occasions; I didn't ever feel I had his full support. After the English test, for example, he told me, "You didn't throw in very well, did you?" And then he added, "I want you to know I'm still not very happy about the decision to bring Mike into the team as a reserve." I couldn't believe what I was hearing. Neil was involved in the group decision, and, as manager, he had the final say anyway. Now he seemed to be edging away from what we'd agreed.

Being the All Black manager is a very political job. Managers write end-of-tour reports where, if you've mucked up, your name goes in Council's "big black book". There have been more than a few All Blacks who've never come back after a bad write-up.

An All Black manager needs to be respected by the players. That is essential. It's not always the case.

LAURIE MAINS

> 'I think it's fair to say the team and coaches lacked confidence in Neil that he would make the decision in the best interests of supporting the team. I don't think it was a major issue, more an irritant.'

In two tours of France I've seen the extremes in management. In 1986 Richie Guy seemed more concerned with what the French officials thought of him than his own team. I can remember having to listen to speeches at 2am after a night game, and Richie not doing a thing about it. We had to be up early the next day but he didn't want to offend their officials. The guys were not impressed.

On the other hand, John Sturgeon was absolutely on our side. Absolutely. After the Nantes test in 1990 he told the French officials that all speeches would have to be completed by a certain time because we had another function to attend.

The time came and the speeches weren't done – apparently we had to wait for the French team who were still on their way. Sturge's attitude was that wasn't good enough: if one team could get to the function on time then both could. So, even though the function was French team-less, Sturge got up and made his speech, handed out the ties and pins and we left.

Sturge wasn't in the least bit bothered. He made his point too – the next day we got an apology from the French camp.

That was management, and that's why the guys warmed to Sturge so much.

> *"Carling has turned, or been turned, into a very commercially orientated young man who knows his value."*
>
> – Jeff Probyn, from his autobiography

IT'S THE LAST PUBLIC act for any team: the end of tour press conference. In Cardiff, it took place after the Barbarians game beneath the stand in a stark and cold room. It suited the atmosphere.

There was standing room only.

I wouldn't call the atmosphere openly antagonistic, but it's fair to say there was only basic courtesy in the exchanges. We got asked some humdrum questions which we answered politely. We wanted to be gone, and we downplayed some unnecessary digs. But then a journo who wasn't part of the usual "rat pack" asked us, "Does it worry the All Blacks that you're leaving the country with a reputation as a dirty side?"

My gut reaction was to get up and go. I'd had enough. I was so angry I pushed my chair back to leave and Laurie obviously felt the same. Realising it would only hurt us if we walked, we both counted to 10 and remained.

"If you writers concentrated on the rugby and not questions like that," I said, not bothering to keep the anger from my voice, "rugby would flourish a lot more over here."

It wasn't one of the great press conferences.

Despite the English loss, the tour was immensely valuable for All Black rugby. Players were successfully blooded, we had a great team spirit, and at times our form reached brilliance.

It was extremely valuable for British rugby finances. We played to capacity crowds, earning more than $12 million in gate receipts for the English and Scottish rugby unions. You couldn't get a seat without digging deeply into your pockets. An official ticket for the England test cost $80 – on the black market it sold for $1500.

So much for the unpopular All Blacks.

Undeniably, the final eight days soured the whole tour. And I have no hesitation in putting the blame squarely on the English media for creating such a lousy atmosphere.

Unfortunately, many New Zealanders think such talk is "media bashing" – nothing more than sour grapes, an excuse for our loss.

That's not the case. The All Blacks, publicly, paid credit to England for their win. What I refer to is our disillusionment at not getting a fair go – at having to put up with the lies and distortions written about us. Constant criticism gets you down.

Perhaps we should have handled some issues better. Who wouldn't with hindsight? If we were prickly at times it was because we were continually getting bagged.

The *Evening Standard*, for instance, listed *as fact* the All Blacks' "10 Tricks of the Trade". They ranged from crooked scrum feeds, psyching out the ref, obstruction – you name it, we did it.

And if people thought we were too sensitive to their criticism, then consider the following reaction to our Twickenham defeat:

> *". . . in the best epic tradition, England had right on their side. They were the good guys in white. The All Blacks had already scarred De Glanville. They now targeted Bracken with the stud and Ubogu with the racist barb. The good guys won. Courage and fair play won. Epic."*
>
> — Eddie Butler, former Welsh captain

"For make no bones about it, an apt metaphor, there were really evil elements in that All Black side . . .
"What awful flaw lurks in the Kiwi psyche which causes them to behave like spiteful, spoilt and sulking toddlers . . .
"What we all cheered at Twickers was not just the winning of a test but the defeat of an attitude . . . an archaic, unsavoury attitude which somehow has survived and festered in the dark bottom right-hand corner of the globe. Get with it, mend your ways, take another look at yourselves . . . or you won't be invited again." – Colin Welland, screen-writer of *Chariots of Fire*

"Persistent All Black fringing and offside meant that the game was a dismal spectacle . . . they seem to set out to prevent the other side playing . . ."
— Martin Humphries, British journalist

"Foul play and cheating are the two factors that can make the game of rugby football unplayable, and the 1993 All Blacks are guilty on both counts. In so doing, they have diminished the proud name of New Zealand and besmirched a great game."
— Clem Thomas, *Rugby World*

". . . they will be remembered mostly as a dirty side. That is sad for them, but I think they deserve it."
— Will Carling, *The Mail on Sunday*

Enough said.

CHAPTER SIXTEEN

A Day in the Life

"If it's not the single biggest sporting event in Sydney this year, it will run close. Tonight's Bledisloe Cup rugby test match between the Wallabies and the All Blacks has created unprecedented interest . . ."

– *Sydney Morning Herald*, Wednesday 17 August, 1994

7.59 am I wake to the sound of the phone: New Zealand calling. I've slept well. I peer outside; another beautiful spring day. Only 10½ hours till kick-off . . . I feel the tension from the moment I open my eyes. Test day never gets easier. Never.

No one outside the team knows this but my left knee has been playing up for weeks. The morning after we get back to Auckland I'm going straight into hospital to have some of the cartilage removed. I hurt the knee in a club game just before the French series.

It hasn't affected my game, it's just sore. I've got through all the tests fine. We haven't made a thing of it; opponents don't need to know. People would be amazed at the knocks some of the guys carry.

Tonight is my 62nd test for New Zealand.

I don't think about it much but I suppose my consistency *is* pretty remarkable. I haven't missed a test since 1986. Of the other

Baby Blacks only Bruiser – and until recently, JK – are still in the team. But I've played twice as many games as Bruiser.

Campo's been around even longer, since 1982. He's an amazing character. He just gets better and better. It is almost 11 years to the day since I played against him in a Colts test in Pukekohe. We're the only players from either of those teams appearing in the test tonight. The Australian Colts won that day. I hope it's not an omen.

The secret of my longevity is that I've enjoyed a good run with health. I think my attitude's helped: the biggest fear for me in rugby is losing – I never worry about getting hurt.

I've had heaps of injuries in my career, but none were too serious. I'm always playing with some part of me in pain. For the past two seasons I've needed operations on my left elbow, because loose bone chips often seize the joint, inflaming it. Both times I was back playing within a week.

Last year Foxy and I visited the young Argentinian schoolboy who suffered a tragic spinal injury in a college game. His courage was an inspiration to us. But I never think about getting hurt like that. I suppose a neck injury is a hooker's main fear, but my attitude is why worry about something that *could* happen? You'd never get out of bed if you think like that. As long as you're physically prepared, you've done all you can. If you're afraid, don't play.

Probably the worst injury I've had was dislocating my kneecap two years ago. Luckily, it came at the end of the season. I don't talk a lot about pain or injuries. To anyone. I just get on with things. I hardly ever go off. If I do I'm really hurting. I had to go off against Waikato in 1991, but that was only a precaution. We were flying out to the World Cup soon after.

It helps that I'm naturally big; I seem to shake off minor knocks other players can't. The guys always reckon that training sessions with me are more dangerous than actual games. I picked up that no-holds-barred attitude from the way Harty coached Auckland.

He made sure we trained as we played. There were never any soft mauls or rucks. It's in my nature to be full-on, so it suited me.

Strength is essential for any rugby player these days. You need to be able to absorb a lot of punishment. At the bottom of a ruck you know you'll get stood on and rucked. You almost wait for it. Because you can't do anything to get out, it's best to accept it. I get badly scraped in most games I play. It hurts, but you don't go squealing about it. I've always got purple and yellow bruises over my back and legs. I bleed a fair bit too. At some stage you'll play with a broken or dislocated finger; it's all par for the course.

BRONWYN FITZPATRICK

'I always touch wood when I talk about injury. Sean's been fortunate, his injuries have tended to be of a cosmetic or superficial nature. He's never out for any length of time, but he gets lots of minor wounds. There are many occasions I'll put a towel over the pillow and next morning it'll be covered in blood. But Sean doesn't consider that an injury.'

I never take painkillers to play. The exception was against Argentina in 1989, but that was because the injury – a torn rib cartilage – was only painful, it wasn't structural. I don't like painkillers because you can permanently hurt yourself as a result. Apparently they're a fact of life in professional sports overseas. Even here in Sydney, you catch talk of league guys in the Winfield Cup only making it from game to game on painkillers. But if you're cheating nature and trying to fast-track the healing process you'll be the one who pays for it when you're older.

Painkillers are quite common in rugby, but their use is kept pretty quiet. I'd estimate 90 per cent of players take them in their careers, and a lot use them regularly.

Look at Mike Brewer. He needs them for every game. Bruiser's been injured so often he must have had needles in every part of his body by now.

By comparison with other sports, I think rugby is drug-free. A few South Africans have been caught out using steroids, and every so often you hear a whisper about a player developing a Schwarzenegger-type physique very fast. I can't see it being a widespread problem because it's such a give-away. There's only so much extra muscle you can put on in a short space of time without arousing suspicion. I don't think it's a problem in rugby today and I don't think it's inevitable it will be, even as the game gets more professional.

10.20 am Enjoy my usual test-match breakfast. Muesli, yoghurt, a bit of toast. Glance through the papers. They are full of tonight's game, it's the number-one sports story: Balmain rugby league club goes out of existence . . . the Aussie Commonwealth Games team . . . all stories are relegated behind the rugby. Great to see.

Peter FitzSimons did a good piece on me in the *Sydney Morning Herald* yesterday. It was intelligent, it was opinionated, it had a sense of humour – but it wasn't malicious. Our journos could learn a thing or two by reading it. But they're so damned negative.

It's sad to admit, but the team have enjoyed being out of New Zealand, away from the aggro. I heard the *Sunday Star-Times* had a go at me but I didn't bother reading it.

The Aussies don't like Loey, that's very clear. He's probably under the most pressure. From the moment we arrived they targeted him. There have been cartoons about him, comments in the press. None of which has had any impact on Loey. When they asked him if he'd changed his style, he said, no, he was still using the same hairdresser.

We've been training twice a day. In the morning we've been doing scrums and line-outs, in the evening we've worked out under lights at the Stadium. They're excellent, the field's in good condition . . . playing at night won't be a problem. The only drag with an evening kick-off is you've got even more time to kill.

GRANT FOX

> 'Fitzy and I have talked about the build-up phase before tests many times. It was always the same. The worst bit comes when the final training is over and you're waiting to get on the field. For 24 hours you're living constantly with a knot of fear in your gut that gets bigger and bigger. And the self-doubt which goes through your mind is unbelievable: you're always thinking, 'Am I good enough? Can I do the job? What if we lose?' '

1.17 pm The nerves are really kicking in now. It's the sixth time in two months I've endured this. It's a huge strain. No wonder the guys are short-tempered occasionally. Everyone's simmering.

We've said it a lot but no one seems to be taking much notice: this has been a killer schedule for the All Blacks. Six tests in nine weeks against the three best teams in the world. It's a lot easier for our opposition. They've all been able to focus their whole season on us – our guys, on the other hand, have had no breather. We can't savour a win or properly analyse our game because there's not enough time. There's always another test to prepare for.

No other All Black side has faced a sequence of demanding tests in such a short time before. It'd be nice if our critics would acknowledge this. For once. It means that for nine weeks we've been living on the extremes of our nerves.

I think we've done remarkably well after such a horror start. We played badly in losing the first test to France. No excuses. We didn't fire a shot all day.

But since then we've been the dominant team in four consecutive tests. It took an act of French brilliance to defeat us in Auckland – we'd controlled that game until the final moments.

And then against South Africa, *for the first time in All Black history*, we went unbeaten through a home series – and we extended our unbeaten run against the Boks to three seasons.

I know you can't blame bad luck, but fate hasn't been kind to us in 1994. If we'd won both tests at Eden Park – which we should have – our season would read at this moment, Played five, won four. We'd be entering tonight's game with our confidence sky-high and every Kiwi back-slapping us onto the field. Instead, we're copping pressure from people who can't see the bigger picture and who keep on relentlessly bagging us.

I hope we have a turn of luck tonight. I think it will be a close game. I'm sure we'll win – but we've got to take our chances.

That's something we haven't always done in 1994. We've let teams off the hook. The classic was the last few minutes against the French at Auckland. We lost concentration . . . we snatched defeat from the jaws of victory.

The draw with the Boks was a case of having them on the ropes and yet not delivering the KO. In terms of public support, it would have been better if we'd drawn with the Boks in Wellington and won in Auckland. Then we'd have been national heroes. To have it the other way around has been a disaster. People act as if we'd lost. As the guys know too well, New Zealanders only remember the last test of a series.

The skill among our guys is there. The skill is *unquestionably* there. The frustrating thing about this All Black team is that we've trained so well and yet been so inconsistent. When we hit our straps, we're awesome. The first half at Wellington against the Boks, long periods of the second French and first South African tests . . . but then we go off the boil somehow.

No wonder our confidence is so brittle.

What we lack is real inner belief. We're aware our record's a bit spotty and that winning is all we get judged on. Still, it hurts when you beat your arch-enemies 2-0 in a series and that's not good enough for the country.

3.38 pm Lying on my bed, staring at the ceiling. I'm in room 324 of the Coogee Holiday Inn. Cream-coloured wallpaper. A big double bed. The TV's on, but I'm not really watching it. Thinking about the Wallabies instead. They have a very good team, well-balanced: a tough tight five, excellent loosies . . . Jason Little . . . Campo . . . the halfback, Gregan, looked good against Samoa. We'll need to watch him.

"Success in rugby was, is, and always will be cyclic."

– Chris Laidlaw, *Mud in Your Eye*

WHY HAS OUR SEASON been so up and down? There's no simple answer. South Africa's presence in New Zealand at the same time we played France was a distraction. Instead of focusing 100 per cent on the French, it was always in the back of our minds that the Boks were in town.

Sunday tests were not a big hit, either. Psychologically they were upsetting to our rhythm. All Black teams are built on maintaining habits, drawing on what's familiar. Sundays are not part of that culture. I hope that experiment never gets repeated.

The French were written off because they lost to Canada. Part of the reason for that was because they weren't properly fit. But on tour they really concentrated on getting their fitness levels up; they trained twice a day. By the time of the tests they bore no resemblance to the bunch that arrived in New Zealand.

The traditional parts of their game functioned as well as ever: their scrum was immensely strong, their flair was there in abundance. They had some exceptional individuals, especially in the loose. Perhaps the key to everything was their discipline. They kept their cool. Later, when everyone saw how easily South Africa lost their rag, the French composure seemed even more impressive.

France were *huge*: a "Jurassic pack". They contested every scrap of ball. Our forwards played well against them – it's not easy against monsters like Merle, who weigh in at more than 20 stone. Yet we still won more possession than they did.

I have no complaints about the outcome of the series. In a nutshell, they took their chances. We didn't. They played exceptionally well to beat us. Our defence was generally excellent – but their two tries were amazing, absolutely out-of-this-world efforts. I don't think any team could have prevented them.

Against South Africa we redeemed ourselves. Except for a disappointing last quarter at Eden Park when we didn't finish them off, we were the superior team throughout the series.

The first test against the Boks was a real battle. They were dishing out a lot of off-the-ball stuff. It was niggly, obstructive play. But they weren't emotionally calm enough to win. I don't think they realised the extent of their shortcomings, either – and I'm sure they underestimated us. In Dunedin our primary goal was to win: and we achieved that. Our rough spots could be fixed. The South Africans overlooked this. They went public with some stupid remarks about our ability, quite remarkable considering they'd lost. Look at the rubbish Venter said after the game about Loey, and what Strauss and company said about our scrum.

Our pushover try in Wellington was the best possible reply.

The Springboks seemed too content to live on past achievements and their tradition. I think they believed that glory would come simply by pulling on the green jersey.

In the second test the All Blacks produced brilliant rugby for the first 40 minutes. Our scrum was totally dominant; that's why I went for a pushover try when we were awarded a penalty. We'd broken them, and even though they came back with a rush, they never mastered us.

Our commitment in the last few minutes was outstanding. When you consider the Springboks' whole tour depended upon them winning in Wellington, for us to shut them out was a superb feat.

For me, the second test was rugby at its zenith. In the last few minutes my legs were like rubber, I was running on empty, but still I pushed on. I wasn't alone – every All Black had played his heart out.

The pace was frantic. The pressure was agony. Every player knew an act of brilliance, or one stupid mistake, held the winning or losing of the test, and the series.

The South Africans were in an absolute frenzy, yelling and shouting at each other. They'd get the ball. Run it. And every time a black shirt would size them up and knock them down.

We out-paced them to the loose ball. Mauled for our lives. Ran and ran and never stopped. I remember telling Cookie, "Wherever the ball goes you run as fast and as hard as you can and get to it first. Give it *everything*."

Our defence was All Black rugby at its very best. The message was absolutely clear: don't let the bastards through.

I remember looking up at the ground clock. It showed six minutes to go. But the referee told the touch judge, "Only three minutes left . . ." When he blew the whistle to signal our victory, the moment was the sweetest of my career. We'd beaten the Boks. A place in history was ours.

At Athletic Park, the All Blacks delivered one of New Zealand rugby's greatest test wins. The crowd were fantastic. We drew such inspiration from their support. Later in the evening, when the All Blacks boarded our bus, a crowd clapped and cheered us on. Everywhere we went that night – and it was a long night – people smiled and thanked us for what we'd done. It was one of the best nights of my life.

After such a high, it was extremely disappointing to receive the criticism we did after the draw at Eden Park a fortnight later.

The success we'd achieved in Dunedin and Wellington was instantly forgotten. People seemed to get more pleasure in shafting us for one average display than enjoying a series victory.

Sadly, I wasn't surprised.

6.00 pm The guys are gathered in the team room. Kick-off is in 90 minutes. No one says a thing. In walks Laurie; he looks serious but relaxed. Well, as relaxed as you can be in his position. He takes off his coat, hangs it on the back of the chair and comes over and shakes my hand. He doesn't say a word, but I know it's his way of showing, publicly, that he's valued my support over the last few days. I appreciate the gesture very much.

> *"If New Zealand's going to win the World Cup, they need a coach, not a Laurie"* – Billboard poster in Auckland

NO ONE'S HAD A tougher year than Laurie Mains. Everyone's had a go at him. Most of the chipping has been mindless, very personal, and the way he handles it so well amazes me.

For the record, Laurie is a very, very good coach. He's the best forward coach I've played under, which, considering he was a fullback in his career, shows that he really knows his stuff.

He's a clever man, a good student of human nature. He knows when to give the guys a boost or a rev-up. Before the decider against the Boks, for instance, he noticed the guys were a bit too casual.

Laurie wasn't happy with them. He bought everyone down to

earth with a thud. We had a bit of a session as he analysed the team and individuals' performances.

"Loey, where were you at that ruck?"

"Cookie, that knock-on cost us 20 metres . . ."

"Bash, you let them off the hook with that kick . . ."

And so on. He went right through the guys, pointing out an area for improvement in everyone's games.

Then, when he'd made sure the conceit was out of us, he said, "What we're going to do in the next test is more of the good things we showed at Carisbrook. There were lots of those . . ." And he outlined the progress we'd made. The guys left the meeting with a much more realistic attitude. A winning attitude.

What a year he's had. I feel so sorry for him. In Sydney he's probably been less uptight than recently. He laughed during the press conference a few times, which the journos made a deal about. I know it's because we're outside New Zealand. Out of earshot of the knockers.

LAURIE MAINS

> ‘Is it worth it? At the end of the day, no it isn't. It's been a huge challenge, there's been an awful lot of satisfaction dealing with players, developing their skills, having a significant part in teeing up a number of them with careers . . . that sort of thing is worth it.
>
> But at the end of the day this has destroyed the life I knew before I became All Black coach.
>
> I had only ever had pleasant memories of rugby. Any disappointments were character-building. But when I finish with the All Blacks, I know that some memories are not going to be pleasant.
>
> The knockers . . . that's not the reason it hasn't been worth it. No, it's because I've given everything to this position. One hundred per cent of my time and effort. Everything.
>
> And I haven't always got back what I put in.
>
> In a financial sense, too, the sacrifice has been enormous. Basically I haven't been revenue-earning for two-and-a-half years. Last year alone, I'd estimate it cost me $130,000 [in lost money] because of the time I put in as All Black coach.’

I know Laurie's biggest disappointment has been the failure of guys he believes in to develop as consistent test players. I know he hates dropping anyone – anyone – but as he tells me, "What do you do if someone's not playing well? There isn't the time to persevere till they hit form."

I think players like Arran Pene and Matthew Cooper are good players, but they discovered this year that the job description of an All Black means you've got to keep on producing *every* match. The cliché "you're only as good as your last game" has real truth to it. So does the selectors' claim they'll go on form. If JK, the most-capped All Black in our history, can get dropped, that shows no one has a divine right to their All Black place.

LAURIE MAINS

> 'One of the things I find tragic is we've been under pressure, but the NZRFU council, as a body, has never supported us.
>
> The non-appointment of a selection panel through to the World Cup was a vote of no-confidence in us. Their non-action was very detrimental and harmful to the team. It opened the door for the knockers to discredit us.
>
> I recognise too there is a deliberate campaign from a group in Auckland to undermine the team. The same thing happened in 1991. The same gang that's having a crack at me undermined Alex Wyllie then.
>
> I find it very disappointing.'

I feel very loyal towards Laurie. He's shown his loyalty to me, too.

In 1992 I hadn't known what to expect – everything about the captaincy was so new. Last season I experienced extreme highs and lows. So this year, when there was early talk in the papers and from the talkback "experts" about my future, I wasn't particularly bothered. The tests were weeks away and the public needed something – anything – to talk about. The way I saw things, it just happened to be me they were using to sell newspapers.

The speculation over my captaincy was a hangover from the UK tour. Clearly, the trip was still a sensitive issue with many rugby people and the All Blacks hadn't been forgiven yet. Laurie's coaching and my captaincy drew a few barbs. When Mike Brewer "unretired", some people wondered if this was a sign he was being tipped as All Black captain. Laurie and I both knew it was just media sensationalism.

That's where Laurie was great. He immediately reassured me. He phoned and said, "Sean, ignore what you read in the newspapers. As long as you're playing good rugby, you're my captain. So don't worry about the speculation."

The public was unaware that I'd done some deep soul-searching over the summer. I knew better than anyone that my form had been inconsistent in 1993. The doubts that I could still compete with the best hadn't entirely gone, even after a few months' break from the game. Mentally, the big change I made before the start of the year was to say, "Bugger it – I'll play the game I know best, the one that comes instinctively . . ."

To do this I needed to be fitter. So I worked out a fitness programme with a private trainer, Mark Patel from Flying Fit gymnasium. It was a six-day-a-week schedule that involved weights and lots of 800-metre runs. I found the weights a lot more demanding than I expected. Mark said I wasn't as powerful as I needed to be. It took a few weeks to build up my strength.

I'm the hardest judge of my form, but I believe it worked. After the Super 10 series I knew I was still competitive, that I still had an edge. In the Super 10 I'd played against Kearns in Sydney and Allen in Natal, and I knew I could still compete at the top.

LAURIE MAINS

'I'd regard Sean's and my relationship as typical of New Zealand men. There's a great deal of respect there, and trust. We don't speak a lot of words.

I think Sean's still growing as a captain. I'm very happy with him.

I endorsed him publicly because I wanted him to know where I stood. I wanted to remove any doubt in Sean's mind.'

6.15 pm We're staying at Coogee because it's close to the ground. The bus trip takes only 10 minutes. Everyone is silent. From my seat, Sydney looks so alive. There are a lot of Kiwis over here; we're getting a lot of waves and salutes. I've been rung by several well-wishers. I spoke to Bronnie three times.

I got a very early indication it was going to be a tough year when, after the first loss to the French, a senior councillor boycotted the after-match without saying a word to us. Later, during my speech, I got booed.

But this time I didn't take it so personally. I understand now that a lot of the abuse directed our way is not at the individual, it comes with the territory.

People ask me if I get upset when ex-players like Andy Haden slag off the All Blacks. It doesn't worry me. If anything, it motivates the team to prove them wrong. You've got to remember that ex-players criticising the All Blacks is not the same as your average, irate talkback caller having a go. Andy Haden has played 117 games for New Zealand. He's been there, done that. It doesn't mean I agree with him. In fact a lot of what he's said recently has disappointed me. I know Andy well, see him socially a fair bit . . . I've told him on more than one occasion to lay off the team. But just because I don't agree with him I don't dismiss any remark lightly, either. He was a very smart player and has a good rugby brain.

I am a lot wiser after the experiences of 1993. I saw those occasions where I had struggled and those times I answered the challenge. I can't stress this point enough: having endured the pits of public scorn and self-doubt after the Lions and UK controversies, the experiences of last year really toughened my public hide. They also taught me not to be so focused on events outside my control. If I am satisfied I've done my best on and off the field, that's all I can do.

Coping with pressure had made me more philosophical about disappointment. I see now there is a bigger picture to everything, and rugby, just like life, isn't about getting your own way all the time. Not even in All Black rugby. It's only when you're young that you think every dream you have will turn out perfectly.

There were other reasons, beyond form, for my more philosophical approach.

In fact, they went beyond rugby, touching most aspects of my life.

Just before the French series I turned 31. The contrast with the previous year showed the extent of the change. For my thirtieth birthday, Bron had thrown a surprise party for me; it was a hoot, a great night. Heaps of friends were there and I really let my hair down.

This time around my 31st birthday fell on a Queen's Birthday Weekend Saturday. I played a rare club game, went to another birthday party that night and the rest of the weekend was enjoyed at my in-law's bach up north. There was just a handful of people around, it was very quiet. Bliss. On Sunday night, Bronnie's father Dan produced a bottle of champagne and a few reds, and after a great meal we all spent the evening talking about everything under the sun.

I understand, better than ever, that I can only be me. I don't know my public image or perception – I certainly can't control it. I don't care. If people want to say something negative about me they may as well say it to my face. I probably won't agree but I'll respect them more than if someone talks behind my back.

It's the old story of being called a so-and-so by someone who's never met you. Someone's heard from someone else that an All Black is stuck up, or loves himself, or this and that . . . and it becomes "fact".

I'm sure it's said about me all the time.

The older you get, the more winning means more – and the less devastated you feel about losing.

I hurt as badly as anyone when we go down, but these days I put defeat into its true perspective – I couldn't have said that until very recently. When I was winning all the time with Auckland and the All Blacks I never appreciated what success really meant. Now that era's gone and world rugby standards have levelled out, victory is more special because it is harder to achieve. When everything clicks, like against the Springboks at Wellington, the elation is total – because you've earned every ounce of triumph.

In recent years I've had a number of setbacks in rugby. They've taught me more about myself, and rugby, than all the combined years of success I had in the '80s. For example, losing the Ranfurly Shield was a major, but when it happened I accepted it. It hurt, but I knew Waikato deserved the glory that day. Being a good loser mattered most to me that night.

It's the same with the All Blacks. I'd love it if every time New Zealand took the field we won. And there hasn't been a single game in my All Black career where I have kicked off feeling less than utterly convinced we would win.

But I think this season's shown that winning every time will not happen any more. When it doesn't, you don't spit the dummy. If you've given your best, you should have no regrets. Disappointment, certainly. But no regrets . . .

I love to meet people who know nothing about rugby, whose emotional well-being isn't tied up in how the All Blacks perform.

I remember one time in Rotorua I was checking into a hotel. The girl behind the counter said, "Sign here please."

"Sure, who's it for?" I asked.

"No one," she said. "It's the guest register."

Soon after becoming an All Black I went out to the Spinal Unit at Otara. It had an indelible impact. Afterwards I told everyone I knew that they should pay a visit to the Unit and be so thankful for the ability to walk and move.

That visit showed me how lucky I am to have good health. At the Unit I saw very clearly that there are problems – and then there are *problems*. An All Black defeat might be the cause for soul-searching.

In the scale of life's troubles, it means nothing.

Over the years I've met many people who have been served a raw deal, yet refuse to give in. Especially in hospitals. I find their response to adversity inspirational. I always walk away with a lump in my throat upon seeing the bravery and courage ordinary people show under some terrible situations.

My nephew Sam has cerebal palsy. He's a marvellous little bloke, always happy, always smiling. So are the kids at Starship Children's Hospital, whom I pop in to see occasionally. No matter how sick or ill they are, they hardly ever moan. Before the third Springbok test this year I remember feeling uptight at the pressure. I'd promised to visit this kid at Starship. When I got there I wondered what on earth I was so concerned about. This youngster had been hit by a car. He'd been told his legs had "gone to sleep forever". He was 10 years old.

And I thought I had worries . . .

I've been very lucky to have such a supportive family. With every game I play, whether it's for Auckland or the All Blacks, the family phones.

Before I was captain and got my own room, it used to be a joke in the team about who was going to room with me because they'd get woken up so early. Mum usually rings around 7-7.30 to wish me luck, and then Dad gets on the phone and tells me to chase "the silly ones", and then my sisters and my brother. I get 10 phone calls sometimes, just from family. Mark always asks the same things – "Now Sean, how're you going to play it today?" or, "Give us some inside information Sean, what are you going to do today?"

"We interrupt this marriage to bring you the football season."
– Australian rugby league sticker

THE ALL BLACKS WERE standing around the bar, shell-shocked. It was only a few hours since we'd trooped dejectedly off Lancaster Park. The first test to the French was now history. And we'd lost. The guys were flat. Morale was low. No one knew exactly what to say . . .

Amid the doom and gloom, Ric Salizzo delivered me a note. It was from Bronnie. I read it and immediately felt better. Bronnie's note read, "Great news. We've hit the jackpot. Grace has just had her first wee in the potty."

It was a typical Bronnie gesture. She'd have hurt as much as me about the result, but she knows there's no point in dwelling on negative things. She always looks for what's positive in a situation, and Grace's "breakthrough" helped put things into perspective. We'd only lost a game, for goodness' sake. But life goes on. My two-year-old daughter had made huge progress. Suddenly, Sunday wasn't such a dark day after all.

Bronnie has been the mainstay of my life. There's no question my career would not have been as successful without her beside me.

We've been married since 1990, but we've known each other for ages.

Rugby's been part of our lives for so long. We've changed with it. Our dreams were very different in the beginning. In 1986, for instance, after my first All Black tour of France, I stayed on to play rugby for a club called Romans in a small town in the south-east, near the Swiss border. Bronnie joined me there and we had our first white Christmas. It was a magical time. No responsibilities; we were young and carefree, everything was new and exciting. We made lots of friends, went skiing, drank a lot of wine, stayed in a beautiful part of the country . . . the rugby was fitted in, somehow. It was part of life – but only a part. It didn't dominate everything, not like it does now.

The more successful I became, the more 1986 faded into a dream. I think that's why we remember it so fondly. Over the years the pressures got bigger, the demands more time-consuming. I've seen more than a few relationships buckle and go under because of rugby's demands, but we've always hung in there. Not only do I love Bronnie very much, she's my best friend. Now that we have a beautiful little daughter I want to start putting in quality time to my family.

They mean everything to me.

I value those rare times when the three of us, as a family, can enjoy simple pleasures. Recently, the three of us went down to the Olympic pool on a Saturday morning. I loved it. I was just one of the many dads playing with their kids in the pool . . . normal living like this was an eye-opener for me. It made me appreciate what I've got to look forward to after rugby.

BRONWYN FITZPATRICK

> ‘We went to the same parties, had the same friends, so it wasn’t a coincidence we met. We started seeing each other soon after. We were both 20. Sean was the same decent, good, straight guy then as he is now. But don’t think we’re talking about the boy-next-door, either.
>
> He told me I was his first brunette.
>
> Sean drove a white mini. The first time he took me out he kept turning up the volume of his radio all the time. It was to disguise the rattles.’

There are no secrets between us. Bronnie has seen the ups and downs, the lot. Unlike some rugby players’ wives or girlfriends, she’s got her own identity. She doesn’t need rugby to make her a “somebody”.

I rely on Bronnie even more now I’m captain. From the moment I step out my front door I’m “the All Black” to the world. When I walk into a dairy, the bloke behind the counter knows who I am. The petrol attendant. The waitress. Everybody. It’s a strain. I’m a human being with moods, inconsistencies. I don’t always react the right way to everything . . . and Bronnie sees this, absorbs a lot of tension. Especially after a test, all I want to do is come home and shut the door to the world, get out of the public eye.

It’s hard on her. She can’t afford to slip up, either. Just as many eyes are watching her.

I know she finds the pressure of a test match difficult to deal with sometimes. From the moment the final whistle goes my time is in demand: from TV, radio and the press for interviews. From Laurie and the team. From officials, sponsors and dozens of other people. It might take two or three hours after a game before we’ll get a moment to chat – and that’ll be at the after-match, with hundreds of people wanting a second of my time.

We’ve talked about getting around this but I don’t see how the system will change. It’s impossible for the All Black captain *not* to be in demand after a test. Not until I get to bed do I have the chance to be away from the public, and that’ll usually be hours after the game.

BRONWYN FITZPATRICK

> ‘Before we got married we had little chat sessions with Dean Rymer. He spoke of the importance of accepting things in life. He said if you don’t accept things that bother you, they can fester, undermine and ultimately destroy a whole relationship. If you accept them, most things are not a problem. I think rugby’s the area I apply this advice to most. Rugby takes up a lot of Sean’s time and it leaves me on my own a lot. I know that it won’t always be this way, so I accept it.’

7.07 pm Kamo is changing on one side of me. Grim is on the other. I'm a player who has to prepare methodically. I wear the same boxer shorts to games. I take my boots out of my bag first, then put my mouthguard in my right boot so I won't forget it. I put my running shoes on, do a few stretches. I've already had a quick look at the stadium. I say a few words, but not many. We've decided to go out a bit early, to spend as much time under the lights as we can. I'm feeling good, feeling confident. Seven minutes to go. I put my boots on.

Tonight's game will be pretty clean, I predict. Tests against Australia usually are. The 1994 French series was incredibly clean too, especially considering a French team was involved.

Australian teams don't really put in the biff or even do much talking. In that respect, they are very different to the Springboks.

The Boks were an arrogant bunch. Even in the first test, with only five minutes to go and them trailing, they were putting more energy into mouthing off than in achieving a win. All day long it had been comments like, "You Kiwis are gutless, just like your wingless bird . . ."

Their abuse didn't bother us. It was boring, that's all – and they played into our hands so easily. It showed where their true priorities were: instead of going for a win by scoring points, they were more concerned in trying to rattle us and put us off our game through verbal intimidation.

All Blacks don't scare that easily.

In the second test they shut up a bit more and concentrated less on the niggle. Well, most of them did.

Johan Le Roux and I did not get on.

When he bit my ear it was a culmination of tension between us that went back to the Super 10 final in 1993. That day he was an idiot. He is one of those blokes who're always trying to prove how tough they are – standing on you all the time, popping off a few cheap shots. Le Roux is the sort of player who, if the referee's watching, stages a dive to get the penalty.

In the first test at Carisbrook, the front row was a pretty interesting place. Le Roux was out to prove to the world what a big, bad prop he was, mouthing off a lot, putting in a bit of slipper. He stomped on me at one stage. So I lashed out at him and he made a big song-and-dance out of it. He wasn't tough; Loey just laughed at him.

There seemed to be a bit of friction in the Springboks; Le Roux's actions weren't that popular with all his team. After the game I spoke to Guy Kebble who told me, "Look Sean, I can't say anything about him now but let's talk after the third test in Auckland, when the tour's over . . ."

Everyone knows Johan didn't make it that far. By then, he'd

bitten through his mouthguard and nibbled on my ear at Athletic Park . . . the rest is history.

Actually, he'd bitten me earlier in the game – on my right arm. It left a mark. To be honest, it threw me a bit. At the time I wondered, "Maybe I should tape my ears . . ."

Le Roux was a strange one. After he'd bitten my ear I told him exactly what I thought of him. He didn't bat an eyelid, he just kept sledging me. In terms of scrummaging ability he wasn't a bad prop. I felt sorry for him in a funny kind of way. He's obviously a loose cannon, but even so . . .

I spoke to him after the test. He shook my hand at the team session we had with the Boks, congratulated me on the win.

But he didn't apologise for biting me. He didn't even mention it. I think he hoped the issue would die a natural death. If so, he made a big mistake.

7.24 pm I lead the All Blacks down the sloping tunnel of the Sydney Football Stadium. My collar is up, as usual. I haven't shaved. As we reach the pitch the crowd's roar greets us. The lights blaze down. It's a warm night, a gentle breeze. I feel an extra shot of adrenalin.

Before any big game you start thinking: "Why do I need this pressure? No matter if we win or lose, I'm out of here." And then, once you've won, you realise, "*This* is why I still play the game. What was I thinking about . . . wanting to give this up?"

Sometimes you don't win.

9.03 pm Australia 20 New Zealand 16

> *"Aussies survive a cliffhanger – All Blacks rue their run of bad luck"* – The *Daily Telegraph Mirror*

So near and yet so far. As I said at the press conference, where the first eight questions were directed straight at me, it was a game of two halves.

We are beaten, but not defeated.

The All Black dressing room is like a morgue. Goldie's very upset. The poor kid blames it all on himself. I tell him he can hold his head high, that not many players could even have made a run like that – but he's beyond caring.

Laurie looks bitterly disappointed.

There's not much talk from anyone. I could not believe our start: if there's one team who you don't want to gift seven points, it's Australia.

10.58 pm I'm standing inside the huge marquee tent, scene of the after-match function. I guess at least 500 people are here, including

many famous faces from the past. Tommy Lawton and I engage in a great conversation. Our years of rivalry have disappeared completely tonight. There's only tremendous respect. Tom's excellent company. We'll probably end up best of friends. Funny how time changes your attitude . . . Some official tugs my sleeve and tells me to go forward. I take a deep breath. It's that moment again, time for my speech.

". . . and finally, to you, Phil, I'd like to congratulate you on your win. As All Blacks, it's the highlight of our careers to play for the Bledisloe Cup. Tonight's game was a credit to both teams because they were prepared to play rugby.

"It was great to be involved. There had to be a winner – unfortunately, it wasn't us. Australia, you deserved your victory but we can go home with our heads held high, too.

"It was a fantastic occasion to be part of, and I thank the Australian people tonight for their support.

"Thank you."

Seven days later . . .

Bronnie, Grace and I are on holiday in Fiji. The pain of the loss is fading fast . . . helped by lying on the beach in 30 degrees of sunshine, and fantastic Fijian hospitality.

We bumped into two Wallabies from last week's game, John Eales and Jason Little. They're on holiday too. We had a laugh or two. It shows what makes rugby so special. Despite the changes taking place, the game still has room for camaraderie, even between opponents.

They're good guys. In fact I'll be seeing them again soon for a Bledisloe "rematch" – we've arranged a game of golf for tomorrow.

This time *I'm* going to win . . .

CAREER HIGHLIGHTS

(to 18/8/94)

Compiled by John Lea

Team	*Games*	*W*	*L*	*D*	*For*	*Against*	*Tries*	*Points*
New Zealand[1]	62	51	9	2	1780	801	8	35
New Zealand[2]	34	33	1	0	1205	347	7	30
Auckland	131	120	10	1	4733	1552	25	107
others	34	25	8	1	896	500	5	21
Total	**261**	**229**	**28**	**4**	**8614**	**320**	**45**	**193**

1 tests 2 other

- From over 100 opposing hookers, Sean has most often opposed Phil Kearns (17 games), Tom Lawton and Warren Gatland (12). Of 28 propping partners his most regular were Steve McDowell (158), Olo Brown (97) and Richard Loe (70).
- After at least 6000 scrums and 4000 line-out throws (first-class), Sean remains virtually indestructible. Test understudies Iain Abercrombie, John Buchan, Warren Gatland, Graham Dowd and Norm Hewitt have one international appearance between them, and that was as a replacement prop (Dowd)!
- Between his 7th and 99th appearances for Auckland, Sean tasted defeat once only: in match 37, vs New South Wales. From 1987 to 1991 he played in sequences of 34 test matches and 38 All Black matches without a single loss.
- Sean has the most first-class appearances in New Zealand by a hooker (Dennis Young with 236 is next), and is second only to Steve McDowell amongst front rowers.
- Sean has played against 21 (of 27) New Zealand provincial unions, in 11 years' play.
- Sean's 62 tests is a world record for hookers, and is currently one match behind John Kirwan's record 63 test appearances for the All Blacks. The next best by a New Zealand hooker is Sean's predecessor Andy Dalton, who played 35 matches.
- Sean's eight test tries is the New Zealand record for a hooker. By comparison, Phil Kearns has 7 in 42 games, Colin Deans 2 in 52, Brian Moore 1 in 55, Philippe Dintrans 1 in 50, Peter Wheeler none in 48 and Bruce McLeod 4 in 24 (next best for New Zealand).
- With 15 tries in all matches for New Zealand, Sean nearly doubles the next best effort from hookers of eight (by Bill Irvine and Hika Reid). His 45 first-class tries are a New Zealand record for a hooker.
- Sean shares (with Grant Fox) a New Zealand record, of playing against 15 different international opponents. The world record of 16 is held by Michael Lynagh.

Afterword

My relationship with Fitzy is very hard to sum up in a few words. Unquestionably, it's based on mutual values.

Fitzy is a mate. A very good mate. There is total respect between us.

Our relationship grew out of our rugby experiences. We went through so much together, on and off the field, that we've developed an intuitive partnership. Today we share a special understanding about so many issues . . .

Fitzy is part of a group of guys who basically started their first class rugby careers together, and whose friendship has endured and gone beyond rugby. The guys I'm talking about are Joe Stanley, Gary Whetton, AJ Whetton, Bernie McCahill, John Kirwan, me, Fitzy.

We all keep in contact whenever we can. We're the sort of guys who play golf together, go to dinner together, go to each other's birthday parties or shindigs of any sort . . . our friendships are equal, no one's more or less than another.

When I think of Fitzy I picture him among those group of guys. I imagine in 20 or 30 years from now that same group will still be mates . . . still enjoying each other's company . . . still having boot parties after a test at the back of Eden Park . . . still as close as ever.

And Fitzy will be laughing as loudly and enjoying life as much as he does now. Only there will probably be more of him then.

Sean's the only one from that group still playing at the top level, which says it all about his ability.

When he retires, rugby will lose a great player. Someone who's been a loyal servant to the All Blacks, to Auckland, to his mates.

There was never a moment we played together when I doubted him. He was one of those handful of players you knew would never let you down.

He is part of a special breed of player. They're born, not made. You never think they might fail – they don't know the meaning of the word. They are committed. They do the job. They are successful.

These sort of players are the best you can meet in rugby. Everyone knows who they are.

Fitzy is one of the best of the best.

Grant Fox
August, 1994

Olympix